*For Norman D'Amours
With best wishes, and
thanks for your support*

John Isbister

THIN CATS:

The Community Development Credit Union Movement in the United States

by John Isbister

CENTER FOR COOPERATIVES
UNIVERSITY OF CALIFORNIA

ISBN: 1-885641-04-4

Copyright ©The Regents of the University of California, 1994

All rights reserved. No part of this work may be reproduced or used in any means without written permission of the publisher.

Cover design by Marianne Post

The research leading to this report was financed by the Center for Cooperatives at the University of California as part of its Competitive Grants Program.

Center for Cooperatives
University of California
Davis, CA 95616

*Dedicated to my father-in-law,
Roy Spafford*

Contents

TABLES vii
PREFACE ix
1. COMMUNITY DEVELOPMENT CREDIT UNIONS 1
    What is a Community Development Credit Union? 2
    Some Community Development Credit Unions 6
    Church-Affiliated Credit Unions 15
    A Statistical Portrait of CDCUs 16
    Appendix: Cooperative Principles and Credit Unions 24

2. THE ORIGINS OF COOPERATIVE FINANCE 29
    Nineteenth-Century Cooperatives 30
    Schulze-Delitzsch and Raiffeisen 31
    The Social Bases of the Early German Credit Unions 34
    Principles of the Early Credit Unions 39
    Quebec's *Caisses Populaires* 48
    The Legacy for American CDCUs 51

3. DEVELOPMENT IN THE UNITED STATES 55
    The Mainstream Credit Unions 55
    The Emergence of Community Development Credit Unions 62
    The National Federation of Community Development Credit Unions 70
    Summary 75

4. WHY ARE CDCUs NEEDED? 77
    Financial Institutions as Intermediaries 78
    An Example on Chicago's South Side 80
    Home Mortgage Lending 81
    Bank Services Besides Mortgage Lending 87
    The Drain of Capital 92
    Legislation 96
    Discrimination 98
    Conclusion 104

5. THE OPERATIONS OF CDCUs 107
    Credit Unions' Financial Statements 108
    A Note on the Data 111
    The Questions 113
    Where Do CDCUs' Resources Come From? 114
    What Do CDCUs Do with Their Resources? 116
    How Do CDCUs Earn Their Income? 124
    How Do CDCUs Create a Spread Between Income and Outgo? ... 137

How are CDCUs Rated by Their Examiners? 144
Conclusions 145

6. THE LENDING PRACTICES OF CDCUs 149
Seven Credit Unions 149
The Loans 152
Central Appalachian People's Federal Credit Union 153
First American Credit Union 155
Mission Area Federal Credit Union 156
Northeast Community Federal Credit Union 157
North East Jackson Area Federal Credit Union 158
Santa Cruz Community Credit Union 158
Watts United Credit Union 160
Business Loans 160
Borrower Ages 164
Borrower Incomes 165
The Importance of the Non-Poor 168
Conclusion 171
Appendix: The Data 172

7. POLICY 175
The Regulation of Financial Institutions 176
The Regulation of Credit Unions 178
The Changing Response of NCUA to CDCUs 181
New Federal Legislation 193
A Community Reinvestment Act for Credit Unions? 197
Policy at Other Levels 200
Conclusion 203

BIBLIOGRAPHY 207

ILLUSTRATIONS

Following page 106

TABLES

Table 1.1 180 Community Development Credit Unions 17
Table 1.2 Total Assets in 180 Community Development Credit Unions 17
Table 1.3 Membership in 180 Community Development Credit Unions 18
Table 1.4 Distribution of CDCUs by Asset Size 19
Table 1.5 Growth in CDCU Assets, 1981—1991 20
Table 1.6 114 Urban Community Development Credit Unions 22
Table 1.7 66 Rural Community Development Credit Unions 22
Table 1.8 Comparison of CDCU Neighborhoods to National Averages 23
Table 2.1 Capital and Liabilities in 948 People's Banks, 1878 42
Table 3.1 Number and Proportion of U.S. Credit Unions by Common Bond 59
Table 3.2 Founding Year of 165 CDCUs 63
Table 4.1 Denial Rates for Applications for Mortgages to Purchase Homes 84
Table 4.2 Denial Rates for Applications for Mortgages to Purchase Homes 85
Table 4.3 Loan-to-Deposit Ratios by Racial Composition of Neighborhoods 94
Table 4.4 Loan-to-Deposit Ratios in Middle-Income Neighborhoods 94
Table 5.1 Balance Sheet 109
Table 5.2 Income Statement 110
Table 5.3 Distribution of Liabilities Plus Capital in 180 CDCUs 115
Table 5.4 Distribution of Assets in 180 CDCUs 117
Table 5.5 Loan-to-Asset Ratios 118
Table 5.6 Dollar Amounts of Outstanding Loans 121
Table 5.7 Loan Types by CDCU Size and Church Affiliation 122
Table 5.8 Average Loan Size for Credit Unions Making Each Type of Loan 122
Table 5.9 Loans Per Member 123
Table 5.10 The Components of Income 125
Table 5.11 Average Interest Rates Charged on Loans 126
Table 5.12 Delinquency and Charge-off Rates 129
Table 5.13 Average Uses of Total Income by CDCUs, 1991 132
Table 5.14 Expense-to-Income Ratios by Church Affiliation and Size 132
Table 5.15 Compensation and Fringes 134
Table 5.16 Staffing in CDCUs 135
Table 5.17 Employees Per Hundred Thousand Dollars in Income 136
Table 5.18 Rates of Return 138
Table 5.19 Cost of Funds 140
Table 5.20 Net Spread 141
Table 5.21 Allocation to Capital 143
Table 5.22 CAMEL Ratios 144
Table 6.1 Seven Credit Unions: Basic Comparisons 151
Table 6.2 Median Values of Loans and Borrower Characteristics 151
Table 6.3 Dollar Amount of Loans by Loan Purpose 152

Table 6.4 Average Size of Loan by Loan Purpose 153
Table 6.5 Comparison of Conventional and VISA Loans,
    Santa Cruz Community Credit Union 159
Table 6.6 Comparison of Conventional and VISA Loans, Mainstream Credit Union 160
Table 6.7 Business Loans in Four Credit Unions 161
Table 6.8 Income of Borrowers 166
Table 6.9 Median Monthly Income of Full-Time Workers 167
Table 6.10 Median Monthly Income by Gender 167
Table 6.11 Average Borrower Incomes Adjusted for Differences
    in Age and Cost of Living 168
Table 7.1 Federal Credit Unions Selected Years 1935-1992 191

PREFACE

This book discusses the history, role, and accomplishments of the country's community development credit unions, or CDCUs. They number only in the few hundreds, and their assets are limited, so they constitute just a small fraction of credit union activity in the country, and a much smaller fraction of overall financial activity. Yet their importance far exceeds their size, since they are the one sector of the financial industry that is devoted solely to the improvement of living conditions in poor communities.

The persistence of desperately poor neighborhoods in the midst of a rich and growing nation is one of the most important challenges, both practical and moral, that face us at the end of the twentieth century. The reduction and eventual elimination of poverty, which had seemed to many people to be a relatively easy task when it was urged on the nation a generation ago by President Johnson, has turned out to be an almost intractable one. By most statistical measures, poverty has risen since 1975, and a whole new generation of young people has been caught in its traps. The causes are complicated, so complicated perhaps as to be beyond our complete understanding.

Yet many facts are clear. Among them is the indisputable proposition that financial institutions, whose business is the allocation of money, influence who gets money and who stays poor. As Chapter 4 will show, the principal effect of conventional financial institutions on poor communities in the United States is not to provide funds for those communities' use, but instead to drain resources out of them.

So the small cooperative community development credit unions are critically important. In their structure and their activities they are an echo of earlier generations of cooperative financial institutions, both in Europe and in North America. Their purpose is to retain a poor community's resources and direct them to that community's own productive use, as well as to attract outside funds in order to enhance those resources. They are small, and even if they were to expand greatly, they would not by themselves eliminate poverty. But they make a particularly important contribution.

I have been working in the CDCU movement as a volunteer since 1979, when I joined the board of directors of the Santa Cruz Community Credit Union. During much of that time, I have known and interacted with credit union people around the country. As a consequence, the methods used in writing this book are diverse. In part, they are conventionally academic. With the help of research assistants I gathered data from the loan files of seven credit unions in the summer of 1991. I analyzed a large data set of the financial statements of the country's community development credit unions, provided for me by economists at the Credit Union National Association. I conducted interviews with credit union leaders at their offices and at national conventions. And I read the small but interesting literature on the subject. In part, however, the methods are more personal than is usual in an academic study. I am not an outsider to the community development credit union movement in the way that most academic authors are to their subjects. I have been working in it so long that I feel just as much a part of it as do any of my informants. Much of what I know about the subject comes not from specific documents or interviews, but from years of conversation and experience, from struggling over financial decisions with my fellow board members to sharing hotel breakfasts with credit union managers at national meetings. Throughout the text I have tried to cite my sources clearly, but in places this has been difficult. Consequently, I would like to apologize in advance to any persons who believe their ideas and information are used in these pages without proper acknowledgement.

The book is intended as a gift to the people who have devoted their lives to the community development credit union movement. They are anything but the fat cats one normally associates with finance. They work for low compensation and little recognition. Even though I have mingled with them for years now, I am still frequently surprised to learn of the dedication and the accomplishments of people I had previously not known. At the risk of excluding some who should be named, I would like to thank the following, all of whom helped to create this study by sharing their experiences and knowledge with me: Carol Aranjo, Leone Baum, Angelina Boone, Marcus Bordelon, Ellsworth Brewer, James Caskey, Raquel Castillo, Michael Chan, Ricardo Garcia, James Gilliam, Tinka Gordon, Mark W. Griffith, Bill Hampel, Everett Harper, Clyde Johnson, Woodrow Keown, Sister Ann Kendrick, Christopher W. Kerecman, David Lewis, Lily Lo, Ruth Lockett, Pearl Long, Erroll T. Louis, Betty Matthiessen, Genia McKee, Robert Mumma, William Myers, Ceretha Robinson, Joyce Rogers, Marc Shafroth, Robert Shipe, Ward Smith, Mary Spink, Caryl Stewart, James Taylor, Kathryn Tholin, Darcine Thomas, Sondra Townsend-Browne, Teresa Trudeau, Jeff Wells, Mardi Wormhoudt, Jann Yankauskas, Karen Zelin and, posthumously, Annie Vamper. Thanks also to the board and staff members of the Santa Cruz Community Credit Union.

I would particularly like to acknowledge not only the help but more importantly the inspiration provided by the joint recipients of the Annie Vamper Award from the National Federation of Community Development

Credit Unions in 1993, Ernest Johnson and Clifford Rosenthal. Johnson, of the Federation of Southern Cooperatives, has devoted his life to the African American credit unions of the rural southeast, and through his talent, hard work, and extraordinarily persuasive powers has become a legend in the community development credit union movement. Rosenthal, Executive Director of the National Federation, developed the organization from a time when there was no money and no salaries, only dedication, to its present state in which it organizes credit unions, provides technical assistance, performs rescue operations on ailing credit unions, initiates programs, brings people in the movement together, and advocates effectively in Washington. Together, the two represent the heart of the movement.

Thanks to a group of undergraduate and graduate students at the University of California, Santa Cruz, who worked as research assistants on the project: Joy Agcongay, Chhorn Be, Christina Cavazos, Javier Tapia, and Robert Thompson. Thanks also to the Center for Cooperatives, which sponsored the research.

And finally, much more than thanks to my wife, Roz Spafford, who encouraged me throughout the project, edited the manuscript, and saved me from at least some of the errors of exposition and judgment that would otherwise have found their way into print. The responsibility for the remaining errors, I am sorry to concede, is mine.

—*John Isbister*

CHAPTER 1

COMMUNITY DEVELOPMENT CREDIT UNIONS

The choice of where we do our business is one of our most significant political and economic tools. The Alternatives Federal Credit Union lets its members determine the social consequences of the uses of our money...The Credit Union invests with a conscience.
—Mission Statement,
Alternatives Federal Credit Union
Ithaca, New York

These mostly small, hardworking and undercapitalized financial institutions are doing extraordinary work in areas deemed unprofitable by the private sector, often with minimal or no support from government, the philanthropic community or other outside sources of assistance.
—Kathryn Tholin and Jean Pogge[1]

In low-income communities throughout the country—in central cities and in rural areas, on Native American reservations and in urban settlement houses, in racially segregated housing projects and in church basements—community development credit unions provide basic financial services to poor people. In total, the CDCUs number only a few hundred—the exact figure is unknown because the definition of a CDCU is rather elastic; and compared to other financial institutions, even other credit unions, they are small and, in some cases, tiny. They are not a large enough component of the country's overall financial system to change, by themselves, the over-

---

[1] Tholin and Pogge, 1.

whelming inequalities of American economic and social life. But for their local communities they make a difference. They offer financial services at reasonable cost and they provide loans to people who frequently could not qualify at another financial institution, or who would have to pay exorbitant rates of interest to a finance company or a loan shark.

Beyond their achievements so far, CDCUs represent a hope, a potential for economic development in communities that need it most. They are nonprofit, cooperative, self-help institutions, relying predominantly upon the resources of local people. They need encouragement and support from the outside, but they do not need to be taken over and directed by outsiders. At a time when the gap between rich and poor Americans is growing, when poverty rates are increasing and racial tensions are simmering, sometimes exploding, they are part of a strategy for change.

In 1993, President Clinton placed the issue of community development banking on the country's agenda. He spoke of how local financial institutions could mobilize a low-income neighborhood's savings, draw in funds from the outside, and lend for housing and small business development to create jobs and income for needy Americans. He proposed legislation to provide seed capital to community development credit unions and to other financial institutions operating in poor communities. His initiative led to some optimism, both that the nation might commit itself in a new way to the fight against poverty and that community development credit unions might play an important role in that fight.

What is a Community Development Credit Union?

Community development credit union is a term used by people in credit unions that serve low-income people to describe their own institutions. It is not an official term, and no precise parameters, definitions, or criteria for inclusion exist. Many, but not all, of the CDCUs belong to a trade association called the National Federation of Community Development Credit Unions.

CDCUs vary widely, but still they share some common commitments, commitments that mean that together they constitute not just a series of separate institutions and not just a sector of an industry, but a movement.

Like every credit union, a CDCU is formally a cooperative: It is owned by the people who conduct their transactions with it, and it is controlled on a one-person-one-vote basis. The people who place their savings in a credit union and who borrow from it become its member-owners, not its customers. They elect the board of directors who, in turn, establish the credit union's policies.[2]

---

[2] See the appendix to this chapter for a discussion of the relevance of cooperative principles to credit unions.

While all credit unions are cooperatives in the legal sense, many CDCUs have more of the spirit of cooperation about them than do most mainstream credit unions. As Chapters 2 and 3 will show, credit unions began in nineteenth-century Europe as institutions committed to social change, to improving the lives of people who were in distress. Most modern American credit unions have abandoned this identity. They provide needed financial services to the employees of a company or to the members of an association, but it is no part of their purpose to change in any fundamental way the social conditions in which their members live. CDCUs, in contrast, bring their members together into a financial cooperative precisely in order to improve their lives and give them new hope. Mainstream credit unions pay attention to the wishes of their members, but they do so much in the way that any business tracks the interests of its customers, in order to develop marketing strategies that will increase revenues. CDCUs, on the other hand, typically stay closer to their members, inviting them to share in the policy direction of the institution. The members provide volunteer help, and the elected representatives typically go out of their way to make decisions that are in the members' interests.

CDCUs are established in low-income communities, usually by low-income people, for the purpose of making a contribution to the economic and social life of the poor.

Every credit union has a charter, issued by either the federal or a state government. Among other things, the charter specifies a "field of membership," or group of people who are eligible to join the credit union. One of the basic features of a credit union is that the field of membership encompasses people who are connected to each other through a "common bond." The field of membership in most American credit unions is defined by employment in a company, or by occupation, or by membership in a voluntary association. In contrast, about half of the CDCUs have a geographical or residential field of membership; all people living or working in a certain area, usually a poor area, are eligible to join. Most other CDCUs have an associational field, for example, all people served by an urban settlement house or members of certain community organizations or churches. But even in these cases, the emphasis is on defining a field of membership for the CDCU that includes people in serious economic need.

There are variations. Some CDCUs, like the one in Santa Cruz, have a mixed membership, combining middle- and low-income people. Self-Help Credit Union covers the entire state of North Carolina. Yet in these CDCUs, as in the others, the primary mission is to improve the living conditions of the poor. The presence of middle-income people in these credit unions helps to generate the resources that in turn are directed towards the poor (this point is developed further in Chapter 6). Most CDCUs have a membership that is predominantly if not exclusively low-income, minority, or disadvantaged in some way.

Like all businesses, CDCUs have their ideologies, but they are not the standard commercial ideologies. Most CDCUs combine a commitment to low-income communities with an explicitly social, or even political, purpose. They care about commercial success too, and commercial success comes hard to CDCUs because of the serious problems caused by dealing with a membership that is predominantly poor. CDCUs need to be profitable in order to survive, but they exist because their leaders want to contribute to social change in their communities.

Ideologies and attitudes differ, of course, from CDCU to CDCU. Some credit union leaders are actively political, viewing their institutions as radical agents of social change. Some CDCUs seem to embody the anger that results from generations of discrimination and oppression. But some CDCU leaders see their mission rather more as one of service to their neighbors who are in need—or even service to those who can provide jobs and housing to people who are in need. Some are not much concerned about the structural transformation of their community and are more focused on the pressing needs of their members as individuals.

CDCUs are a private-sector initiative. In contrast to most anti-poverty, welfare, and community development agencies, they are not sponsored by or controlled by the government. They are owned and controlled by their members on a private, voluntary basis.

This point needs stressing at a time when government social programs of all sorts have become suspect. The 1980s and 1990s have seen a reaction against the public programs of the New Deal and the War on Poverty that were rich in promise but seemed to many people to be less effective in reality. In fact, many of those public programs were completely effective, transforming the social landscape of the country. Nevertheless, the very idea of direct government action to eliminate poverty and rescue the central cities has fallen into disfavor.

To be sure, CDCUs have connections to the public sector. They are chartered by state or federal government agencies and, like all businesses, they must operate according to the commercial laws of the land. They are insured, examined, and regulated by government agencies. Government regulations influence the character of the CDCUs, up to and including whether they can be started in the first place and whether they can survive. Government programs sometimes provide resources for them. The question of government policy towards CDCUs is reviewed in Chapter 7. CDCUs do not depend, however, upon government funding or upon government personnel.

The most important defining feature of CDCUs is that they mobilize their communities' own resources for the needs of local people and for local economic development. Since they lend to the people who make deposits, they represent a form of community self-help.

As Chapter 4 will argue, one of the most serious problems in many low-income communities is that resources flow out of them. Conventional financial institutions contribute to the outflow; their branches accept deposits from people in the neighborhood, but they return very little of the money as loans. As a consequence, whatever savings exist in low-income communities tends to be siphoned off into the wider world of finance.

CDCUs plug up this outflow. In almost every case, their charters restrict their membership to a small local area. They accept deposits from people in this area, and, since they are constrained to lend only to members, they pump the money back into the area, to people who can make productive use of it. It must quickly be said that not all of the deposits in a CDCU are immediately recycled back into the community. Most CDCUs have excess funds that are not yet loaned out. These are invested in other financial institutions where they earn interest for the credit union. Almost all of these investments are made outside the local area. In most CDCUs, however, investments total much less than loans, and so it is accurate to say that for the most part CDCUs act to recycle local savings for local use.

Many CDCUs also act as a conduit for funds to come into the local low-income community from outside the area. One source of outside resources is the Revolving Loan Fund of the National Credit Union Administration (NCUA), which makes low-interest deposits of up to $200,000 in some specially designated credit unions and which has recently agreed to expand the program. Some low-income credit unions are permitted by the NCUA to accept outside, "non-member" deposits in an amount not to exceed 20 percent of their assets (and exceptions to this limit can sometimes be negotiated). The non-member deposits are a way for socially responsible investors to direct funds into poor communities. A number of churches, foundations, corporations, and even banks have made these kinds of deposits in order to contribute to socially worthwhile projects while at the same time earning a return on their assets.

CDCUs can, therefore, have just the opposite effect from the one that financial institutions such as banks normally have upon a poor community. CDCUs keep local resources local, and add to this by attracting outside funds.

CDCUs lend their funds for constructive purposes in poor neighborhoods. Different CDCUs define those purposes differently. Some follow the tradition of other American credit unions and restrict themselves almost totally to personal, consumer lending. They make loans for automobiles, for home improvements, for appliances, for vacations, for education, for consumer items, for debt consolidation, and for other needs that individuals have. The CDCU is frequently the only conventional lender in the community that will deal with the local, low-income people. In the absence of the CDCU, people are forced to borrow from pawnshops, finance companies, loan sharks, and used car dealers. All of these sources tend to charge much higher interest rates than the members can obtain at the CDCU.

Other CDCUs go beyond consumer lending, to commercial business lending, and also to mortgages. CDCUs that make this choice are hampered by many state and federal regulations, because credit union laws and regulations are written with the expectation that credit unions will remain committed predominantly to consumer lending. But more and more CDCUs have shown an interest in developing the expertise to make broader, "community development" loans. They understand that their members' welfare depends upon access not just to consumer finance, but to decent jobs and affordable housing. Some CDCUs are affiliated with community development loan funds, which are unregulated, uninsured agencies specializing in affordable housing and sometimes in small business loans. The lending performance of CDCUs is examined in Chapter 6.

Most CDCUs are committed to the development of their members as people, not just as savers and borrowers. They depend to a certain extent upon volunteers, and they give their volunteers responsibilities and experience that are often valuable to them as they struggle to improve their lives.

Since CDCUs have so many goals aside from profitability, and since they operate in poor neighborhoods which have largely been abandoned by other conventional financial institutions, it will come as no surprise to learn that many of them face serious obstacles to commercial success. The financial statements of CDCUs are analyzed in Chapter 5. With some exceptions, CDCUs face higher rates of delinquency and default on their loans than do other credit unions; they have higher expenses and lower net margins. The great majority of them are successful enough to survive and grow, however, and they retain a cushion of reserves that is sufficient to see them through hard times.

Some Community Development Credit Unions

CDCUs can be introduced best by describing a few of them briefly. The descriptions are based on interviews with leaders of the various credit unions as well as visits to some of them.

The main office of the Central Appalachian People's Federal Credit

Union[3] is located in Berea, Kentucky, on the western edge of the southern Appalachian mountains. Three staff members work at old desks, surrounded by rows of file cabinets of various colors and states of disrepair.

The town of Berea is a center of Appalachian culture and education. Berea College, which dominates the town physically, was established just before the Civil War by abolitionist Christians for the purpose of educating the mountain people, and it continues that mission today. The southern Appalachian region is one of the most beautiful in the country, and rich in culture, but its people are among the most disadvantaged in terms of income, poverty, employment, housing, and health.

The credit union operates throughout the mountain region in 20 counties that stretch into Tennessee and Ohio as well as eastern Kentucky. Membership totals 2,000, with $2 million in assets. The field of membership includes people affiliated with about 35 community organizations and businesses in the region. Each of the affiliated organizations functions as a branch of the credit union. A person in each affiliated organization is available to counsel members, provide them with forms, help them with the loan application process, send in payments, and check with the Berea office on the status of their accounts. Many of the transactions are made by telephone calls between the branches and the main office; as a consequence the credit union is able to reach far across the mountains and hollows that isolate Appalachian people. The credit union makes only personal loans, but it is affiliated with a community development loan fund that does small business lending in the mountain region.

The board of directors and the credit committee are both made up of local people who meet frequently and take their responsibilities seriously. They look to the manager of the credit union, Marcus Bordelon, for guidance, but he is reluctant to give too much of it, since he wants the credit union to be a real cooperative, a vehicle for local control and for the education and development of the members.

The Southwest Germantown Association Federal Credit Union[4] of Philadelphia is located on the first floor of a building formerly occupied by a branch of the Fidelity Bank. When Fidelity closed its branch, as many banks have done in poor neighborhoods, it invited the credit union, then in a cramped brownstone, to take over the building. At first, the credit union had to refuse, since it lacked the resources even to maintain the building. Eventu-

---

[3] Thanks to Marcus Bordelon, Genia McKee, Joyce Rogers, and Jann Yankauskas for telling me about the credit union and for their hospitality when I visited.

[4] Teresa Trudeau, manager of the credit union and board member of the National Federation of CDCUs, described the institution to me.

ally, however, a cooperative plan was worked out with another community organization, a grant was obtained from the William Penn Foundation to cover the building's expenses, and the credit union moved in.

The credit union has assets of just under $2 million, membership of about 2,500 people, and a staff of 3. It serves the historic Germantown neighborhood, once the temporary location of President Washington's White House when Philadelphia was suffering from an epidemic of yellow fever. It is now a mixed-income and mixed-race neighborhood, with the mix changing continuously in the direction of poor and African American. The poverty rate is triple the level for all of Philadelphia and unemployment is typically high.

The credit union was founded in 1977 by a group of people concerned about high unemployment and the refusal of banks to lend in their neighborhood. As is typical with most CDCUs, the organizers had almost no background in or knowledge of financial affairs; what they had was a commitment to their neighborhood. They were particularly attracted to the credit union form since neighborhood people were already familiar with cooperatives organized for other purposes such as food buying and babysitting.

Southwest Germantown FCU makes loans for as little as $20 and as much as $20,000. In partnership with the city, it makes "action loans" of up to $15,000 for home improvements. The manager, Teresa Trudeau, maintains that it is very important for the credit union to be distinct from the banks, for the staff and board to know the members and understand their problems in a way that banks do not. "We could not be who we are if we were bank-like," she says. It is important to keep the credit union mission at the forefront, she says, and to help "the little people."[5] "If a person comes in and asks for a $20 or a $50 loan, they need it; they're not asking me for that money to squander it, they need it for some good reason, like school clothes for the kids or a prescription." She says that the credit union helps people who would never be able to get help elsewhere. Furthermore, the members understand that they are being supported by their neighbors.

Self-Help Credit Union[6] in Durham, North Carolina, is the country's largest community development credit union with over $35 million in assets in 1992 and a field of membership that stretches across the state, but it does not look like a financial institution at all. At its main office in Durham there is no lobby, no stream of members flowing in and out, just a suite of offices.

---

[5] "The little people" was the trademark phrase of the late Father Matthew Fogarty, one of the early and most influential leaders of the CDCU movement.

[6] I have learned about Self-Help mostly from presentations by and conversations with Everett Harper, and from printed material circulated by the Center for Community Self-Help. The Center has been in the news frequently, in connection with the President's initiative for community development banking.

In spite of its size in assets, Self-Help does not actually have many members, just over 1,700 at last count. The explanation is that Self-Help is not a traditional credit union at all, but rather a component of a community economic development agency.

The parent agency is the Center for Community Self-Help, a nonprofit institution that receives tax-exempt grants, and that in turn sponsors both the credit union and a community development loan fund called the Self-Help Ventures Fund. The entire complex of institutions concentrates on housing and commercial lending, with particular emphasis on what they call "socially or economically disadvantaged constituencies," in their case, low-income, rural, minority, and women borrowers.

The fact that the Center has two lending agencies allows it to segment its loans in an interesting way. The credit union, which is chartered by the state government and whose deposits are insured by the National Credit Union Administration, must adopt a more conservative stance in its lending than the Ventures Fund. Self-Help's plan is that the credit union should concentrate on loans that would not be made by a traditional bank but which would be viable with a slight liberalization of bank lending criteria. It should also make loans in cases in which traditional lenders appear to be discriminatory. But it should not fund commercial start-ups or other high-risk activities. Those are reserved for the Ventures Fund. Because deposits in the Ventures Fund are not insured by the government, the Fund does not have to answer to strict federal regulations; it is therefore free to be at least somewhat more adventurous in its lending. The tightening of federal member business loan regulations for credit unions in 1991 (described in Chapter 7) has made this plan harder to implement, however, and since that time the majority of the business loans have had to be channeled through the Ventures Fund.

When President Clinton introduced his community development banking initiative on the White House lawn on July 15, 1993, one of the speakers was Tim Bazemore, the African American manager of the Workers Owned Sewing Company in Windsor, North Carolina. He described how Self-Help had lent the workers the money to buy out the company and save their jobs in the early 1980s, and then go on to become the second-largest private employer in Bertie County.

Self-Help serves the entire state of North Carolina and receives deposits from throughout the state. It can do this because its charter permits it to accept as members any people or institutions who are members of the Center for Community Self-Help, the parent association, and the Center is a statewide organization. It has succeeded in attracting many large, "socially responsible" deposits from institutions that want to make a contribution to community development in the state while at the same time earning a return on their money. Other credit unions that try to follow this strategy have to classify such funds as "non-member deposits" because the investors are not in the credit union's field of membership, and because federal regulations severely restrict non-member deposits. Because of its charter, however, Self-Help can enroll the investor as a member and thereby avoid the limitation on outside deposits.

The D. Edward Wells Federal Credit Union[7] sits in the main square in the heart of the African American community of Springfield, Massachusetts. Its building, a former bank, was bought in 1991 by a group of friends of the credit union, who rent it to the credit union. It is a community credit union; its field of membership includes "the brotherhood" of Springfield, which the credit union's board interprets as meaning the entire population of the city. It was founded, however, in 1958 as a church credit union, drawing its members from the Mount Calvary Baptist Church, and for years it operated out of the church building. Many of the credit union's members are still from Mount Calvary and that church is the credit union's biggest supporter.

The credit union has 2,700 members and 3 employees. The manager, Carol Aranjo, says that most people have joined out of a sense of ethnic loyalty (the credit union is the only African American financial institution in Massachusetts), out of a commitment to the church community, and out of a desire to be treated fairly. They are well aware of the difficulty that minorities have in getting loans at conventional financial institutions, and they know that they will be treated fairly at Wells.

Loans are in relatively high demand at Wells, and consequently most of the deposits are loaned out to the members. Many of the loans are made without collateral, on the personal signature of the borrower. In the case of car loans, the credit union takes a lien on the vehicle. The credit union has been troubled by a fairly high and fluctuating delinquency rate on its loan repayments, largely due to layoffs and other longstanding economic problems in Massachusetts.

Wells has a youth credit union, begun in 1988, which children in the community aged 7 to 17 are eligible to join.[8] The youth credit union has its own board of directors and officers, its own tellers and loan committee. It is open for transactions one day a week after school; it accepts deposits from the children and makes small loans for purposes such as buying bicycles or birthday presents. The Wells model of a youth credit union has been replicated by many other CDCUs.

---

[7] For the description of the credit union I am in debt to Carol Aranjo, manager of the credit union and Chairperson of the National Federation of CDCUs.

[8] On the youth credit union, see Jerving.

While Wells is no longer strictly a church credit union, its roots are still in the church. Ms. Aranjo is a champion of all sizes of church credit unions. The spirit of the credit union movement should be flexible enough, she argues, to welcome an institution of just a hundred members and a few thousand dollars, provided those people want to join together and help each other. In many minority communities the church is the most important institution, and it simply makes sense for the church to provide the common bond for financial self-help. She regrets, therefore, the pressure that many small, church-based credit unions face from their examiners to liquidate or merge into a larger institution.

The main office of First American Credit Union[9] is in Window Rock in northern Arizona, the capital of the Navajo Nation. A branch is located in Casa Grande in the southern part of the state. First American was founded in 1962, chartered by the State of Arizona. At that time it was called Navajo Tribal Employees' Credit Union, its field of membership being the 1,500 employees of the tribe as well as members of the governing Tribal Council. In 1965 the name was changed to Navajoland Credit Union, and the charter expanded to include everyone working or living on the Navajo Reservation. In 1983, the name was changed again, to First American, and the charter amended to include members of all Indian tribes whose headquarters were located in Arizona. With $26 million in assets and 10,000 members in 1992, it is the largest Native American credit union in the country and one of the largest CDCUs.

First American serves a poor community. While some Indians on the reservation are economically comfortable, the incidence of poverty, unemployment, welfare dependence, disease, and alcoholism is significantly higher than in the rest of the country. For years, the credit union operated out of a dilapidated trailer whose doors and windows would never quite shut. Now, however, it is housed at the main crossroads of Window Rock, in a modern building with a spacious foyer and computerized services. Three tellers in the smart, attractive uniforms of the credit union meet with members in the foyer and take loan requests over the phone, while another half dozen employees work at terminals in the back office.

The credit union's successful transition from a small, marginal operation with high delinquencies and an uncertain future into a strong, growing institution is due in part to its board of directors which was able to identify the policies that needed changing, and in part to the leadership of its manager since 1974, Robert P. Shipe. Shipe grew up in the credit union movement; his father had been director of both the Credit Union National Association and

---

9 Thanks to Robert P. Shipe, manager, and Angelina Boone, collections officer, who welcomed me warmly on a visit to Window Rock.

the Arizona Credit Union League.

The credit union's leaders decided that the most important priority was to spread the loan money as broadly as possible among the members. As a consequence, the institution makes only small, personal loans. Once they have established a line of credit, members can borrow in amounts as small as they wish up to their credit limit, just by making a phone call. In effect, their line of credit at First American operates like a credit card. To qualify for a line of credit, they must be employed and they must sign up for automatic payroll deduction to make their loan payments.

Watts United Credit Union[10] is located in a small suite on the first floor of a two-story office building at the corner of Wilmington Avenue and 103rd Street in the heart of the Watts district of Los Angeles. Across Wilmington is the large 102nd Street Elementary School, and across the road from that is a row of boarded-over and barred shops. It is a poor neighborhood, and the site of two of the worst urban disturbances in modern American history, in 1965 and 1992. During the 1992 episode, the credit union's manager, James Taylor, stayed in the office for three straight days and nights. When the protesters came by and threatened the building, Taylor, a tall and distinguished-looking African American man, walked out front and, he says, spoke quietly to them, saying, "You're looking at the owner, please pass on," and they did.

Watts United was chartered as a response to the 1965 uprising, as part of a program to bring some hope of economic progress to local residents. Taylor recalls the credit union at that time as being a kind of "experiment," to see if people on welfare would pay their debts. Many of the loans in the early years were for $50, to tide people over between welfare checks. In some cases, he says, it was a struggle to get people to understand the difference between a grant and a loan, and the fact that the latter had to be paid back; but in the end the borrowers made good on those $50 loans and the credit union was in a position to grow. Even today, the credit union restricts itself to personal, consumer loans, many of them now for automobiles. It does not yet make business loans.

All Watts residents are eligible to join the credit union. By 1992, Watts United had over 2,000 members, approximately two-thirds African American and one-third Latino (reflecting the shifting demographics of Watts), with assets totalling $1.5 million. Initially the credit union's expenses were paid by a sponsoring agency, the Westminster Association, but it has been on its own for many years now. It is in a particularly strong financial position, with a ratio of reserves to assets of 12 percent in 1992, remarkably high for a CDCU.

---

[10] James Taylor, the manager, welcomed me to the credit union in 1991, and since then he has kept me posted frequently on the progress of the institution.

The Santa Cruz Community Credit Union[11] occupies an old, two-story stucco building in downtown Santa Cruz, California. When the Loma Prieta earthquake destroyed much of the commercial area of the city in October, 1989, it fortuitously spared the credit union. But even though the building was preserved, the leaders of the credit union nevertheless feared for the institution's financial future. Members might withdraw their funds, they thought, both because the downtown area was almost inaccessible and also because they would need their money for rebuilding. Businesses that were damaged might default on their loans. The credit union people need not have feared. In the weeks and months following the earthquake, the assets of the credit union grew as never before. Members added to their deposit accounts and new members joined. The tellers in the front office often heard variations on the same story: "This community needs help, and I know the credit union is committed to helping, so this is where my money is going." By the summer of 1990, the credit union's assets had grown by almost 50 percent, to about $18 million.

The credit union was founded in 1977 by a group of activists in Santa Cruz who had long been active in movements for environmental preservation and for expanding social services for the poor. From the beginning, the credit union had a political purpose, to serve as an agent of change in the county, to promote economic democracy, and the interests of poor and moderate-income people.

The emphasis in the Santa Cruz credit union is on community development, by which is meant support of local small businesses, nonprofits, other cooperatives, and affordable housing projects. For years, the credit union's goal was to lend 60 percent of its resources for community development purposes and just 40 percent for personal purposes. With the growth in assets and the restrictions on commercial lending by the examiners, the 60-40 policy had to be abandoned, but the community development portfolio continues to grow. The credit union has provided part of the financing to make possible several low-income cooperative housing complexes. It made the initial loans for an organic juice company that eventually developed a strong market position throughout northern California. It has supported Latino farmers in the southern part of the county who provide employment to some of the poorest people in the area. It has a strong record of supporting women-owned businesses and worker-owned collectives. It has become the lender of choice for businesses in the community that identify themselves as "progressive."

At the same time that it has stressed community development lending,

---

[11] My information on the Santa Cruz Community Credit Union comes from my experience on its board of directors.

the Santa Cruz credit union has pushed to expand financial services to its members. It is closer to being a full-service financial institution than most CDCUs are, with many different types of savings and checking accounts, automated teller machines and automated transactions services over the telephone, credit cards, money orders, traveler's checks, and other products. Its board has wanted to be able to demonstrate that the credit union could be a force for progressive social change, without having to ask its members to sacrifice in terms of convenience or return.

North East Jackson Area Federal Credit Union,[12] or NEJA, is housed in a trailer that sits on a rural route, surrounded by woods and peanut fields, on the front lawn at Mrs. Pearl Long's house outside Marianna, Florida. It is in the state's northwestern panhandle, just ten miles from the Alabama border and fifteen miles from Georgia.

NEJA is a small credit union, with about $650,000 in assets at last count and one full-time employee. Its 800 members are all African American, many of them farmers. It was founded in 1965 by the Office of Economic Opportunity, as part of the Johnson administration's "war on poverty." The founders were participants in the local civil rights struggles, and they saw the credit union as a way of freeing themselves from dependence on the white financial institutions of the region. Many of the other OEO credit unions begun at that time received financial and administrative support from a local community action agency, but NEJA was on its own from the beginning. It has therefore had to rely on volunteers most years, and only recently has been able to afford any paid help at all. The founders of the credit union included Mrs. Long's late husband, Gye Long. When he died in 1979, she took over the leadership. She is an unpaid volunteer, but she spends most days in the trailer taking care of the members' business.

NEJA has almost had to close several times, because of high delinquency rates on its loan repayments as well as low income. But each time it has managed to survive, thanks in part to the help of Ernest Johnson. Johnson, a civil rights veteran and director of credit unions for the Federation of Southern Cooperatives/Land Assistance Fund, advises, shepherds, and nurtures rural Black credit unions in the southeastern states. Over the years he has spent many weeks at NEJA reconciling the accounts, helping the board of directors develop policies, and doing battle with the federal examiners.

NEJA specializes in making crop loans to farmers, loans of between $5,000 and $20,000 with terms of about a year, for the purpose of allowing the farmer to buy seed, chemicals, fertilizer, and equipment. The credit

---

[12] I would like to thank Ruth Lockett and Mrs. Pearl Long for their gracious welcome when I visited NEJA. Ernest Johnson gave me further information of the credit union.

union provides better terms than the farmers can get from the local banks or from the suppliers.

Church-Affiliated Credit Unions

Many credit unions in the United States are affiliated with churches, their fields of membership being the members of a single church or, in some cases, the members of a number of churches (often of the same denomination) in a geographical area.

In mid-1991 there were 911 church credit unions, with a membership of 1.1 million people and total assets of $3.2 billion. The Baptist and the Roman Catholic churches have the largest number of credit unions.[13] No facet of American society is more segregated than the churches, and consequently most of the church-affiliated credit unions are ethnically homogeneous. Most that are CDCUs are African American. This is a result of the fact that the church is such a central institution, and church membership such an important part of one's identity, in many low-income African American communities.[14]

Not all church credit unions should be considered CDCUs. They serve their parishioners with basic banking services, but have no wider purpose of meeting the needs of low-income people or of community economic development. Some of them, however, explicitly consider themselves to be CDCUs, and others, which operate in predominantly low-income communities, perform much the same function as non-church CDCUs. Perry Henderson estimates that there were 191 black church credit unions in 1990,[15] and many of them regarded themselves as CDCUs. Other church credit unions operated in low-income Asian immigrant and Latino communities.

In 1991 the National Federation of Community Development Credit Unions conducted a "Church-Based Credit Union Study," funded by the Trinity Grants Program, followed by a "Church Credit Union Development Project," begun in 1992.[16] The study found that the leaders of the church credit unions saw themselves as providing a service essential to the mission

---

[13] National Federation of Community Development Credit Unions, "Interim Report: Church Credit Union Development Project."

[14] For a discussion of credit unions associated with African American Churches, see Henderson.

[15] Op. cit., 30.

[16] See "Interim Report: Church-Based Credit Union Study," 1990; "Final Report: Church-Based Credit Union Study," 1991; and "Interim Report: Church Credit Union Development Project," 1992 — all issued by the National Federation of Community Development Credit Unions, New York.

of the church. The church, they believe, is a community of people helping people, and the credit union is a concrete expression of this.

The D. Edward Wells Federal Credit Union, described above, originated in a Baptist congregation. A quite different example of a church CDCU is Family Federal Credit Union in Wilmington, California, near Los Angeles. It was chartered in 1983 and is affiliated with Holy Family Roman Catholic Church. Many of the church's—and the credit union's—members are immigrants from Latin America, attracted to the church because it offers masses in Spanish and because it sponsors an array of social services, dealing with food, jobs, children, housing, and immigration. The credit union is part of this broader program, helping immigrants establish a stake in their new country.

Tables 1.1, 1.2, and 1.3 in the next section show that church-affiliated credit unions represent about 30 percent of the country's CDCUs. They are predominantly urban, and mostly small in terms of both assets and members. Although small, they have the potential to be very important, particularly in low-income, urban, African American areas where the church is frequently the most intact, coherent voluntary institution.

A Statistical Portrait of CDCUs

This section paints a different sort of picture of the country's community development credit unions, using statistical information from the institutions' financial statements and census data from their neighborhoods. It shows the number, membership, asset size, and growth rates of the CDCUs, divided into different categories. It then looks at the income, poverty level, and racial composition of the neighborhoods in which they are located.

Comprehensive information about CDCUs can be culled from the semi-annual "call reports" that each federally-insured credit union files with the National Credit Union Administration (NCUA). At various times, researchers have selected the CDCUs from this large data set in order to develop a statistical profile. The set used in this study consists of 180 CDCUs reporting as of December 31, 1991.[17]

Additional information about CDCUs comes from an extensive survey questionnaire sent to about 400 low-income credit unions in 1986 as part of a joint study by the National Federation of Community Development Credit Unions and the federal Department of Health and Human Services.[18]

---

[17] For an explanation of how these credit unions were selected, see "A Note on the Data" in Chapter 5.

[18] Gore, Rosenthal, and Smith, a study prepared by the National Federation of Community Development Credit Unions and the Office of Community Services, Department of Health and Human Services.

Table 1.1
Number of Credit Unions by Category

180 Community Development Credit Unions
(Dec. 31, 1991)

	Church	Non-Church	Total
Assets up to $500K	35	54	89
Assets >$500K	19	72	91
Urban	47	67	114
Rural	7	59	66
NFCDCU	22	69	91
Non-NFCDCU	32	57	89
Total	**54**	**126**	**180**

Table 1.1 shows the distribution of the number of CDCUs by asset size, urban or rural location, membership in the National Federation, and church or non-church affiliation, at the end of 1991. Table 1.2 shows the CDCU assets in the same categories and Table 1.3 the members of the CDCUs. The three tables, plus Tables 1.4 and 1.5 were compiled by the author from the call reports.

Table 1.2
($ in Millions)

Total Assets in 180 Community Development Credit Unions
(Dec. 31, 1991)

	Church	Non-Church	Total
Assets up to $500K	6.6	9.7	16.3
Assets > $500K	26.0	260.5	286.5
Urban	29.4	155.4	184.8
Rural	3.1	114.8	117.9
NFCDCU	20.8	175.5	196.3
Non-NFCDCU	11.8	94.7	106.5
Total	**32.6**	**270.2**	**302.7**

Table 1.3
(Thousands)

Membership in 180 Community Development Credit Unions
(Dec. 31, 1991)

	Church	Non-Church	Total
Assets up to $500K	10.4	16.4	26.7
Assets > $500K	19.2	143.2	162.5
Urban	25.9	89.5	115.4
Rural	3.7	70.1	73.9
NFCDCU	18.6	97.4	115.9
Non-NFCDCU	11.0	62.2	73.3
Total	**29.6**	**159.6**	**189.2**

CDCUs are only a small portion of the credit union industry. At the end of 1991, the 180 CDCUs identified in these tables constituted just 1.3 percent of the country's 13,977 credit unions. Their 189,000 members were only 0.3 percent of the total credit union membership of 62.4 million. And their assets, $302.7 million, were a smaller portion yet, just 0.12 percent of total credit union assets, which stood at $244.5 billion.[19]

Table 1.1 shows that half of the CDCUs have less than a half million dollars in assets, and half more. A half million dollars is a very small size for a financial institution. With a gross rate of return of roughly 10 percent per annum, a credit union of that size generates an annual income of just $50,000, and that sum has to be divided among dividend payments to the savers, salary and other operating expenses, provision for loans that go into default, and reserves for the institution. There is not much to go around in a half million dollar credit union—and many CDCUs are much smaller than a half million, as Table 1.4 below shows.

About a third of the CDCUs are rural. Credit unions were classified by the author as rural if they were located in the countryside, or if they were located in a small town and their field of membership included a significant rural population. The majority of the CDCUs are urban, and of these, most are located in the centers of the country's large cities.

Half of the credit unions included in this data set are affiliated with the National Federation of CDCUs and half are not. Those that are affiliated tend to be somewhat larger.

---

[19]The industry-wide data are from Credit Union National Association, *Operating Ratios and Spreads: Year-End 1991*.

Table 1.4 allows a more detailed look at the size of the country's CDCUs. It shows the percentage distribution of the CDCUs by asset size, and, for comparison, the final column shows the size distribution of all credit unions in the United States as of December 31, 1991.

Table 1.4
(Percentages Total to 100)

Distribution of CDCUs by Asset Size
(Dec. 31, 1991)

Asset Size ($ in Millions)	All	Urban	Rural	Church	Non-Church	All CUs in the US
0.0 – 0.1	16	17	15	22	14	–
0.11 – 0.25	21	17	27	28	18	–
0.26 – 0.5	13	12	14	15	12	–
0.0 – 0.5 (total)	49	46	56	65	43	16
0.51 – 1.0	19	20	18	20	19	11
1.01 – 2.0	14	18	9	9	17	13
2.01 – 5.0	11	12	8	6	13	19
5.01 – 10.0	2	1	5	0	3	14
10.01 – 20.0	3	3	3	0	4	10
20.01 – 50.0	1	1	2	0	2	10
50.01 +	0	0	0	0	0	7

Almost half of the CDCUs had assets of less than a half million dollars at the end of 1991, compared to only 16 percent of the almost 14,000 credit unions in the country. Only 6 percent of the CDCUs had more than $5 million, compared to 41 percent of all credit unions. Within the CDCUs, the rural credit unions tended to be smaller than the urban, and the church-affiliated credit unions smaller than the secular. Taken as a whole, and with a few exceptions, community development credit unions are very small financial institutions.

In recent years, CDCUs have grown at rates roughly comparable to the rates of growth of other credit unions in the country. Table 1.5 shows annual growth rates for five- and ten-year periods ending in 1991. The rates are for the total assets of 152 CDCUs that existed throughout the decade. For comparison, the growth rate of assets in all federal credit unions over the same periods is shown.[20]

---

[20] The figures in the last row of Table 1.5 are simply the growth rates of all credit union assets, not matched to the CDCUs by size of credit union. Thus the figures are dominated by the largest credit unions in the country, credit unions larger than any CDCUs. See National Credit Union Administration, *1991 Annual Report*.

Table 1.5
Average Annual Percentage Growth Rates

Growth in CDCU Assets, 1981–1991

	1986–91	1981–91
Assets up to $500K	4.5	6.0
Assets >$500K	9.8	14.7
Church	4.4	8.9
Non-Church	8.2	13.8
Urban	10.3	14.1
Rural	8.3	13.6
Total CDCUs	9.4	13.9
All U.S. Federal CUs	8.2	12.3

Table 1.5 shows that the larger CDCUs grew faster than the smaller ones, the non-church faster than the church, and the urban a little faster than the rural. The calculated CDCU growth rates that are shown in the table have a bit of an upward bias,[21] and it is likely, therefore, that the true CDCU growth rates were even closer to the industry rates than the table shows.

Tables 1.6, 1.7, and 1.8 explore the income and racial characteristics of CDCU members. This is quite hard to do, and numerous difficulties arise in the interpretation of these tables. The problem is that credit unions keep no comprehensive records of the income and race of their members. Income but not race is recorded by borrowers on their loan applications, but this information remains in the loan files and is not compiled and revealed by the credit unions.

The strategy used in this section is to look at the characteristics not of the members themselves, but of the populations living in the neighborhoods where the credit unions are located.[22] This information is easily available from the national census. The procedure is valid to the extent that the credit union members are representative of the neighborhood population.

Two principal problems exist with this method. First, the author had to use the 1980 census, since the detailed compilations from the 1990 census were not available at the time the research was done, and therefore the infor-

---

[21] They are based on the records of 153 credit unions that existed continuously over the decade 1981-1991. Yet over that same period the total number of CDCUs fell. Using the same methods for identifying CDCUs as were used in 1991, there were 222 CDCUs in 1981, 219 in 1986, and 180 in 1991. In other words, of the 222 CDCUS that could be identified in 1981, 72 had been liquidated or merged by 1991, and only 27 new ones had been chartered.

[22] Thanks to Chhorn Be for her help in compiling the data on CDCU neighborhoods.

mation is dated. Second, the information on the rural neighborhoods is not at all comparable with the information on the urban neighborhoods. In these tables the rural income levels are significantly higher, and the poverty rates and non-white proportions significantly lower, than is doubtless the case for the actual CDCU memberships.[23] Nevertheless, Tables 1.6 through 1.8 give at least an indication of the characteristics of the CDCU members.

In 1980, the median family income in the country was $19,917, the poverty rate 12.4 percent, and the non-white population 15.1 percent of the total. Table 1.6 shows that the 114 urban credit unions serve neighborhoods that were significantly poorer than the rest of the country, with higher poverty levels and non-white populations. All of these tendencies are accentuated in the case of the church-affiliated credit unions, most of which are in African American, central-city neighborhoods.

Table 1.7 shows similar information for the 66 rural CDCUs, although, as noted above, Table 1.7 is not directly comparable with Table 1.6. It does show, however, that the rural CDCUs are located in relatively poor and non-white communities.

Table 1.8 compares the CDCUs' neighborhoods to the national averages. In the case of the urban CDCUs, 90 percent are in neighborhoods whose median family income was less than the national median family income in the 1980 census, and 40 percent are in neighborhoods whose me-

---

[23] In the cities, the census presents information by census tract. The tracts are quite small neighborhood areas, with generally just a few thousand people. Census tracts are not specified for most rural areas or small towns, however, and so in the case of the rural credit unions the neighborhood was taken to be the small town, or in some cases the county, in which the institution was located. Thus the information on rural populations is not directly comparable to the information on urban dwellers in Tables 1.6, 1.7, and 1.8. In particular, a naive use of these tables would seem to indicate that the rural credit union members are somewhat better off than the city dwellers. As Chapter 6 shows, this is probably not the case. There is another difficulty in comparing the rural and urban areas. Central cities tend to be quite segregated by race and by income levels, while rural areas are not. Nevertheless, many of the rural credit unions serve a specific racial or income group. One may compare, for example, the St. James AME Credit Union in Newark, New Jersey, an urban, church-affiliated organization, with NEJA, the North East Jackson Area Federal Credit Union, located outside Marianna, Florida. St James is an African American church, and the membership of the credit union is almost totally African American. This is reflected in the census tract in which it is located, where in 1980, 95.1 percent of the population was non-white (compared to the national average of 15.1 percent), the median family income was $5,417 (compared to a national average of $19,917), and 68 percent of the people were living in poverty (compared to the national average of 12.4 percent). In the case of the Florida credit union, the closest neighborhood described by the census is Jackson County, where the 1980 population was 33.7 percent non-white, with a median family income of $13,212, and 23.9 percent of the population in poverty. One expects that the Newark census tract figures reflect the St. James membership reasonably accurately (although no doubt some church members commute from a distance), but the Jackson County figures do not reflect NEJA's membership at all closely. In fact, the NEJA members are entirely African American and, as Chapter 6 shows, quite poor. In sum, the figures for the urban credit unions in the tables probably reflect those credit unions' memberships fairly well, while the rural figures represent significant overestimates of the members' incomes, and underestimates of the poverty levels and the proportion that are non-white. The rural figures are included nonetheless because, even with those significant biases, they show that the rural credit unions are in relatively poor communities.

dian family income was less than half the national median. The other urban numbers are even more striking. Almost two-thirds of the CDCUs are in neighborhoods with greater than twice the national average poverty rate, and three-quarters are in neighborhoods with twice the national average of non-white population. The rural figures show a similar picture, although, again, they are not directly comparable with the urban figures.

Table 1.6
(Average Neighborhood Characteristics, 1980)

114 Urban Community Development Credit Unions*

	All	Church	Non-Church
Median family income	$12,348	$10,792	$13,458
Persons in poverty	31.7%	37.6%	27.4%
Non-white	64.2%	79.6%	53.3%

* Source, 1980 Census of Population.

Together, Tables 1.6, 1.7, and 1.8 demonstrate that CDCUs are located in neighborhoods that are significantly poorer and more non-white than the rest of the country. On the reasonable assumption that their members come largely from the surrounding neighborhoods, it is clear that they serve people who are in particular need.

Table 1.7
(Average Neighborhood Characteristics, 1980)

66 Rural Community Development Credit Unions*

	All	Church	Non-Church
Median family income	$13,558	$15,717	$13,298
Persons in poverty	24.1%	18.6%	24.7%
Non-white	36.4%	22.2%	38.1%

* Source, 1980 Census of Population.

Other sources of information confirm this. Chapter 6 reports the results of extensive sampling in the loan files of seven CDCUs, conducted by the author and several research assistants. The reported incomes of the borrowers were quite low in most of the credit unions. A 1986 survey by the National Federation of CDCUs asked the managers of 400 low-income credit unions to estimate their members' incomes. While the estimates were probably based on rough impressions from loan applications, still, in a year in which the national median household income was $23,618, and the median household income in all of the country's credit unions was $32,360, the low-income credit unions reported that 75 percent of their members' household incomes were under $20,000, and 44 percent were under $10,000. They reported that 14 percent of their members were unemployed, 20 percent received public assistance, and over 60 percent were non-white.[24]

Table 1.8
(Percentage of Credit Union Neighborhoods)

Comparison of CDCU Neighborhoods to National Averages*

Neighborhood Characteristic	Urban	Rural
Median family income < $9,959	40	15
Median family income < $19,917	90	92
Poverty rate > 24.8%	66	38
Poverty rate > 12.4%	88	82
Non-white population > 30.2%	76	55
Non-white population > 15.1%	83	78

* Source, 1980 Census of Population.

Information from a variety of sources makes it clear beyond a doubt, therefore, that the members of CDCUs are much poorer than Americans generally.

In summary, community development credit unions are a very small component of the nation's financial structure, but their growth is keeping pace with the growth of other credit unions. The majority of CDCUs are secular; a minority are church-affiliated. The majority are urban, a minority rural. They serve people who are poorer than other Americans, and their members are largely, although not exclusively, non-white.

The next two chapters explore the history of community development credit unions.

---

[24] Gore, Rosenthal, and Smith.

Appendix: Cooperative Principles and Credit Unions

This chapter asserts that credit unions are cooperative institutions, and so they are. Some difficulties arise, however, in applying the classical cooperative principles to the credit union form.

As Chapter 2 will discuss, credit unions developed in the nineteenth century as a part of the more general European cooperative movement. Many of the original German credit associations had close connections to other kinds of cooperatives, particularly of producers. While there were tensions between the different types of cooperatives and their leaders, there was also a good deal of mutual support. In twentieth-century United States, however, credit unions developed apart from other cooperatives.

Over the years, a set of cooperative principles has emerged from the experiences of the cooperative movement. They are sometimes referred to as the Rochdale Principles, since they were derived from the practices of the consumer cooperative that was founded in Rochdale, England in 1844. In fact, however, the Rochdale pioneers never established a definitive set of principles to guide their store; the closest they came was a very long list of rules, some of them completely specific to their own situation. It was left to contemporary and later writers to try to codify the Rochdale experience into principles. These principles have been widely accepted within the various cooperative movements, but they have changed considerably over time. The International Cooperative Alliance brought some order to the subject in 1931 by adopting seven principles that a committee of inquiry thought to have been at the heart of the Rochdale store almost a century earlier. In 1966 these principles were amended by the ICA into a group of six that were "to be considered as essential to genuine and effective cooperation practice both at the present time and in the future as far as can be foreseen."[25] They are:

1. Open, voluntary membership. There is to be no discrimination and no coercion in joining the cooperative. All who are able and willing to participate are welcome.

2. Democratic control, or one person, one vote. Voting is by person, not by number of shares held.

3. Strictly limited rate of interest on share capital. Members buy shares in the cooperative in order to provide the capital it needs, not in order to speculate on profits.

4. Patronage refund. Surplus earnings, above the return to shares and above the funds set aside for the cooperative's reserve and for

---
[25] Bonner, 309.

common services, are returned to the members in proportion to their patronage, or transactions with the cooperative. The patronage refund is a way of protecting the financial stability of a consumer cooperative while keeping costs to the members low. The cooperative initially charges the same price on goods as other stores; if it makes a profit, however, the patronage refund has the effect of reducing prices retroactively.

5. Member education. A cooperative has the responsibility to educate its members in the principles of cooperation, both economic and democratic.
6. Cooperation among cooperatives. Just as individuals cooperate within an institution, so do the institutions cooperate among themselves, to develop the cooperative movement.

The first two principles define the cooperative as a democracy, the second two ensure that the cooperative's earnings are used for its members' benefit, and the last two provide for the development of the cooperative movement.

The adoption of these principles by the ICA did not end the controversy about the definition of a cooperative because a number of cooperative associations violate one or more of the rules. As an example, the first principle, open membership, is difficult for many producers' cooperatives to adhere to, and impossible for a workers' or a housing cooperative. A less constraining set of guidelines has been proposed by the United States Department of Agriculture, as defining cooperatives:[26]

1. Services at cost to member-patrons.
2. Democratic control by member-patrons.
3. Limited returns on equity capital.

The USDA guidelines eliminate the first, fifth, and sixth Rochdale Principles, and interpret the fourth, the patronage refund, more broadly as simply services at cost. Yet even this broader set of principles is of almost no relevance to a worker cooperative, with the exception of the provision for democratic control. And financial cooperatives—credit unions—adhere to the first two USDA guidelines but would appear to violate the third.

How well can credit unions fit within these defining cooperative principles? The first two ICA principles present no problems. Credit unions are voluntary associations, open to everyone within a defined field of membership, with the exception of those who have demonstrated that they are inca-

---
[26] Schaaf, 12.

pable of or unwilling to undertake the necessary responsibilities. They are democratic organizations, with a board of directors elected by the members.

The third and fourth ICA principles seem problematic for credit unions. People who deposit money in the credit union become the owners of the credit union, and the tradition in the United States is that the deposits are consequently called "shares." The rate of interest on share capital is not fixed and strictly limited, as the third ICA principle would appear to call for. Members receive a variable dividend on their shares, a dividend which is not fixed by contract but which depends instead upon the surplus earnings of the credit union. This would seem to violate the very idea of a cooperative, that the proceeds of the business should not accrue to capital but rather to the members.

The interpretation of the third and fourth principles in a financial cooperative is, however, ambiguous. The fourth principle is that the surplus earnings of the cooperative should be returned to the members in proportion to the transactions they have conducted with the association, thus in effect retroactively reducing the price of those transactions. But a principal way in which members transact business with a credit union is by depositing funds in it. The other principal way of conducting business is by borrowing. And credit union law permits the surplus earnings of a credit union to be returned to the members in proportion to their deposits, and/or in proportion to the interest that they have paid on their loans. Thus the distribution of the surplus could be seen to be a patronage refund, and not a variable return on shares. If the structure of a credit union is interpreted generously, therefore, the institution can be seen as falling well within the classical definition of a cooperative.

In fact, however, the ICA principles are strictly appropriate only for a consumer cooperative, while most other types of cooperatives have to stretch a little or a great deal to fit completely under their tent. The USDA principles are completely appropriate for agricultural producer cooperatives, but not for all others.

It may be impossible to find a set of principles that would comprehend worker cooperatives as well as all of the other types. The difficulty is that the basic purpose of a worker cooperative is to generate income for its members, not to provide services at cost. The following three principles will probably suffice to describe the other types of cooperatives, and to distinguish them from other forms of business organizations:

1. Ownership. A cooperative is an institution owned by the people who use its services.

2. Democracy. Control is exercised on a one-person-one-vote basis.

3. Services are provided to the members at cost.

If these three principles are the essence of a cooperative, then the nineteenth-century German "people's banks," and also the modern credit unions that evolved from the German antecedents, fit well within the cooperative movement.

28 THIN CATS

CHAPTER 2

THE ORIGINS OF COOPERATIVE FINANCE

Credit unions were born of adversity.
—Jack Dublin[1]

The credit unions, if they are to win lasting success, must absolutely not get themselves mixed up with charity cases; for they are not designed to support the poor, but what is more important—to prevent poverty.
—Hermann Schulze-Delitzsch[2]

The credit granted by the [Schulze-Delitzsch] cooperative unions should be eminently a "productive" credit, to be employed in carrying on or extending one's business, and not to be eaten up in unproductive consumption.
—Richard T. Ely, 1881[3]

Most community development credit unions in the United States were formed within the last several decades. A few were founded in the 1940s, but the first major development came with the War on Poverty in the 1960s. The history of cooperative financial institutions goes back much earlier, however. The first American credit union was established in New Hampshire in 1909, and before that the first credit union on the North

---

[1] Dublin, 142.

[2] Quoted in Tucker, 50.

[3] Ely, 220.

American continent appeared in Levis, Quebec, in 1900. The North American credit unions trace their roots, in turn, to the cooperative credit societies that were begun in Germany in 1850 and grew rapidly throughout Europe in the second half of the nineteenth century.[4]

It is useful to consider the historical evolution of credit unions, and not just for reasons of antiquarian curiosity. The early cooperative credit societies had a distinctive purpose; they were established in order to protect groups of people whose livelihoods were threatened by economic forces over which they had no control. As credit unions grew and prospered, however, their social contexts, their structures, and even their basic purposes changed, never abruptly but slowly and relentlessly. From agents of social change they evolved into institutions that provided a useful service to members, but they did not challenge the economic and social structures in which they were embedded. In fundamental ways, modern CDCUs are rejecting many of these recent changes and are attempting to return to at least some of the original principles of the credit union founders.

Nineteenth-Century Cooperatives

Credit unions are cooperative financial institutions. While in the late twentieth-century United States most of them stand quite separate from other types of cooperatives, in mid-nineteenth-century Europe they were part of the cooperative movement more generally.

Cooperatives began as a response to the excesses of free market capitalism. Capitalism broke apart the traditional bonds that had connected people to their workplaces and to rural and urban communities. These bonds had often been exploitative—for example, the bond between a lord and his serf—but they had created what seemed at the time to be unbreakable connections between people. The capitalist, industrial revolution shattered those bonds, creating individual workers, or "hands," who were free to sell their labor for whatever it could bring, but for whom the society as a whole had no specific responsibility. Industrial capitalism brought with it individual freedom, both the freedom to rise above the ocean and the freedom to sink beneath it. It brought newly-prosperous mill owners and traders, and it brought stinking cities, child labor, epidemics, and early death.

To a large extent, therefore, the history of social movements in nineteenth-century Europe is a history of attempts by people to join together, to combine their resources to create safe havens against the onslaught of individualism. Some aspects of the movements were reactionary, in the sense that they were defensive and ultimately futile attempts to preserve social

---

[4] The history of American credit unions and their predecessors is outlined in Moody and Fite.

relationships that were inexorably passing. Other parts were progressive, pointing the way to forms of collective organization that would thrive in the twentieth century. Among these social movements, all of which were at the same time reactionary and progressive, were the beginnings of the welfare state, the beginnings of trade unionism, and the beginnings of cooperatives.

Cooperatives appeared in different sectors. The leaders of the various cooperative associations knew of each other and had some personal connections, but the movements they established were separate, and they led to quite different types of cooperatives in the twentieth century, including communal societies as well as consumer, producer, worker, housing, and financial cooperatives.

Robert Owen's community at New Lanark in Scotland and his subsequent colony at New Harmony in Indiana were early examples of planned communal societies in which all components of social life—not just work, purchasing, selling, or borrowing—were organized collectively. The early utopian socialist experiments such as Owen's failed eventually, but they had a strong influence on twentieth-century communes, ranging from the highly structured Israeli kibbutzim to back-to-the-earth settlements of young Americans in the 1960s and after. The other types of nineteenth-century cooperatives, more limited in scope than the communes, can point to a more continuous chain of success. Modern consumer cooperatives trace their origins to the Rochdale, England, cooperative store, founded in 1844. Producer cooperatives, formed predominantly by independent farmers, were created throughout Europe and later North America, for the purposes of purchasing supplies jointly and/or selling produce. Worker cooperatives—firms owned and controlled by their laborers—arose in France and Italy, and to a lesser extent in other countries of continental Europe.

At the same time that consumer, producer, and worker cooperatives were first appearing, financial cooperatives originated in Germany. Initially they were associated with producer cooperatives.

Schulze-Delitzsch and Raiffeisen

Two visionaries were responsible for the founding of the German credit unions, F. Hermann Schulze-Delitzsch (1808-1883) and Friedrich Wilhelm Raiffeisen (1818-1888).[5] The Schulze-Delitzsch credit unions, called Volksbanken, or people's banks, were urban, while the Raiffeisen credit unions, called loan associations, were rural. Both types of associations grew substantially in the second half of the nineteenth century in Germany; both created national organizations and both spread to other countries of conti-

---

[5] On the origins of cooperative credit in Germany, see Ely; Wolff; Tucker; and Aschhoff and Henningsen.

nental Europe. They shared a number of characteristics, but in some important respects they differed.

Schulze-Delitzsch was at times a judge and a liberal political leader from a part of eastern Germany that was originally in Saxony but was incorporated in his lifetime into Prussia.[6] Moved by the distress of his countrymen in the economic crash of 1846-47, he searched for ways to improve the lot of craftsmen and shopkeepers. His first project was a cooperative insurance fund for craftspeople; his second, a cooperative leather-buying club for shoemakers. Both were producers' cooperatives, associations of independent producers who joined together for certain limited commercial goals. The shoemakers discovered that if they bought their leather in bulk they could achieve a price reduction of about 15 percent, even after paying the administrative expenses of the buying club. They faced a barrier, however; they lacked the funds to make the bulk purchase. They required credit, and had no access to it. As a consequence, Schulze-Delitzsch turned his attention to the question of credit.

At this point, he made the first of many decisions that were to have an important impact on the subsequent development of the credit union movement. The shoemakers' buying cooperative could have extended its operations into the area of credit, but Schulze-Delitzsch decided that the two functions, purchasing and credit, should be kept completely separate. The shoemakers would get the best price on their purchases of leather if they paid cash, if the seller did not have to assume any risk. The risk inherent in borrowing should be isolated in a separate institution. Schulze-Delitzsch therefore established the first people's bank in 1850 at Delitzsch, the precursor to what is now known as a credit union. Thus the pattern was set for the credit union movement to develop separately from the more general cooperative movement.

The main problem to be confronted was the source of the funds. Those in need of loans, the craftsmen and artisans, did not have surplus savings to lend to each other. Schulze-Delitzsch's first solution to this problem was to solicit the equivalent of $140 in capital from several of his well-off friends, who were given the title of honorary members. The funds were then available for lending to those who needed them, called the beneficiaries, with the proviso that the beneficiaries were required to contribute five cents a month to the capital of the institution.

This first scheme was not successful, but in its structure it anticipated

---

[6] Born Hermann Schulze, he added Delitzsch, the name of his home town, to his surname when he became a member of Parliament at Berlin, in order to distinguish himself from the many other Schulzes he encountered in political life (Tucker, 29). The account of Schulze-Delitzsch's banking innovations from 1850 to 1852 in the paragraphs that follow comes from Tucker.

the later cooperative credit associations. Two features distinguished it from the charitable loan associations that existed at the time in Germany. The borrowers were required to be members of the association, not just customers of it, and they were required to save as a condition of borrowing. So from the beginning, the Schulze-Delitzsch banks were cooperatives established for the purpose of saving as well as borrowing.

The first Delitzsch people's bank failed because a number of the loans were not repaid, and because the honorary members, the benefactors of the bank, gradually withdrew. Schulze-Delitzsch was absent for about a year on a judicial assignment in another town; he returned to discover that the only remaining members were the beneficiaries and that the bank had collapsed.

He then turned to the example of a similar financial cooperative, founded, also in 1850, by a colleague in the nearby town of Eilenburg. At Eilenburg, wealthy patrons were not allowed; the only members were working and small business people, each of whom was required to make a more substantial contribution to the bank's capital.

In 1852, then, Schulze-Delitzsch founded the people's bank in Delitzsch, the model on which subsequent credit unions would be based. The initial requirement was an entrance fee equivalent to $2.50, and each member pledged eventually to purchase a $12.00 share in installments. In other words, there was considerable emphasis upon member savings. The funds saved by the members were still insufficient to meet the loan demand, however, and so the bank had to borrow additional money. The decision was made not to depend upon the charity of wealthy benefactors, but instead to borrow on commercial terms from regular banks and depositors.

In order to secure these loans, the association adopted the principle of unlimited liability. Under normal corporate law, the doctrine of limited liability means that an investor is liable only for the amount of his or her share investment, and cannot be held personally responsible for the debts of the corporation. Under unlimited liability, as practiced in the Schulze-Delitzsch banks, the members were collectively responsible for the outside debts. With the pledge of unlimited liability, the cooperative was able to secure all the loans it needed.

The Schulze-Delitzsch people's banks were democratic unions, each member having one vote. They were regarded as non-profit institutions, and as such were not taxed.

Schulze-Delitzsch spent the rest of his life, until his death in 1883, promoting his people's banks. From his seat in the Prussian House of Representatives, and then in the German Reichstag, he advanced the legal framework for cooperative banking. He wrote books and newspaper columns advocating the banks. He organized the Universal Federation of German Cooperative Societies, of which the largest number of member organizations were his people's banks. The banks grew in number to more than a thousand by the end of the century, and membership was more than half a million.

Friedrich Wilhelm Raiffeisen's rural loan associations began at the same time as those of Schulze-Delitzsch and developed more slowly, but his movement eventually became considerably larger.[7] Raiffeisen, born in poverty, rose to become mayor of several towns in the western Rhineland area, but he retired in 1863 at the age of 45 because of poor eyesight. Both before and after his retirement, he devoted most of his energy to the development of institutions to help small farmers. Like Schulze-Delitzsch's first efforts, Raiffeisen's initial institutions were based upon the charity of the well-to-do. In 1849 in Flammersfeld, where he was mayor, he organized a union of 60 wealthy citizens who held themselves jointly liable for borrowed funds which they in turn lent to poor farmers. This model was repeated several times, but Raiffeisen eventually lost faith in it. Under this scheme it was the wealthy patrons, not the poor farmers, who controlled the institution, and while the institution was useful to some of the farmers, it was not a cooperative. In 1862, Raiffeisen turned to the organizational structure that had been pioneered by Schulze-Delitzsch, and founded the first German rural credit cooperative. The Raiffeisen movement expanded quickly in the 1880s, and it eventually became substantially larger than the Schulze-Delitzsch movement.

The Social Bases of the Early German Credit Unions

The Schulze-Delitzsch and the Raiffeisen banks were both directed towards people who were being victimized by the economic changes in nineteenth-century Germany. They were established for the purpose of changing social relationships. One should not leap from this to the conclusion, however, that they always represented the interests of poor people, for their role was rather more ambiguous than that.[8]

Their leaders were not poor people. Schulze-Delitzsch was born into a substantial family in a small village, and was well educated in preparation for a career in the law and politics. Raiffeisen came from a once well-off background—his father had been a minister and village mayor—although his father's alcoholism and early death left the family in difficult circumstances. Interestingly, the subsequent founders of national credit union movements—Luigi Luzatti and Leone Wallemborg in Italy, Louis Durand and Charles Rayneri in France, Alphonse Desjardins in French Canada, and Ed-

---

[7] The material on the Raiffeisen rural loan associations comes primarily from Wolff.

[8] On the social bases of the early German cooperative associations, see Fairbairn and Rudin.

ward Filene in the United States—were men of commerce or the professions.[9] Credit union movements were not founded by the poor.

To understand the role of the early cooperative credit associations, it is helpful to know something about how German society was changing in the middle of the nineteenth century. The Germany into which the credit associations were introduced was socially backward by comparison with England, France, and the United States in the same period. Not only was the population poorer, its social structure was much closer to medieval feudalism. The country of Germany did not even exist. A unified state was created under Prussia by Count Bismarck's wars of 1864, 1866, and 1870. Prior to that time, "Germany" consisted of a series of rival principalities. While the strict feudal division of labor of earlier centuries had broken down somewhat, the remnants were still very strong.

Until the beginning of the nineteenth century, production in the German towns was organized in rigid guilds, membership in which was compulsory for craftspeople. The guilds enforced detailed rules about apprenticeship, product design, working hours, and all other aspects of economic and even social life, for the purpose of achieving security and equality for the guild members. In the countryside, the land was controlled by the nobility and worked by the semi-free serfs. Between those two classes was a "petite bourgeoisie" of small-scale commercial and professional people, dependent upon the powerful landholders. The legal basis of feudalism was abolished only at the beginning of the nineteenth century. Freedom of trade was allowed in the cities, and in the countryside serfdom was replaced by land ownership. It was one thing to change the legal system, however, and quite another to transform the social system. In the towns, the guilds still survived well into the nineteenth century, and artisans still carried on their trades. In the agricultural sector, serfdom was replaced by overwhelming debt in many cases, since the newly independent farmers were required to pay for their land. In England, feudalism had been dissolved by the industrial and commercial revolutions, but in Germany the artisan and peasant populations still predominated. Barrington Moore has made the argument that fascism emerged in twentieth-century Germany because industrial technology was imposed on a social structure that was still feudal.[10]

If mid-nineteenth-century Germany was still influenced by feudalism, however, that feudalism was not secure; it was under sharp challenge by the forces of corporate capitalism. The new freedoms of movement and associa-

---

[9] See Rudin.

[10] Moore.

tion were eroding the guild and peasant economies. Large-scale production in factories was threatening the livelihoods of the urban artisans, and commercial farming was beginning to squeeze out the small farmers and peasants. The clash between two economic systems — the feudalism of the past versus the capitalism of the future — was leaving victims in its wake, people whose way of life, while never comfortable, had at least been secure in the recent past.

The cooperative credit movement was a response to this social conflict. It was an unclear and ambiguous response by people who could not fully understand the character of the social change that was buffeting them. In part, the movement can be understood as an attempt to restore the certainties of the feudal world, but in part it was an attempt to soften the hard edges of corporate capitalism. It was not primarily a movement of poor or working-class people, but of threatened intermediate classes. A German historian, Erwin Hasselmann, writes:

> ...the first German attempts at cooperation were made by farmers, peasants and artisans whose outlook was typically middle-class and whose main concern...was the defense of their independent middle-class existence against the overpowering competition of large scale capitalist enterprises.[11]

Schulze-Delitzsch was a man of strong humanitarian bent. He was by no means a revolutionary, however; as Fairbairn shows, he saw his people's banks as a way of forestalling radical social movements. He actively opposed working-class cooperative movements,[12] whether of producers or consumers, finding them too radical. The members of his banks were not the urban poor, but rather the class of craftspeople whose livelihoods were under attack. They were in danger of losing their shops and falling into poverty, but they were not poor. The contemporary English writer Henry Wolff, while an admirer of most aspects of the people's banks, nevertheless sensed that they were not established for the benefit of the poor in the way that the English consumer cooperatives were. Referring to the share requirement that was a condition of membership, he wrote:

---

[11] Quoted in Fairbairn, 69. Note that Hasselmann uses the term "middle-class" not in the modern American sense of comfortably salaried employees, but to refer to the feudal classes of artisans and producers who were situated socially between the aristocracy and the serfs.

[12] Ibid.

> ...it is altogether contrary to our idea of co-operation, that the humblest classes, the working men proper, should be excluded and bidden to wait outside until they have accumulated sufficient funds to qualify themselves for membership...There are working men, no doubt, in the Schulze-Delitzsch associations; but only in very small proportion...The bulk of the members is nearly everywhere made up of small tradesmen, small landowners, and men of similar independent or quasi-independent position...[13]

Schulze-Delitzsch should not be libeled as the reactionary that some of his countrymen were, however. He was not calling for the restoration of the feudal guilds and manors. He was rather of the school of the English classical economists, believing in capitalism, technology, markets, and competition. Like the classical economists, he believed that the public welfare was best promoted by a large number of small enterprises, not by a few monopolistic giants. He saw the loans made by the people's banks as a way of promoting small-scale capitalism.[14] Of course, small-scale capitalism was destined to lose out to large-scale corporate capitalism by the end of the nineteenth century, but to argue for it was not at all the same as to argue for the restoration of feudalism.

Raiffeisen was more backward looking than Schulze-Delitzsch. It is true that his rural loan associations were accessible to a poorer group of people because they imposed no share requirements on members. Rudin argues, however, that in Germany, as later in France and then in Quebec, the leadership of most rural cooperative credit associations was largely in the hands of the petite bourgeoisie, the men of the professions, commerce, and the church. Their motive was to keep small farmers on the land, because their own social position depended upon the continued existence of a subservient agricultural class.[15] They really did yearn for an earlier era, in which they imagined their own positions were more comfortable.

In keeping with this backward, quasi-feudal orientation, Rudin argues, the Raiffeisen associations were imbued with a conservative, moralistic, Christian ethic, quite different from the secularism inherent in modern business. It was an ethic which glorified hard work and sober habits as well as deference to authority. It called for neighborly love. An important feature of the Raiffeisen associations was that they were usually restricted to a single

---

[13] Wolff, 102.

[14] Tucker, 51-55.

[15] Rudin, op. cit.

rural parish, and were sponsored by and reinforced the position of the pastor.

The Raiffeisen associations were also imbued with the sexism and the anti-Semitism that were endemic to German rural life. They did not allow membership by married women because they were restricted to people who were independent. As to their anti-Semitism, they did not have the explicitly racist political agendas that some other German rural cooperative groups had. But they saw their mission as that of combating usury, and the usurer they identified was the Jew. A pastor in the province of Kurhessen who led a Raiffeisen association said in 1881, "How much do the Jews here want to take part in our cooperative? I will never offer them my hand, for that would violate the purpose of the cooperative."[16] Completely blind to the implications of what he was hearing, the good English cooperator, Henry Wolff, wrote in 1893 of his travels in Raiffeisen's area, "...from one and all, here, there and everywhere, have I heard the self-same, ever-repeated bitter complaint, that the villages were being sucked dry by the 'Jews.' Usury laws, police regulations, warnings and monitions have all been tried as remedies, and tried in vain."[17] In 1903, a German political leader remarked, "As far as I know, all Raiffeisen men are anti-Semitic."

Thus humanitarian motives were mixed with class self-interest and racism in the early German credit unions in ways that were complicated. The credit unions were partially a reactionary attempt to restore a social order that was being defeated, and they were partially a progressive attempt to provide resources for people who were threatened by the new capitalist order. They were partially a self-interested movement by people of some position who felt those positions threatened, and partially a disinterested movement on behalf of the poor. The ambiguous class basis and ideology of the early credit unions are relevant to this study, because in some ways today's community development credit unions are echoing the principles of the founders—although not necessarily consciously—and rejecting some of the deviations from those principles that have been made by modern mainstream credit unions. CDCUs focus on community development, and many of them lend for the purpose of promoting small businesses. They attempt to bring outside resources into their communities. Their leaders are committed to social change. They would do well to remember, therefore, that when these ideas were put into practice in an earlier era they were accompanied by attitudes and practices that are frightening, at least from the perspective of the twentieth cen-

---

[16] On anti-Semitism in the rural credit unions, see Peal. This quote, and the last one in this paragraph, come from this source.

[17] Wolff, 112.

tury. The German cooperative loan associations led to modern credit unions, but the anti-Semitism they professed led to the Holocaust.

Needless to say, rural Alabama and central Philadelphia in the 1990s are very different places from a German agricultural village or town of the 1850s. So the parallels are not exact, but they are suggestive. No evidence exists at all that modern CDCUs are anti-Semitic, but they may need to guard against ethnic chauvinism that merges into discrimination. They are certainly not trying to restore a feudal order, but they may need to remind themselves at times that all of their members have equal rights. CDCUs have been strongly influenced by the Civil Rights movement and by other egalitarian movements for social change, and it was often for that reason that their founders chose the form of a cooperative credit union, with its promise of democracy and universality. Still, the danger exists that the narrowly-defined common bond of a credit union can lead to parochialism.

Principles of the Early Credit Unions

The bank that Schulze-Delitzsch reorganized in 1852 had a set of six principles,[18] and these principles stayed at the defining core of his movement:

1. The exclusion of charity. The bank was to be operated as a business.
2. The joint and unlimited liability of all members for the bank's debts.
3. Outside funds to be borrowed by the bank on the basis of this joint liability.
4. Loans made only to those who could use the funds productively.
5. Regular contributions by the members to the bank's working capital.
6. A broad membership, not limited by area, occupation, or class (this principle was added later).

The first four principles, but not the last two, were eventually adopted by the Raiffeisen loan associations. A consideration of these principles will help to show the relevance of these early credit unions to the community development credit unions of today.

---

[18] See Tucker, 48.

The first principle—the exclusion of charity and its replacement by business practices—was central to the associations. Without this principle, they would not have developed as cooperatives. It is doubtful that they would have developed much at all since the scope of charity is inherently limited, while in the century and a half since the founding of the movement, people's own resources have grown at an extraordinary rate.

That both movements began by depending upon charity is, however, telling. Both Schulze-Delitzsch and Raiffeisen turned naturally to people of their own class to help alleviate the social distress they saw around them. And their friends came through, motivated, one suspects, both by compassion and by self-interest. It was only after the experience of depending upon the charity of the rich that both movements decided to exclude charity. The rich were too fickle, the founders discovered. They might withdraw their funds at any time, if repayment problems arose or if the political fashions of the moment took a reactionary tilt. The people's banks excluded charity not because help was unneeded but because the need was too great to depend upon dilettantes. People in distress would have to obtain the resources they needed not by supplication but by contractual agreement.

Today's CDCUs do not reject "charity." They sometimes receive grants from foundations, and they often receive deposits from socially responsible investors that are at below-market interest rates and therefore have a component of charity. Charity never dominates, however; CDCUs are first and foremost private businesses whose success depends upon their ability to keep their income in balance with their expenses. While they do not adopt the first German principle exactly, they are still business entities run on commercial principles.

The second and third principles, adhered to by both German movements, were that the members were jointly and completely liable for the repayment of the funds that were borrowed by the association. This was at the heart of the organizations.

It was completely clear to both Schulze-Delitzsch and Raiffeisen that groups of small, struggling artisans or farmers required outside funds.[19] Whether or not they could contribute some capital themselves, the amounts they would be able to provide would not be sufficient to meet their needs, and they would have to look beyond their own resources. Self-sufficiency was not an option. A principal purpose, therefore, of the early people's banks was to draw outside funds into communities that needed them—not as charitable donations, but as loans to be repaid.

This purpose is foreign to most modern American credit unions. They

---

[19] See Tucker; Wolff.

are permitted to borrow outside funds, under strictly defined terms, but few make much use of this. Under current laws, most are expressly forbidden from accepting non-member deposits, deposits from people and institutions that are outside their fields of membership. An exception is made in the case of a small number of low-income credit unions which are permitted to accept non-member deposits in an amount not to exceed 20 percent of assets (occasionally, higher waivers are granted). These exceptions are insignificant, however, compared both with the use that the German pioneers made of outside funds, and with the potential that CDCUs could make of outside funds were they permitted to do so.[20]

Once the German credit unions had excluded charity from the well-to-do as a source of outside funds, they had no option but to borrow money on commercial terms from banks and other lenders and depositors. Borrowing required the pledging of some form of security, however, and this the members lacked as individuals. They came to the conclusion that the associations could have access to the funds they needed only if the members jointly pledged to repay those funds. In 1866, Raiffeisen wrote:

> *The members' most important duty, upon which the existence of the societies is based, is liability. In order to obtain the credit-worthiness for the funds needed by the societies for their operation it is inevitable that liability be shared by the members on the basis of solidarity, and that among them all be liable for one and one for all.*[21]

Unlimited liability did not mean that each member was responsible for each other member's loan from the cooperative. An individual loan to a member was the responsibility of that member, and in some cases it was also the responsibility of one or more co-signers. Unlimited liability applied rather to the loans and deposits that the association received. Even here, however, the members had some protection. If a cooperative loan association was unable to pay back a loan to a creditor, the creditor could institute legal proceedings against the association and might force the credit union into bankruptcy. Such a procedure did not, however, place the individual members in a state of bankruptcy. If the association could not pay off its loan, then a bankruptcy court would allocate responsibility for repayment among the individual members.[22]

What unlimited liability really meant, therefore, was that a member

---

[20] The topic of non-member deposits in CDCUs is taken up in more detail in Chapter 7.

[21] Quoted in Aschhoff and Henningsen, 20.

[22] For an explanation of unlimited liability in the German credit societies, see Ely, 215-216.

could be held responsible for his fair portion of the cooperative's borrowed funds, a portion that might exceed his holding of shares—but it did not mean what unlimited liability means in modern American law, that each member could be held responsible for the entire loan. In other words, unlimited liability was a risk for the members, but not an unmanageable risk.

By joining a loan association, members assumed unlimited liability for funds borrowed not only from outsiders but also from other members. The distinction between shares and borrowed funds in the early German people's banks was not quite the same as the distinction between member shares and non-member deposits in modern American credit unions. In a credit union today, all of a member's deposits—in a savings account, a checking account, a money market account, or any other form—are called shares. Non-member deposits, when permitted, are made by people and institutions that are outside the credit union's field of membership. In contrast, in the original German credit unions, a member might be required to purchase one share, and in fact was usually restricted to purchasing only one share. In addition to this, members could make savings deposits which were separate from their share. The legal status of these savings deposits was similar to that of the association's borrowed funds: they carried a fixed contractual rate of interest and the association's members assumed unlimited liability for the obligation to repay. As opposed to the fixed interest rate on the savings deposits, each year the association declared a variable dividend on the shares, a dividend that in many cases was quite high.

As an example of the relative magnitudes, Table 2.1 shows the capital and liabilities for 948 Schulze-Delitzsch people's banks in 1878.

Table 2.1
(Percentages)

Capital and Liabilities in 948 People's Banks, 1878*	
1) Member shares	22.2
2) Reserves	3.0
3) Savings deposits	26.1
4) Borrowed from private individuals	44.9
5) Borrowed from banks and unions	3.8
Total	**100.0**

*Calculated from the table in Ely.

According to the German way of accounting, the capital of the banks consisted of the first two items, amounting to just one quarter of the total. These were the shares held by the individual members, plus the reserves that were held by the members collectively. The liabilities of the bank, the last three items, were three-quarters of the total. These included the funds owed to the members (item 3) as well as the funds owed to other private individuals and institutions (items 4 and 5). The members pledged unlimited liability in the repayment of all three categories.

In a modern American credit union, the first three items would constitute the capital because there would be no distinction between the first and the third items; all would be counted as shares.

The great advantage of unlimited liability was that it provided the security that a group of people with scant means needed if they were to bring significant funds into their community. Without unlimited liability, the loans would not have been forthcoming. Unlimited liability implied risk for the members, and as a consequence existing members were careful about whom they admitted to the association as new members. New members could be admitted only when the existing members were convinced of their character, their industry, and their commitment to back up their debts. Schulze-Delitzsch wrote:

> *Your own selves and characters must create your credit, and your collective liability will require you to choose your associates carefully, and to insist that they maintain regular, sober and industrious habits, making them worthy of credit.*[23]

The concept of unlimited liability did not spread from the German cooperative banks to the rest of the world. In modern American credit unions, unlimited liability would be completely unnecessary for two reasons: first, because they are permitted to borrow only in an amount up to 50 percent of their unimpaired shares and capital, and second, even when a few of them are allowed to accept non-member deposits, those deposits are insured by the National Credit Union Share Insurance Fund, just as the member deposits are. But the doctrine of unlimited liability was dropped well before the cooperative credit movement hit American shores.

Cooperative credit spread from Germany first into Italy, spearheaded by a young scholar, Luigi Luzzatti. Luzzatti adopted most of the features of the German people's banks, but he rejected unlimited liability since he judged that Italian people would not accept it. As the movement expanded into

---

[23] Moody and Fite, 4.

Switzerland, Austria, Belgium, and other countries, new laws permitted the associations to adopt limited liability—the legal doctrine that members are liable to lose their share contributions but no more—and most chose to do so.

Even within Germany a reaction arose against unlimited liability, and when the cooperative law was amended in 1889, associations were allowed to opt for limited liability. Schulze-Delitzsch fought against the abandonment of what he thought was the central feature of cooperative credit, but he lost the battle. He argued that joint liability improved the ability of an association to borrow at lower cost. He also argued that unlimited liability led members to pay closer attention to the affairs of their association.

He was met with the argument that while unlimited liability might once have been necessary for cooperatives to secure loans, this was no longer true. Credit unions now had sufficient capital and sufficient reserves to secure a loan adequately, without putting their members' individual assets at risk. Furthermore, since member capital was growing, outside loans were no longer as essential as they once had been. These arguments were advanced by the leaders of the larger and more secure cooperative banks at the time.

Both observations were doubtless true, but they can be seen as steps in the gradual transformation of cooperative credit from an agent of social change into a convenient service for the middle classes. The cooperative banks became more highly capitalized as their members participated in the economic expansion of the times and became better off. As their own resources grew, they had less need of loans from the outside. For both reasons, unlimited liability became less of an advantage and more of a hindrance as credit unions tried to persuade people to join. Eventually a credit union became, almost by definition, a closed community, a community in which members pooled their own resources for the purpose of making loans to one another. This actually became the strength of the credit union movement, that it was a means by which communities could use their own assets to support themselves.

At the same time, however, credit unions lost some of their relevance to people whose economic positions were threatened. People who were in danger of losing their livelihoods did not have the resources they needed even when what resources they had were pooled. As credit unions moved away from unlimited liability, then, they began a gradual migration away from a social-change movement to a predominantly middle-class institution.

I would not propose that today's community development credit unions return completely to the old German notion of unlimited liability. Such an idea would not be accepted and it is unnecessary. The desirability of bringing outside funds into a poor community has not disappeared, however. Modern CDCUs could serve as a conduit for outside funds were they not impeded in this function by federal regulations. I think, therefore, that a careful consideration of the German example might lead CDCUs in some creative directions. For example, a new category of member shares might be designated which would not be federally insured, which would be used as collateral against loans to the credit union from outsiders, and which might receive a higher return than the normal dividend rate.[24]

The fourth principle of the people's banks was that loans were to be made only to those who could use the funds productively. Loans were not to be used for personal, consumer purposes. Rather the Schulze-Delitzsch and Raiffeisen loans were almost exclusively what one today would call small business loans—for working capital, cash flow, seed, materials, tools, small buildings, and so forth. This was what the small farmers and artisans needed, and furthermore such loans were the most conservative, sensible ones that the credit union could make. A loan for a productive purpose, if invested wisely, would generate the income with which the loan could be paid back. In contrast, consumer loans were thought to be "unproductive" and even frivolous, and were to be avoided. As early as 1850, Schulze-Delitzsch wrote:

> Do not forget that your object should be to borrow to produce, that is, to give a plus value to the money you have borrowed so that you may be able to pay it back with interest and some profit. But never borrow for consumption, as is frequently the case with wage-earners who render themselves liable to default. Let your union be strictly a credit association among producers, and small producers if possible.[25]

The emphasis on business lending should be understood in the context of the class structure within which the cooperatives found themselves, as discussed in the previous section. The purpose of the associations was to combat the destructive growth of large-scale corporate capitalism that left a trail of human victims in its wake. The early credit union pioneers may have thought they were fighting this new order by trying to restore an idealized version of feudalism or (like Schulze-Delitzsch) they may have been trying to promote decentralized, small-scale capitalism. They must frequently have been confused about their ultimate goal. In any case, the pressing need was to provide large numbers of ordinary people with tools, equipment, and other means of production. Consumer lending would have been beside the

---

[24] I am grateful to Clifford Rosenthal for suggesting that CDCUs might think creatively about ways of using the liability of their members to advance their communities' interests.

[25] Quoted by Herrick, 272.

point; it would have contributed nothing to the particular struggle at hand. Henry Wolff, the contemporary English cooperative leader who thought that Schulze-Delitzsch's people's banks were too little concerned with the poor, was equally critical of their neglect of consumer lending:

> *Schulze, when adopting co-operation as a form, did not at the same time adopt with anything like sufficient fullness what we now everywhere recognize as the co-operative principle—to wit, consideration, above all things, for the* consumer.[26]

This sharp difference of opinion between Schulze-Delitzsch and Wolff about the proper use of credit union loans reflects the difference between the German and the English class structures in the nineteenth century. While capitalism was just beginning its entry into German society and was still confronted with the independent artisans and peasants whose position derived from the medieval era, by the late nineteenth century capitalism had completely transformed English society. The majority of the English people were by this time members of the working class who labored for wages for an employer. The society with which Wolff was familiar was one divided quite sharply into capitalist producers on the one hand and wage employees, who used their earnings for consumption, on the other. Hence his conviction that an institution dedicated to improving the lot of the victims of the economic system should concentrate on consumption. A bank that specialized in small business loans in England would have left the working class completely untouched.

While Wolff criticized Schulze-Delitzsch for ignoring the laboring classes, he himself and the English cooperative movement are vulnerable to the charge of ignoring the truly poor in England. Fairbairn points out that the English cooperatives did not organize the "dangerous poor" of London, people who were unemployed or semi-employed, but rather the working poor of the northern industrial cities.[27] It is doubtful that a consumer cooperative would have been of much help to the dangerous poor.

The nineteenth-century dispute between the proponents of production-oriented and consumer cooperatives is interesting in view of the role of credit unions in the United States, which do almost no business lending. In 1991 only 1.3 percent of the dollar amount of American credit union loans

---

[26] Wolff, 105 (emphasis in original).

[27] Fairbairn.

were directed to member businesses.[28] It would not be too much to say that mainstream credit unions in the United States are by definition consumer lenders. They are a component of an economic system in which most people are salary or wage employees of companies and other organizations. One reason why the early German credit unions are such an interesting model for today's community development credit unions is, however, the current dearth of good employment opportunities in poor American neighborhoods. In many low-income areas the issue of jobs is at least as important, if not more important, than consumer finance, and therefore some low-income credit unions are turning back to small business loans as a way of generating an employment base. As they do so they are returning, whether knowingly or not, to the old German model.

The fifth principle—regular contributions by members towards the cooperative's working capital—was important to the Schulze-Delitzsch associations but not to Raiffeisen's. Raiffeisen's banks did not require any member contribution until the German cooperative law of 1889 made member shares mandatory. At that point the Raiffeisen societies instituted a share requirement much smaller than that of most of the Schulze- Delitzsch banks. The issue of shares was a point of acrimonious contention between the two movements.

The Schulze-Delitzsch associations had a relatively high membership fee as well as a rule that each member had to purchase a share at a substantial price. Most members purchased their share in small amounts, over time, and thus the bank operated as a cooperative savings club. This was deemed important for several reasons. To protect the soundness of the bank, the aim should be to have one-half members' capital, matched by one-half borrowed funds, although few banks ever reached this portion of member capital. The other reason for requiring share purchases was to encourage the accumulation of wealth by the members.

Raiffeisen's institutions placed much less emphasis on member shares than did Schulze-Delitzsch's. The principal reason was that the membership tended to be significantly poorer in the former than in the latter. Most members of the Raiffeisen banks could not have come close to affording the entrance fee and share that was required in the urban credit unions. Wolff argued that the Raiffeisen institutions were much closer to the true cooperative spirit because they related to the needs of genuinely poor people. Furthermore, he argued, the Schulze-Delitzsch banks violated cooperative principles by paying a substantial dividend to members on their share. At times the dividend rate got as high as 20 percent. The purpose of a cooperative, he

---

[28] Credit Union National Association, 1991 Operating Ratios and Spreads, Mid Year Edition, Table 3.

argued, should be to provide service at cost to people who need it, not to promote financial speculation in shares.[29]

Whether or not Wolff's opprobrium is deserved, the urban Schulze-Delitzsch institutions were indeed different in their orientation from their rural Raiffeisen counterparts. The former served independent business people who could afford to provide some of the capital for the bank. The small farmers who were the members of the Raiffeisen banks were close to the bottom of the social and economic scale in the rural villages and could provide very little of the needed funds.

The dispute over member shares, which so divided the two German movements, is scarcely an issue in today's American credit unions. There is no question but that the great majority of a credit union's funds, if not all of them, must be provided by the members. Yet few credit unions set a membership requirement so high as to exclude poor people, as many of the Schulze-Delitzsch banks did.

The sixth principle, adopted at a later date by Schulze-Delitzsch's institutions, but never by Raiffeisen's, was that the membership should be broad and inclusive of different occupations, classes, and areas. This is consistent with the differences just noted. The Schulze-Delitzsch members were on the whole better off, with more resources, than their rural counterparts. The principal threat to their institution was that a price fall or some other particular event might threaten a group of businesses in the same sector. A hedge against this danger was to have a varied membership, so that one sector's hard times might be balanced by another sector's good fortune. The poorer Raiffeisen members had to be more concerned with just staying solvent in normal times. Because of the feature of unlimited liability, they needed to know, and be able to trust, their fellow members with their collective debt. As a consequence, Raiffeisen institutions were generally confined to just a single rural parish, or occasionally two.

As noted in the previous section, the confinement of a Raiffeisen association within a parish served the additional purpose of reinforcing the social position of the people in authority in that small area, including but not confined to the pastor.

Quebec's *Caisses Populaires*[30]

The credit union idea entered the United States in the early twentieth century not directly from Europe but indirectly from the Province of Quebec

---

[29] Wolff.

[30] The source of most of the material in this section is Rudin's excellent study, *In Whose Interest?*

in Canada. It was from a Canadian, Alphonse Desjardins, that Edward Filene and Pierre Jay learned the rudiments of cooperative banking.

There is a certain irony to this circuitous route, for Quebec in 1900 was a far more backward, agrarian, and feudal society than Germany or any other western European country at the same time. New England, in contrast, was a completely commercial, capitalist region, with barely a trace of the old European class system. A credit union could not possibly serve the same purpose in both societies. And yet the Americans believed they communicated well with the French Canadian and that in large measure they adopted his principles.

Desjardins (1854-1920) was a parliamentary (or "Hansard") reporter, taking verbatim notes in legislative debates, first in the provincial Legislative Assembly in Quebec from 1879 to 1890, and then from 1891 to 1915 in the federal House of Commons in Ottawa. While working in Quebec, he lived across the St. Lawrence River in the town of Levis, and even after moving to Ottawa he kept Levis as his home base. Levis became the site of the first credit union, or *caisse populaire* (in English, people's bank), and eventually the center of the provincial movement.

While listening to the debates in Ottawa in 1897, Desjardins was struck by the speech of a member of Parliament from Montreal, Michael Quinn, who described the victimization of his constituents by loan sharks. "There was one notable case in Montreal within the last few days," said Quinn, "in which a man obtained a loan of $150, and was sued for, and was compelled to pay in interest, the sum of $5,000, for the loan of $150.[31]

Desjardins spent the next three years learning about the European people's banks, corresponding with their leaders, and forming a planning group in Levis. The Caisse populaire de Levis opened for business in 1900 in Desjardins' house. Since he was absent much of the time in Ottawa, it was managed by his wife, notwithstanding the fact that as a married woman she was ineligible for membership. The movement spread slowly over the next few years, until enabling legislation was passed by the Province of Quebec in 1906. Thereafter, Desjardins spent his time promoting new *caisses*, starting about 200 by the time of his death in 1920. The movement gathered speed in the 1940s, and eventually became one of the strongest financial sectors in the province. By 1986 there were 1,400 *caisses*, with aggregate assets of $23 billion. Fully one-third of the savings of Quebec's population were held in the *caisses*.[32]

---

[31] Quoted in Rudin, 9.

[32] Ibid., x.

The journey of the *caisses* from their humble beginnings to their powerful present position in Quebec's financial sector was not simply a matter of growth; it was also a matter of class transformation. Rudin has shown that Desjardins and his associates occupied a place in Quebec's society at the turn of the century similar to that of Raiffeisen in Germany's a generation before. The founding members of the early *caisses* were invariably men of a certain social position, particularly in rural areas. At Levis, for example, the organizing group was made up not predominantly of the workers who constituted the majority of the town's population, but of professionals and people of commerce. Their status was under attack from the forces of large-scale capitalism that were invading their communities, and they sought to defend their positions through the use of the *caisses*. As members of the French Canadian traditional elite, they were hostile not only to capitalism, but to the English who were the purveyors of capitalism. One of the attractions of the *caisses* was that they were completely controlled by the French, whereas the banks that were spreading their tentacles throughout the province were controlled by English Canadians. Almost every *caisse* was supported by a parish priest, and only French Catholics—not English-speaking Protestants or, needless to say, Jews—were welcomed as members. "Do not forget that each member must receive the approval of the board of directors," wrote Desjardins in 1910, "this is your guarantee against the invasion of Protestants that you fear."[33]

In other words, Desjardins' *caisses populaires* played the same role as the German loan associations. Desjardins and many of his associates were genuine humanitarians, concerned for the well-being of their countrymen. At the same time, and without contradiction in their minds, they were participants in the battle for the survival of the French Canadian people, not only their survival as a linguistic group but their survival as a separate society based on a rural, feudal class structure, dominated by the unreconstructed clergy.

Quebec changed in the twentieth century, from a closed, defensive, rural, feudal, clerical society to an open, capitalist, secular, well-educated, urban, and dynamic society. The change was mirrored by a struggle within the *caisses*. By the end of the Second World War, a group of business-oriented liberals took control of the institutions and transformed them into one of the principal financial components of the startling capitalist growth that transformed the province. As they did so, however, a group of more traditional *caisses* stayed closer to the original vision of Desjardins and split from the main movement.

All this was to happen, however, long after the conversations between

---

[33] Ibid., 11.

Desjardins and the Massachusetts leaders in the first decade of the twentieth century that led to the founding of the first American credit unions. The *caisses populaires* that Desjardins described to Jay and Filene were small institutions based for the most part in a parish. They were operated as democracies, with each member having a vote. They were ostensibly open to all, although in fact all of the members were French-speaking Catholics. With the blessing of the clergy, they promoted traditional social and spiritual values. They made small loans for business purposes, discouraging and generally even rejecting loans for consumption. They encouraged regular savings by their members.

The Legacy for American CDCUs

Modern American CDCUs can look back to the origins of the cooperative credit movement for precursors and lessons. They cannot and should not emulate the early credit unions in all particulars, but they can learn from their experience. The most striking points of comparison are:

- The goal of social change. The German and Quebec cooperative credit associations were established to help rescue groups of people who were under assault by changing economic and social conditions. The nature of those conditions is different in the United States of the late twentieth century, but the ultimate goal of bringing people together in the struggle for their betterment against long odds is the same. In this respect, the early associations and the CDCUs share a purpose that has been largely forgotten by most American credit unions.

- The importance of attracting funds from outside the community. For all of the Schulze-Delitzsch and Raiffeisen associations, this was central. It has been abandoned as a goal by most modern American credit unions because it is not needed. Those credit unions serve mostly middle-class members who collectively have enough savings to meet their own needs. But CDCUs operating in poor communities need to return to the German tradition by attracting non-member deposits.

- Independent control, not charity. The German cooperative banks began as charities, but soon converted to the form of independent associations controlled by their borrowers and savers. While they accepted outside funds, they did so on a commercial, contractual basis, without yielding authority to the outsiders. So also the strength of CDCUs is that they are owned and controlled by

- their members who, for the most part, are low-income people. It is important that, as CDCUs deal with government regulators and outside investors, they not surrender this control.
- Loans for a productive purpose. History shows that the most important use of borrowed funds in a poor community depends upon the class and employment structure of that community. Where established employers are providing jobs, as in late nineteenth-century England, low-income people need access to credit for consumption. Where employers are scarce and people must fend for themselves, as in Germany at the same time, the priority need is for business loans. Today's CDCUs find themselves in both positions. Some of their members have jobs with incomes, albeit low ones, and need access to loans at reasonable rates for consumer purposes, lest they fall into the clutches of informal-sector loan sharks and other high-interest lenders. But most of their communities lack good jobs, and so business loans are also important.

Some of the points of comparison between today's low-income credit unions and the early associations are ambiguous:

- Access of poor people. The Schulze-Delitzsch banks included for the most part business and crafts people who were not at the bottom of the social ladder, and they actually excluded the poor by setting a share requirement for membership. The Raiffeisen associations attracted poorer people, in part because they set no requirement for saving. The dilemma is one that frequently faces CDCUs. To survive at all, they must attract their members' savings, but to meet their social purpose they must be relevant to the needs of people who have little if any savings. CDCUs reject either of the rather extreme German solutions—no poor people, or no savings—and instead they continuously face trade-offs and compromises as they try to meet the twin goals of access on the one hand and commercial viability on the other.
- Unlimited liability. This feature was critical to the success of the early associations, as the way of securing outside loans, but it is not used by today's credit unions. The need for drawing outside funds into poor communities still exists, however, while the flow of such funds is impeded by federal credit union regulations. It is possible that a creative use of members' liability could increase the availability of outside monies.

And some of the early features are simply inapplicable or objectionable to today's CDCUs. Among them:

- Romantic, reactionary politics. To a certain extent, the original institutions were established in order to preserve a feudal, hierarchical, clerical world. That world has long passed in the United States and the CDCUs have no connection to it.

- Racism and chauvinism. The early associations accepted the ethics of their time, and this often included anti-Semitism and discrimination against women. While there may be an occasional and well-justified expression of ethnic pride in some of today's CDCUs, they are not racist, and many of their leaders are women.

CHAPTER 3

DEVELOPMENT IN THE UNITED STATES

The founders of credit unionism in the United States possessed a combination of idealism and practicality characteristic of many American reformers. They believed that if people joined together in cooperative spirit and action they could solve the old problems of scarcity of credit and exorbitant interest rates.
—J. Carroll Moody and Gilbert Fite[1]

Even mainstream credit unions are becoming a 'working people's alternative,' since they are so often associated with the workplace. The unemployed, the underemployed, and those in service sector jobs generally don't have access to a credit union of their own.
—Episcopal Church statement[2]

By joining a CDCU, poor people seeking loans can make their case to a neighbor who understands their problems.
—National Federation of CDCUs

The Mainstream Credit Unions

A decade after the *caisses populaires* were started in Quebec, credit unions were introduced into the United States.[3] Three people were particularly responsible for the first American credit unions: Alphonse Desjardins,

---

[1] Moody and Fite, xi.

[2] Episcopal General Convention.

[3] The most complete account of American credit union history is Moody and Fite. It concentrates on developments at the organizational center of the credit unions, the Credit Union National Association. Unless otherwise noted, the material in this section is drawn from this source.

Pierre Jay, and Edward A. Filene.

Desjardins started the first two American credit unions, in St. Mary's parish, New Hampshire, in 1908, and in St. Jean Baptiste parish in Lynn, Massachusetts in 1910. Both were *caisses populaires* of the type that he was founding at a fast clip north of the border. The members were French Canadians who had emigrated to New England within the previous generation. The local leader in each case was the French-speaking, Catholic parish priest.

Desjardins' role in the history of American credit unions stems not so much from the institutions he personally founded, however, as from the influence he had on the thinking of Jay and Filene. Jay, a descendant of the first Supreme Court chief justice, John Jay, was appointed Commissioner of Banking in Massachusetts in 1906. He learned about the European people's banks and about the *caisses populaires*, corresponded and visited with Desjardins, and then drafted the country's first credit union enabling law which was passed by the Massachusetts legislature in 1909.

Filene, a department store owner in Boston, first became interested in cooperative credit during a visit to India in 1907. Upon his return he began to take initiatives in founding credit unions, lobbying for favorable legislation, and developing a national organization of credit unions. For thirty years, until his death in 1937, he was the leading force behind the credit union movement in the country. Among many other achievements, he founded and funded the institution that became the Credit Union National Association or CUNA, the principal trade association of credit unions in the country. In 1920 he hired Roy F. Bergengren, and then paid his salary for many years, as managing director first of the Massachusetts Credit Union Association, then of the Credit Union National Extension Bureau, and finally of CUNA.

Since Filene was Jewish, the credit union movement entered the United States without the stench of anti-Semitism that had marred it in Germany and in Quebec. One of Filene's purposes was to dispel the bias that Jews were usurers. In a statement that one could be forgiven for finding ambiguous, a Boston rabbi who was associated with Filene wrote that Jewish support of the credit union movement "helps to make the people realize that not all Jews are alike, that not all are bad, that not all are money lenders or usurers."[4] Anti-Semitism was not completely banished from American credit unions, however. The author was told that for years, although no longer, CUNA Mutual Insurance Company had an unwritten rule that Jews could not be hired.

---

[4]Ibid., 33.

As the initiative for credit union development passed from Desjardin's hands to Filene's, the spirit of the institution began to change. Cultural nationalism and religious identity were no parts of Filene's purpose. He had a liberal, universal vision of the potential of credit unions; they could be useful to all working people.

In contrast to Desjardins, Schulze-Delitzsch, and Raiffeisen, Filene saw credit union members principally as employees, not independent producers. As early as 1909 he wrote,

> *As a large employer, I have long felt that some provision should be made by which people of small means can, in case of necessity or distress, borrow at reasonable rates of interest and under thoroughly honest and fair conditions.*[5]

Filene did not follow Desjardins' initiative of organizing credit unions in parishes but instead urged that they be organized among the employees of different companies.

As the American credit union movement developed, the emphasis on lending for a "productive purpose," which had been central to both the German and Quebec credit unions, disappeared. The Massachusetts Credit Union Act of 1909 called for loans for useful and beneficial purposes, not production. Useful and beneficial can be defined in broad terms, and in time they came to mean consumer purposes. In 1915, Filene wrote out a list of eight credit union principles.[6] On the subject of lending, the principles included rigid exclusion of thriftless and improvident borrowing, small loans with frequent partial repayments, and the use of character and industry as the main basis of securing credit. There was no hint that business or productive loans should be favored.

Filene's ideology had some similarities and some differences from the views of both Henry Wolff and Hermann Schulze-Delitzsch, described in Chapter 2. Like Wolff, the English cooperator, Filene saw potential credit union members as people whose incomes were low but who were employed. They did not need jobs; jobs were provided by the capitalist employers, of which he was one. They needed credit at reasonable rates to finance consumer purchases. Unlike Wolff, however, he believed in capitalism, and did not see cooperatives as challenging the capitalist structure of business in any way.

Schulze-Delitzsch had believed in capitalism also, but the version he fa-

---

[5] Ibid., 25-26.

[6] Ibid., 37.

vored was the small-scale capitalism of the English political economists, with many independent entrepreneurs confronting each other in competitive markets. The German people's banks existed in large measure to provide the capital for those small enterprises so they could hold out against the destructive power of large corporations. Filene had nothing against small-scale operators, but he was equally comfortable with large companies. The credit unions he foresaw would help companies of all sizes, not by providing their capital, but by providing the needed service of low-cost consumer loans to their employees and thereby improving the level of satisfaction within the work force. Class conflict was not a part of Filene's vision; to the contrary, he saw credit unions as a means for bringing employer and employee together.

In common with the *caisses populaires*, but in contrast to the German people's banks, the American credit unions were not established for the purpose of drawing outside funds into the members' communities. The funds to be lent would come from the members themselves. The 1909 Massachusetts act defined a credit union as "a cooperative association formed for the purpose of promoting thrift among its members." The question of unlimited liability for loans to the credit union did not, therefore, arise.

From its early beginnings in New Hampshire and Massachusetts, the credit union movement grew enormously. Every state passed laws permitting the chartering of credit unions, and in 1934 the Federal Credit Union Act was passed. Both the states and the federal government examined and regulated credit unions. Federal examination began in 1934, and in 1970 it was lodged in an independent agency, the National Credit Union Administration (NCUA). Federal share insurance came much later than deposit insurance for the banks, in part because of active opposition from within the credit union movement—many credit union leaders were opposed to paying for the insurance, and also to the increase in government control of their operations that insurance would lead to. By 1970, however, share insurance was imposed. The number of credit unions grew steadily from the early days, reaching a peak of about 20,000 in the early 1970s. By the early 1990s, the number of credit unions had fallen to about 14,000, mostly because of mergers; nevertheless, the number of credit union members continued to grow, reaching about 60 million. At the end of 1992, the combined assets of federally chartered credit unions plus federally insured state chartered credit unions totalled $261 billion.[7] State leagues and corporate central credit unions were formed in each state to provide services to credit unions.

As credit unions grew in the United States, they retained some of their

---

[7] National Credit Union Administration, *1992 Annual Report*.

early features, but developed in new ways as well. The great majority continued to define their field of membership by a place of employment or an occupation. A much smaller number were based on membership in an association such as a cooperative, a labor union, or a church, and a smaller number yet had a geographic field of membership. Table 3.1 shows the distribution of credit unions by common bond at the end of 1991.[8]

Table 3.1

Number and Proportion of U.S. Credit Unions by Common Bond
(December 1991)

Common Bond	Number	Proportion
Occupational	10,203	73.0%
Associational	2,014	14.6
Residential	937	6.7
Multiple groups	796	5.7

In a formal sense credit unions remained cooperative institutions, with each member having a vote in the election of the board of directors. As they grew bigger, however, they ceased to rely upon the work of volunteers as they had in the early days, and came to depend upon both paid staff and professional management.

A high proportion of the lending in American credit unions was for personal purposes, and the preponderance of this was for consumption. In 1991, as noted earlier, just over one percent of credit union loan dollars outstanding were used for a business purpose, while the remaining loans were all personal, including mortgages.[9]

At the end of the twentieth century, as at the beginning, most Americans are employees, and need loans to finance consumer purchases, especially of durable products. There is a big difference, however, between the typical American employees who were members of credit unions in 1910 and today. In 1910, they could reasonably be called members of the working class, people who were just at the edge of subsistence. Today, they are more appropriately called members of the middle class. As noted in Chapter 1, the median income of a credit union household now exceeds the median income of all households in the country. Of course, the incomes and living standards of employees varies widely throughout the country and within communities,

---

[8] Credit Union National Association, *Operating Ratios and Spreads, Year-End 1991*, 66.

[9] Ibid., 21.

but the majority are comfortable. Just as the center of the American population has moved from working class to middle class, so too the credit unions that serve them have changed their orientations. From agents of social change, they have gradually transformed themselves into institutions providing a useful service to the middle classes.

One way of seeing this change is in the gradual transition in terminology, from "credit union movement" to "credit union industry." A "movement" implies change, resistance to authority and power, and transcendent ideals. As ambiguous as their motives were, the early credit union pioneers all had visions of social movements. Most credit unions, however, gradually transformed themselves into more ordinary business institutions, whose success was measured by their financial statements more than by the quality of their members' lives. They became one more competitor in the financial marketplace. Their members no longer had to fear victimization by the local loan shark, but instead had access to many different sources of credit, of which the credit union was just one. People who chose to work in credit unions were no longer necessarily making a commitment to the betterment of intolerable conditions among their neighbors, but instead were often seeking an attractive career path.

Yet the change from movement to industry was not smooth, consensual, or even complete. At many points in their history, credit unions faced critical decisions in which the philosophical issues, the soul issues, were central. Among them, one of the most important was the removal of Roy Bergengren from the position of managing director of CUNA in 1945. With Filene's support, Bergengren had built and coordinated the movement since 1920. He was a practical visionary. He retained a clear sense of credit unions as a movement and as a part of a larger movement. He saw them as cooperatives, working together with other cooperatives to change the economic system. In 1938, towards the end of the Great Depression, he wrote:

> ... *there must be some reorganization of economic society on a cooperative basis. . . . Capitalism in most of its aspects has failed, and in the long run we cannot develop economic democracy on the principle of dog eat dog and the theory that the shrewdest, the most unscrupulous, the smartest of our number, should survive at the expense of all of the rest of us.*[10]

Moody and Fite show that this attitude became increasingly uncomfortable for many credit union people. They came to dislike even mentioning

---
[10] Quoted in Moody and Fite, 193.

that credit unions were cooperatives, let alone part of a broader cooperative movement, lest they seem to be critical of the corporate system. Their sponsors were, after all, the companies whose employees comprised their fields of membership. Bergengren saw this opinion as short-sighted, and contrasted it to his view:

> One group thinks of the credit union as a personnel activity in industry. As such, it takes care of the short-term credit problem of employees on a humane basis, and performs a useful function which is appreciated by both employee and employers. The other concept is that cooperation is a sort of circle made up of segments, and that the credit union is one of the segments, and therefore a part of the cooperative whole.[11]

Bergengren's enemies in CUNA portrayed him as incompetent to run a large organization, and after years of conflict finally succeeded in forcing his withdrawal in 1945. The conflict over Bergengren was repeated a quarter century later in 1971, when CUNA's then managing director, J. Orrin Shipe, was fired by the board of directors. By that time, power at the national level had shifted markedly to the CUNA Mutual Insurance Company, which was operated on strict commercial principles. On the basis of a series of interviews, Moody and Fite concluded that the cause of Shipe's dismissal was that he believed in credit unions as a movement, while the majority of the CUNA board saw them as an industry. The crisis of capitalism that was associated with the Depression was long gone, and Shipe did not follow Bergengren's lead in seeing credit unions as part of an alternative to a dying capitalist system. But he had the missionary spirit of the movement's founders. He wanted CUNA to work with low-income credit unions, with small credit unions, and with credit unions in poor countries. He saw credit unions as an instrument for changing the lives of people in need. His critics wanted CUNA to help credit unions become full-service financial institutions, capable of competing against the banks for the deposits of middle class Americans.[12] As in 1945, the "industry" proponents emerged victorious over those who favored the "movement."

The transformation of the credit union ethos is not complete; even today the practical issues of the credit union "industry" have to compete with the idealism of the "movement." But for the most part, credit unions in the United States are a standard, if relatively small, component of the nation's

---

[11] Ibid., 215.

[12] Ibid., p. 279. Also based on conversations with Shipe's son, Robert P. Shipe, manager of First American Credit Union on the Navajo Reservation in Arizona.

financial system, catering to the savings and borrowing needs of middle-class employees.

The historians of American credit unions, Moody and Fite, take the position that this evolution was inevitable and even desirable:

> In the 1960s the [credit union] movement joined the War on Poverty by seeking to establish credit unions in the black ghettos where rates of unemployment were high and incomes low, as well as among Spanish-Americans and poor whites. These efforts were generally unsuccessful, even with federal aid. By the very nature of credit unions their benefits were confined mainly to those with jobs because a member had to have money to invest and means to repay loans. This meant that credit unions had little to offer the hard-core, unemployed poor who did not need loans so much as grants or jobs.[13]

The leaders of the community development credit union movement disagree.

The Emergence of Community Development Credit Unions

Community development credit unions represent a departure from the mainstream credit union industry, a departure that harkens back to the earliest days of the credit union founders. Their purpose is social change, the improvement of the living conditions of people in need. CDCUs certainly constitute a movement.

The first American CDCUs, as distinct from mainstream credit unions, were founded in Black, Southern, rural communities in the late 1930s and the early 1940s. A few of those early CDCUs have lasted to this day, including about ten in eastern North Carolina.[14] The oldest surviving CDCU is Bricks Community in Enfield, North Carolina, which even today is tiny, with under $200,000 in assets and just one full-time employee. The early North Carolina CDCUs were created by working people who were enmeshed in the plantation system, whose incomes were very low, and who lacked access to credit on any but the most exploitative terms. Here and there, other community credit unions were started in the 1950s; for example, one credit union in New Mexico brought together miners who were Spanish speaking with min-

---

[13] Ibid., 334-335.

[14] I would like to thank James Gilliam of St. Luke Credit Union in Windsor, North Carolina, for his insights into the credit union history of his state.

ers who were Polish speaking.[15]

Table 3.2[16] shows the chartering year of 165 CDCUs that were in existence in early 1993—the dates range from 1937 to 1993. Many more CDCUs were founded but later failed or merged; the table shows only those that have survived.

Table 3.2

Founding Year of 165 CDCUs

Year	Church	Non-Church	Total
1935-39	1	1	2
1940-44	1	6	7
1945-49	1	3	4
1950-54	4	8	12
1955-59	12	5	17
1960-64	12	4	16
1965-69	4	37	41
1970-74	1	15	16
1975-79	0	12	12
1980-84	4	18	22
1985-89	1	8	9
1990-	1	6	7
Total	**42**	**123**	**165**

Low-income credit unions appeared at a fairly slow rate from the end of the Second World War through the early 1960s; church-affiliated credit unions predominated during this period. The largest number of surviving CDCUs date from the late 1960s. In fact, the number of credit unions serving low-income populations exploded in that period. By one estimate, 400 were formed. Three different groups converged to promote these credit unions: CUNA, a group of activists in the civil rights movement, and the federal government's Office of Economic Opportunity (OEO).[17]

---

[15] Thanks to Ricardo Garcia of the College of Education in the University of Idaho, the son of the credit union's organizer, who told me about life growing up in the miners' credit union.

[16] Most of the data in the table comes from the call reports that were introduced in Chapter 1 and will be analyzed fully in Chapter 5. The survey of 400 low-income credit unions in Gore, Rosenthal, and Smith shows roughly the same distribution of chartering dates. The figures for the 1990s come from the National Federation of CDCUs.

[17] Most of the information that is used in this section on the CDCUs that were founded in this period comes from Robinson and Gilson. Other sources are Livingston and National Federation of Community Development Credit Unions, "The OEO Credit Union Experiment: Implications for Community Development Banking." My thanks to several veterans of the OEO credit unions who talked with me about their experiences, including Ernest Johnson, Pearl Long, and James Taylor.

A few people within the CUNA management—people who still believed in credit unions as a movement—had begun to consider the credit needs of poor urban and rural communities in the late 1950s. In 1958, CUNA instituted a broad study of the credit needs of the poor, and on the basis of this study it organized and funded two experimental rural credit unions, one in Texas and one in Nebraska, in 1961. In 1964 it added five urban credit unions in poor neighborhoods, this time allocating $50,000 to defray the start-up costs. The credit unions were intended to meet people's needs for small loans, for purposes such as car and home repair, medical expenses, and education. A technical specialist from CUNA kept watch over all of these experimental credit unions, and reported that they were finding success hard to come by. In 1966, CUNA was forced to spend another $50,000 to keep the credit unions solvent, but in that same year it joined forces with the Office of Economic Opportunity to effect a major expansion in its program.[18]

The Black civil rights movement of the 1960s also played a role. One of the weapons that members of the white southern establishment had during the period of the demonstrations for racial equality was that they could cut off virtually all credit to people who were identified as activists. Simply joining in a march with Martin Luther King, Jr., for example, could result in a person's losing department store and agricultural credit. Ernest Johnson recalls that civil rights leaders raised this problem in discussions with federal officials. They were encouraged by those officials to cooperate with the OEO in the setting up of cooperative, self-help lending institutions that could mobilize the savings of local Blacks and thereby allow the Blacks to avoid the necessity of interacting with credit institutions that were dominated by whites.[19]

Some of the African American credit unions that were established in the late 1960s are still run by people whose first active public involvement was with the civil rights movement. Pearl Long of NEJA Federal Credit Union in northern Florida, then a school teacher and now retired, recounted to the author stories of the demonstrations that the credit union founders participated in and of the risks that they took.

The strongest force behind the establishment of CDCUs in the 1960s was the federal government. The War on Poverty was announced by President Lyndon B. Johnson in his State of the Union address in January 1964. The government set up the Office of Economic Opportunity (OEO) to coordinate a range of programs designed to raise the living standards of the one-

---

[18] This paragraph is based on Robinson and Gilson.

[19] This paragraph is based largely on conversations with Ernest Johnson, who, in addition to his credit union duties, is a member of the Southern Christian Leadership Conference.

third of Americans whose incomes fell below the poverty line. In 1966, with the encouragement of civil rights leaders, the OEO joined in a working partnership with CUNA to found credit unions in poor rural and urban locations throughout the country.

Some of the OEO credit unions still exist today. Most of them failed, however. By 1975 just half of the original 400 were still active, and by the 1990s only ten percent had survived. The experience of the OEO credit unions, and the reasons for the failure of so many of them, are worth consideration at a time when the federal government is once again taking the initiative to bring financial services to poor communities. To anticipate, the OEO history shows not that government intervention into low-income financial markets is necessarily doomed, but that particular federal policies in the 1960s, policies which both were and are avoidable, were responsible for the problems with the program.

Most, although not all, of the OEO credit unions were sponsored by a Community Action Agency (CAA). The CAAs were institutions established for the purpose of empowering local poor people, advocating for the rights of the poor, and providing some direct services such as food and nutrition, family planning, day care, emergency shelter, etc. The credit union was an additional activity undertaken by the CAA. Only about one-third of the new credit unions received direct funding from the OEO; the funding was generally in the form of salaries for up to three staff members. The remaining credit unions received encouragement and some technical assistance as they started up, and many of them were provided with space in the CAA facility.

From recent interviews that Ceretha Robinson and Anne Gilson of the Woodstock Institute have conducted with staff and board members of the early OEO credit unions, and from documents prepared at the time, it appears that many of the credit unions succeeded in lending money and providing financial services to poor people. The loans were often very small, for purposes like buying food, paying medical bills, consolidating debts, and buying school clothes. The credit unions were places where people could cash checks and buy money orders without paying exploitative fees at liquor stores and similar establishments.

To a large extent, however, the OEO experience represents an enormous and costly case study in how the government should not sponsor financial institutions for the poor. On the whole, concludes the Woodstock Institute report, it was a top-down effort, not the result of local grass-roots organizing, and in retrospect it seems as if failure were almost built into it by design.

The arithmetic of growth and self-sufficiency was never fully confronted by most of the planners of the OEO credit unions. Some of the credit unions were given grants to pay for three staff members in the hope that they would eventually be able to cover those expenses out of their earned income. But three staff salaries plus other office expenses might total about $40,000 annually. If the credit union was earning a spread on its assets of 8 percent,[20] it would need total assets of a half million dollars to generate $40,000 in earnings, and even then it would have nothing to put aside for reserves and capital growth. But deposits of a half million dollars were unthinkable for most OEO credit unions operating in poor communities. After several years' operation, many of them were still struggling to bring in their first $100,000 in member savings. The consequence was that many of their leaders never took seriously the possibility of becoming self-sufficient and operated as if the grants would last indefinitely. When the grants were abruptly cut off in the early 1970s, some of the credit unions collapsed in short order.

Other OEO credit unions received no grants to cover expenses, and in the long run they may have been more fortunate, since they were forced from the beginning to rely upon their members' own volunteer efforts. But they too faced problems that eventually forced many of them into liquidation or merger. All of the sources of information on this period are in agreement that one of the most serious problems facing the OEO credit unions was inadequate training. Although the OEO provided some training through CUNA, it was never enough to meet the needs fully. In spite of CUNA's interest in the OEO credit unions at the national level, few individual credit unions or state leagues offered the newcomers any assistance. As a consequence, many credit unions operated with informal and incomplete accounting systems and made serious errors in their business management. At times, loans were not tracked, payment delinquencies were allowed to accumulate, funds were not prudently invested, and expenses were allowed to rise.

Other problems were of a more sociological or cultural nature. Veterans of the OEO credit unions told the Woodstock Institute's interviewers that many of the members of the credit unions were enmeshed in the welfare system and had developed a sort of grants mentality; they apparently did not fully understand that the loans they received from the credit union had to be repaid.

The connections that the credit unions had to the CAAs, while helpful in some ways, were a handicap in others. Some of the Woodstock Institute's informants recalled that the CAA leaders tried to use the credit union for patronage. Others said that the CAA leaders wanted to establish a relationship of dependency between community members and the institution and

---

[20] A spread of 8 percent would result from average net earnings on assets that were lent or invested of 13 percent, minus dividend payments to the members on their savings deposits of 5 percent. These are fairly typical rates for the period.

that this brought them into conflict with the credit union whose mission was to foster independence. When government funds for the CAAs dried up in the 1970s, some of the CAAs exploited the credit unions by charging relatively high rents for the use of the facilities.

It appears that the CAAs were generally not appropriate sponsors of credit unions, since their focus was largely on the delivery of and advocacy for social welfare, not on community economic development and certainly not on banking.

A reading of the Woodstock Institute's interviews leads one to the conclusion that the root problem was that the credit unions were initiated by the OEO in Washington, and then by the staff of the CAAs. They were not for the most part a response to local community organizing, and many therefore failed to develop a group of volunteers who were committed to their ongoing success. When hard times came, the OEO credit unions had few resources on which to fall back.

Two public policies of the early 1970s signaled the end for many of the OEO credit unions. First was the cutoff of subsidies to the credit unions, along with the reduction in support to the CAAs, as the new Republican administration of President Nixon retreated from a commitment to the War on Poverty. Many of the OEO credit unions were not self-sufficient by that time.

The second problem, ironically, was the requirement, imposed in 1970 by the NCUA, that all deposits in the country's credit unions be insured. The NCUA Share Insurance Fund, which provided most of the deposit insurance for the country's credit unions, imposed financial criteria for eligibility; credit unions were required to maintain a certain level of capital, or reserves, in order to protect themselves against losses—and thereby to protect the insurance fund. Most of the OEO credit unions, however, could not meet the capital standards. After considerable protest and negotiation, they were given a grace period of two years to come into compliance with the insurance regulations, but even this concession was not enough for a number of them which were eventually forced to close their doors.

Those in the country's credit unions who feared increased government regulation as a result of the insurance requirement were correct. After 1970, federal and state regulators substantially increased the rigor of their examinations and held credit unions to higher standards of performance and safety. A number of OEO credit unions which survived the trauma of the early 1970s nevertheless failed eventually because they could not meet the examination requirements.[21]

---

[21] Chapter 7 discusses in more detail the dual effects of the increasingly rigorous examination standards. CDCUs which could meet the standards emerged stronger. But examiners often had no understanding of the particular difficulties that poor people's credit unions faced, and ended up closing institutions that could well have survived and made a contribution to their communities.

The legacy of the OEO period is not entirely negative. Loans and other services were provided even by the institutions that did not succeed in the long run. Lessons were learned. And most importantly, some of the credit unions overcame all the handicaps and survived. In African American communities in the rural southeast, over a dozen CDCUs founded by the OEO still sustain their struggling communities. One in the Florida panhandle, North East Jackson Area Federal Credit Union, makes crop loans to small farmers. Others provide a full array of small consumer and business loans. A small credit union in south central Iowa meets the credit needs of people associated with the still existent community action program. In the poorest area of Los Angeles, Watts United Credit Union, sponsored by the OEO in the wake of the 1965 riots, makes consumer loans to low-income people, many of them on welfare. Approximately 40 CDCUs from the OEO period are still functioning, still making a contribution.

All of the surviving OEO credit unions are still relatively small—none of them over $5 million in assets, many under $1 million. But they are important beyond their size. Their staff and board members and volunteers come from the local communities and understand well the financial problems that their neighbors are facing. Moreover, the OEO credit unions are a critical part of the CDCU movement as a whole. While the newer CDCUs exceed them in number, still the OEO institutions provide continuity and a sense of history that the low-income credit union movement would otherwise lack. Their experience gives some reassurance to the other people in the movement that obstacles can be overcome and that their own credit unions can last into the indefinite future.

Chapter 7 will outline President Clinton's new proposal for federal support of what he calls Community Development Financial Institutions, including CDCUs. As that chapter shows, the new plan is designed to avoid the problems inherent in the OEO approach. The President's proposal anticipates that most of the support to poor people's financial institutions in the 1990s will be in the form of capital or reserves, not in the form of subsidies for operating expenses; thus the institutions will not be seduced into operating beyond their means. The program will be administered not by a poverty agency lacking expertise in finance, but by its own separate administration. It will offer support to existing community financial institutions which have a track record of performance, as well as to start-up institutions which have demonstrated community involvement.

From the perspective of the 1990s, therefore, it appears that one of the important legacies of the OEO period is that it has provided the experience to help design an effective public-private partnership in support of community development in low-income areas.

New CDCUs continued to appear in the 1970s and the 1980s.[22] By then the government had backed off from organizing and chartering low-income credit unions. The newer credit unions were initiated by a variety of local groups and grass-roots organizations, not by federal officials. Each of these more recent CDCUs has its own unique story. Some were organized by activists who had tried to promote change in their communities in the 1960s and who turned to CDCUs at a later date because they seemed to be an institution with some chance of permanence. Some were spinoffs of existing community organizations. A few were sponsored by churches, particularly in African American neighborhoods, although the pace of new church CDCUs slackened in the most recent period. In the 1980s especially, CDCUs were organized by groups of people in response to the closing of bank branches in poor neighborhoods; in some cases the organizers of the CDCUs were able to use the Community Reinvestment Act to pressure the departing banks into contributing resources, for example, buildings, equipment, deposits, or in a few cases, even staff.

The newer CDCUs appeared in all parts of the country and among varied population groups. Most were urban, although a few—including two of the most innovative, Central Appalachian People's Federal Credit Union in Kentucky and Community Trust Federal Credit Union in Florida—were rural. Some were in predominantly African American neighborhoods, as had been many of the earlier CDCUs. But others arose among different ethnic groups, including Latinos, Asian Americans, and Native Americans, as well as in predominantly white low-income neighborhoods. Some were in desperately poor areas, but others were in mixed-income communities where the resources of middle-income members could be used in support of lower-income members.

Most of the earlier CDCUs had had a straightforward mission, namely to meet poor people's unmet credit needs and to provide a safe place to save. Some of the newer ones developed new ideas about how to operate a savings and lending cooperative. Among them were several of the credit unions described in Chapter 1: Central Appalachian People's in Kentucky, with its dozens of branches spread throughout the mountains; Self-Help in North Carolina, with its statewide charter and its exclusive focus on business and housing lending; and Santa Cruz Community in California with its commitment to community development lending. There were others. In Apopka, Florida, Community Trust Federal Credit Union, chartered in 1982, succeeded in organizing migrant farm workers, many of whom did not speak English. While

---

[22] The author's understanding of the history of CDCUs from the 1970s to the present comes from his own involvement in the movement, from discussions with CDCU activists, and from reading documents that were generated over the years by the credit unions.

banks had seldom been willing to lend to poor migrants before, Community Trust took the risk. It found that most—but not all—of its members paid back their loans, even when they were in a distant part of the country. Over the years Community Trust has faced serious problems, and the NCUA threatened to liquidate it in 1991-92, but it has survived. In Ithaca, New York, Alternatives Federal Credit Union, chartered in 1978, has devoted much of its attention to real estate lending to low-income borrowers.

While some new CDCUs were appearing, however, the NCUA showed increasing reluctance to grant new charters, and it liquidated or merged many existing CDCUs. This was part of its general policy to reduce the number of small credit unions. As Table 7.1 in Chapter 7 will show, the pace of new chartering fell to almost zero by the early 1990s, while liquidations and mergers continued at quite a high rate, so that the number of credit unions in existence fell sharply from a peak in 1970. NCUA's policy followed from its view that people's needs for credit union services could best be met by expansion of the existing larger credit unions, that small credit unions were likely not to be viable in the long run, and that they were more expensive than it was worth to examine and regulate.

But the NCUA's view was simply incorrect in the poorer neighborhoods of the country. For the most part, these neighborhoods did not have existing large credit unions which low-income people could join. The credit unions were not physically located in those neighborhoods, and in any case most low-income people did not have the jobs or belong to the organizations that would have made them eligible for credit union membership. The consequence of the NCUA policy was therefore to restrict very severely both the growth of CDCUs and the access to credit unions of any kind by low-income people.

In the early 1990s, this policy appears to be changing. In 1992, for example, seven new CDCUs were chartered. These included South Central People's in the area of Los Angeles which had been severely damaged in the disturbances in April of that year, and Central Brooklyn, described by its founder, Mark Griffith, as the world's first "hip-hop credit union." New CDCUs were set up in Omaha, Nebraska and in Denver, Colorado, and new charters were expected in Camden, New Jersey and Washington, D.C. A charter was granted to a Korean Catholic church in Oakland, California. In response to President Clinton's call for a new emphasis on community development banking, the NCUA was once again willing to entertain charter applications from poor communities, provided that they were well thought out.

The National Federation of Community Development Credit Unions

The CDCU movement has been assisted by a trade association, the National Federation of Community Development Credit Unions. The Federation was incorporated in Washington, D.C. in 1974, but its origins go back a few years earlier to 1970 and 1971 when a group of limited-income credit unions got together to deal with the problems created by the new federal requirement for share insurance. The credit unions were successful in their negotiations with the government and decided to make their association permanent.

Initially the Federation had no income. It was simply an association of credit unions, and the central work was done on a volunteer basis. It received its first small grant in 1977 and in 1979 it began a three-year period of substantial grant support. The Community Services Administration, successor to OEO, provided the Federation major funding, reaching a peak level of a half million dollars in 1981. The funding was in support of technical assistance that the Federation provided in conjunction with the government's revolving loan program for low-income credit unions, a program that will be described more fully in Chapter 7. At first the Federation shared responsibility for the training with the National Center for Urban Ethnic Affairs, but in 1981 the NCUEA staff was folded into the Federation. At that time the Federation's staff numbered about a dozen.

The period of government largesse passed quickly, however. The grant expired on September 30, 1982, and most of the staff members left. Two, the Executive Director, Jim Clark, and Clifford Rosenthal, who had joined the staff in 1980, stayed on, drawing just a day or two of salary a week, and tried to hold the Federation together. A few months later, Clark left and the Federation was in danger of closing. Rosenthal managed to pull together a few small grants, however; in the fall of 1983 he hired Annie Vamper of the National Credit Union Administration, and the two began the uphill task of reconstructing the organization.

In 1984, the organization started to grow again. Rosenthal obtained several grants—initially from the New York Foundation and from the New York Community Trust—in support of credit union organizing in the city of New York, in areas that had been abandoned by banks. The Federation helped to establish a credit union on the Lower East Side of Manhattan, and worked in a half dozen other areas of the city. Meanwhile the membership of the Federation consisted of between 50 and 100 CDCUs from around the country. While the grants were directly in support of community work in New York, they helped to pay modest salaries for Rosenthal and Vamper, who in turn were able to spend part of their time coordinating the national movement.

In the long run, however, it was clear to the staff and board of the Federation that a national movement could not be carried on the back of organizing grants in just one city. As early as 1982, when federal support was ending, the

Federation decided upon the strategy of a capitalization program. The idea was to attract deposits and loans from "socially responsible investors"— foundations, churches and other organizations that were prepared to earn less than the maximum possible return on their funds, provided the money was put to work on behalf of a good cause. The Federation would act as an intermediary, soliciting the deposits and placing them in CDCUs, while taking a cut of about a percentage point to cover its own expenses. Since most of the Federation's member credit unions were certified by NCUA as serving low-income people, they were able to accept non-member deposits. The deposits raised the spread or net earnings rate of the credit unions, and in some cases they also increased the capacity of the credit unions to make loans to their members.

The capitalization program grew slowly at first, reaching only $100,000 in 1986. In that year, however, the Federation received a major deposit from the John D. and Catherine T. McArthur Foundation, and assets rose almost overnight to about $1 million. That proved to be the turning point in the program; thereafter, substantial support was obtained from the Presbyterian and Roman Catholic churches, from the Ford Foundation, and from a number of other socially responsible investors. In 1993, the capitalization program stood at $4 million and was growing, although it was still a long distance from its ultimate goal of $20 million.

During the middle and late 1980s, the Federation struggled to establish its own credibility as a representative voice to be taken seriously on the national scene. A breakthrough occurred in 1985, when it was invited by the White House to do a study of the role of credit unions in capital formation in low-income communities.[23] The study presented new data and developed new arguments about the actual and potential importance of CDCUs. Thereafter the Federation was turned to increasingly for its views, and it found that its views were often heeded.

Consequently, and in spite of the fact that its resources were exceedingly limited, the Federation become an effective advocate with the Congress, White House, and NCUA. For most of the 1980s, its principal goal was to restore the revolving loan program to low-income credit unions that had been eliminated in 1981. It also lobbied in favor of increased technical assistance to CDCUs, relaxation of the restriction on non-member deposits in CDCUs, greater sensitivity on the part of federal examiners to non-white and low-income communities, and the chartering of new CDCUs. It took a leading role in proposing what became President Clinton's initiative on community development banking. Its staff developed close working relationships

---

[23] See Gore, Rosenthal, and Smith.

with some of the board and staff members of the NCUA.

In the late 1980s and early 1990s, the Federation continued to obtain grants to support its technical assistance and training programs. It still emphasized its work in New York City. Programs there included job training for low-income individuals to prepare them for entry level jobs in credit unions, and technical assistance for low-income housing and small business development. It won a large grant from the Ford Foundation to set up networks of CDCUs—for mutual support and technical training—in four separate areas: the cities of New York, Philadelphia, and Chicago, and the state of North Carolina. It also obtained grants first to study minority church-based credit unions, and then to set up a support network for them. In 1992, with the assistance of a major grant from the DeWitt Wallace-Reader's Digest Fund, it started a program of children's credit unions in eleven CDCUs, based on the model developed at the D. Edward Wells credit union, described in Chapter 1.

Another important activity of the Federation has been to provide help to community groups trying to organize and secure charters for new credit unions. As noted above, beginning in the 1970s, both federal and state regulators became increasingly reluctant to see new credit unions start. Faced with this resistance, the task of the Federation became harder each year, up through the early 1990s.

The Federation represented the CDCUs in developing working relationships with other types of progressive financial institutions operating in poor neighborhoods, including community development loan funds, community development banks and microenterprise lenders.[24] With representatives of these institutions, it formed the Coalition of Community Development Financial Institutions which argued for President Clinton's community development banking initiative and had an influence in shaping it.

Over time the Federation succeeded in attracting as members increasingly greater proportions of the credit unions located in low-income areas of the country, but this trend was countered by the overall reduction in the number of CDCUs. In the 1990s the trend turned upwards; by 1993, the Federation had 109 member credit unions in 30 states plus the District of Columbia and American Samoa. It holds an annual meeting which representatives of the member credit unions attend. In addition to providing training seminars and business sessions, they offer an occasion for the people in these institutions to meet and learn from one another.

As the programs of the Federation have grown, it has developed enough

---

[24] For descriptions of the loan funds and the microenterprise lenders, see Stevens and Tholin; and McLenighan and Pogge.

sources of income to expand its staff. Member credit union dues rose from $21,000 in 1988 to $33,000 in 1992, but the dues represented a smaller and smaller portion of the Federation's total income, just 3 percent in 1992. The bulk of the Federation's income comes from grants, contracts, the spread on the capitalization program, and CUNA. In 1993, the Federation's staff had risen to 10 people. Most were non-white, reflecting the Federation's overall membership.

The most important development in stabilizing the Federation was its merger with CUNA, the Credit Union National Association, in 1991. The Federation had grown up outside the CUNA umbrella, and many of its members were suspicious of or even hostile to CUNA. CUNA was seen to represent the large and mainstream credit unions, mainly white and middle class, that had largely forsaken the mission of social change that was central to the CDCUs. A number of CDCU leaders told the author in interviews that they had encountered a certain lack of cooperation from the credit union leagues in their states.[25] By the turn of the decade, however, it was becoming clear that both sides would benefit by closer organizational cooperation. From CUNA's side, it was facing increasing skepticism from Congress that credit unions deserved tax exemption and other legal benefits that derived from their status as cooperatives. The country's credit unions were looking more and more like banks, and the Congress was increasingly considering treating them just like banks. So, at least in the opinion of board members of the National Federation who talked with the author, CUNA wanted to be able to say publicly that its members were serving a social purpose well beyond that provided by the banks, and the CDCUs were perfect for this. In addition, CUNA had embarked upon Operation Moonshot, to raise the country's credit union membership from about 60 million people to 100 million. To do this, it would need to make major inroads into poor communities, and the CDCUs could be a help in this. The Federation, for its part, needed ongoing, permanent organizational and financial support. Its staff salaries were low, and completely vulnerable to the changing fashions of foundation support. Affiliation with CUNA promised to bring with it salary support for the staff, plus medical and retirement benefits, plus access to the enormous technical resources that CUNA had available. The concern, from the Federation's side, was to retain its autonomy in terms of setting policy, while enjoying the benefits of CUNA affiliation.

Long negotiations produced an agreement under which the Federation's

---

[25] The leagues are the trade associations in each state that represent most or all of the state's credit unions. They provide technical assistance and in some cases operate a central financial facility. The state leagues are affiliated with CUNA on the national level.

offices would stay in New York rather than move to CUNA headquarters in Madison, Wisconsin, and the Federation's board of directors would retain responsibility for the organization's policy. At the same time, the affiliation provided that part of the executive director's salary would be paid by CUNA, and that the position would report, for some purposes, to a CUNA vice-president. As the partnership worked out, in 1992 CUNA covered 19 percent of the Federation's operational expenses.

Summary

By the early 1990s, then, CDCUs had reached a position of reasonable stability and were prepared for expansion. Some of them had been in existence for 50 years. They had survived the roller coaster of the late 1960s and early 1970s when hundreds were chartered but many soon failed. They had made it through the 1980s, when almost any program in the country dealing with poor people was viewed with hostility by many in positions of public authority. Liquidations and mergers of CDCUs continued throughout the 1980s and early 1990s, and the CDCU movement had figuratively held its breath in the late 1980s when no new CDCUs were chartered. But most recently the chartering of new CDCUs has begun again, and interesting innovations in cooperative community finance are springing up around the country. The trade association, the National Federation of CDCUs, is stronger than ever, continuously inventing and implementing new programs. CUNA, representing the whole credit union industry, has taken a new interest in CDCUs, and backed that interest with support. NCUA has begun to consider CDCUs as rather more of an asset, and rather less of a bother, than it once did. There is a new interest by the federal government in promoting community development banking, to be discussed in detail in Chapter 7, and this interest is likely to translate into substantial real support.

No one imagines that the hard times are over. Institutions that work with the poor will always be in a tenuous position. More CDCUs will be liquidated and the chartering of each new one will be a struggle. But overall, the CDCU movement was in a much stronger position in the early 1990s than it was a decade before.

Why does the success of the CDCUs matter so much? To answer this question, Chapter 4 turns to the issue of how ordinary financial institutions treat poor communities in the United States.

CHAPTER 4

WHY ARE CDCUs NEEDED?

I was born in Lee County, Alabama in a small town where poverty and ignorance were accepted as a way of life. People in Lee County worked hard but earned little, especially people of color....My own family had no access to credit from banks or from other sources. We were victimized by loan sharks who operated through finance companies and businesses, as these were our only sources for credit.
—Ernest Johnson, CDCU specialist[1]

In many American cities the most accessible financial institution is a check cashing facility. In some areas these institutions charge as much as 10 percent just to cash a government check. People who want to save have no place to go; businesses have no access to capital.
—Senator Bill Bradley, D-NJ[2]

It has been our experience that the voluntary initiatives of banks have been entirely insufficient to address fair access to credit and that regulators have been undependable in enforcing the Community Reinvestment Act.
—Gilda Haas, Communities for Accountable Reinvestment[3]

---

[1] John Ernest Johnson. "Low Income Credit Unions: Failures that Lead to Success." Master's thesis, Antioch University, Yellow Springs, Ohio, 1991.

[2] Testimony before the U.S. Senate Banking Committee, July 15, 1992.

[3] Testimony before the Subcommittee on Housing and Community Development and the Subcommittee on Consumer Affairs and Coinage of the U.S. House of Representatives Committee on Banking, Finance and Urban Affairs, May 7, 1992.

Financial services and financial institutions are seriously lacking in low- and moderate-income neighborhoods in the United States. The existing conventional financial institutions—banks, savings and loan associations, and even credit unions—have not provided the services that are needed. To a large extent, the financial tasks in poor areas have been left to the informal sector—to check cashers, liquor stores, pawnshops, finance companies, and loan sharks—and this has left poor communities at a severe disadvantage.

The evidence shows that fewer loans are available to residents of poor communities than to people and businesses in middle- and upper-class areas. Banks are more likely to deny loan applications from the poor. What is true of the poor is doubly true of the non-white; even among the poor, racial minorities have less access to loans than do whites. These assertions are well documented in the case of home mortgage loans; in small business and consumer lending the available information is less comprehensive but suggests the same conclusion. There are fewer branch offices of financial institutions in poor communities than in other areas and recent branch closures have exacerbated the discrepancies. Many of the poor have to turn to currency exchanges or check cashers to conduct the simplest of financial transactions; these institutions charge relatively high fees and offer limited services and no insurance protection. The branches of conventional financial institutions that do exist in poor communities serve largely to drain resources out of those communities rather than bring capital to bear on pressing problems. The federal legislation that has been designed to address these sorts of problems is largely, if not completely, ineffective. The extent to which the problems are the consequence of active discrimination and racism, or rather the consequence of the impersonal functioning of normal capitalist markets, is not clear, but it may not matter very much. What matters is the severe lack of financial services in poor communities. Community development credit unions—which offer essential financial services to poor communities at reasonable rates—are therefore critically needed. This chapter discusses these issues.

Financial Institutions as Intermediaries

Financial institutions such as banks and credit unions are a key to economic development. They function as the intermediaries between savers on the one hand, and consumers and investors who can make productive use of loans on the other hand.[4] They pool the savings of a large number of people,

---
4 For the classic analysis of financial institutions as intermediaries, see Gurley and Shaw.

and subsequently lend those savings at a rate of interest sufficient to cover the cost of funds and their own expenses.

At first blush, financial institutions might not seem to be very critical players on the economic scene. They do not generate significant savings of their own; they simply allow for the pooling of other people's savings. They do not invent new technologies, buy equipment, start businesses, or build houses; they simply lend to other people who perform these tasks. One might well ask why financial institutions are needed at all. Why do the people with excess funds, the savers, not simply lend directly to the people who need extra funds, the borrowers—and thereby avoid the expense and bother of the intermediary altogether?

The answer is that financial institutions provide significant services to savers that individual borrowers could not provide and significant services to the borrowers that the savers could not provide. Most savers are in no position to evaluate the creditworthiness of a loan applicant or make informed choices between different applicants. Few savers are prepared to assume the risk inherent in lending to a borrower. Instead, they deposit their funds in a financial institution where, in most cases, their savings are completely guaranteed and the rate of return is secure. The borrowers, for their part, would find it tedious and expensive in the extreme to approach a large number of small savers in order to put together a large loan. They would find it difficult to persuade savers to tie up their funds for the length of time the borrowers wish to keep the money. Instead, they approach a single financial intermediary, which is likely to provide all of the funds needed for a reasonable length of time. The intermediary builds up long-term assets (its loans) which are suitable to the borrowers, and balances them with short-term liabilities (its deposits) which are attractive to savers.

Financial institutions provide the important service, therefore, of connecting savers and borrowers. They are a channel through which a society's financial resources are converted to productive use. They are not the only channel. Governments amass funds through taxation and use them for purposes that are decided upon in the political process. But within the private sector of a capitalist, market economy such as the United States, banks and other financial institutions are the principal mechanism for gathering funds and directing them.

As a consequence, the financial sector has a great deal of power. Through its lending policies, it determines the uses to which a society's funds will be put. This is not to say that each individual financial institution has a great deal of power. Many thousands of banks, thrift institutions, and credit unions operate in competitive markets. If one of them decides not to engage in a particular kind of lending, that niche may be filled by another institution. But taken as a whole, the financial sector influences the sorts of investments and expenditures that will be undertaken and the overall direction of economic development. Some sectors, communities, and people are amply provided with funds while others are starved—whether because they lack productive investment opportunities, or because they appear untrustworthy to the lenders, or because of outright and arbitrary discrimination.

The failure of banks and other financial institutions to serve poor communities adequately is therefore a matter of great concern to those communities.

An Example on Chicago's South Side[5]

A testament to the importance of financial services in a poor community exists on the south side of Chicago in the contrast between two predominantly African American neighborhoods, South Shore and Woodlawn. In the mid 1970s, both were depressed, low-income areas with high unemployment and a decaying housing stock. Woodlawn was well known to the outside world as the area in which Saul Alinsky developed his techniques of grass-roots community organizing in the 1960s. The Woodlawn Organization (TWO) was a model of local people taking the issues that beset their neighborhood into their own hands, confronting the power structure, and working for constructive change. South Shore did not enjoy this kind of community organization.

By the 1990s, however, the contrast between the two areas was dramatic. Woodlawn was almost completely devastated, with block after block of abandoned apartment buildings and many vacant lots where buildings had burned. South Shore, on the other hand, was thriving, with block after block of rehabilitated housing and a viable commercial sector.

How did South Shore succeed and The Woodlawn Organization ultimately fail? The full answer is no doubt complicated, but one difference between the two neighborhoods stands out easily. In 1973, the South Shore Bank was formed to buy out a local bank and to direct funds into the local neighborhood for housing rehabilitation. South Shore Bank was a community development bank, a bank with stockholders and established to make a profit, but with the additional purpose of rescuing its neighborhood. Rather than drain funds from the neighborhood, it became a conduit for channeling outside funds into the neighborhood. The bank made local real estate loans on the express condition that the property be rehabilitated. These were properties that Chicago's banks had consistently declined to finance. South Shore

---

[5] Much of the information in this section comes from the author's visit to South Shore Bank, along with other members of the National Federation of CDCUs, in May, 1992. For descriptions of South Shore Bank, and the associated financial institutions controlled by the holding company, Shorebank Corporation, see among others Satin, Quint, and Houghton.

Bank initially provided mortgages on single family units. Within a few years, it had demonstrated that such lending was profitable and other Chicago lenders moved in to compete. At that point, seeing no further need in the area of single family structure mortgages, South Shore began to finance the purchase and rehabilitation of apartment buildings. Between 1973 and 1991, it financed the rehabilitation of 30 percent of the neighborhood's rental housing units. Still later, it moved into small business lending.

South Shore Bank uses the deposits of community people for the development of the local area. It also serves as a vehicle for channeling outside funds into the local community; about half of the deposits come from outside South Shore, while almost all of the loans are made within the target area.

In Woodlawn, on the other hand, there was no institution devoted to development finance and consequently no way of directing capital into the community. The Woodlawn Organization was a marvelous example of community organizing but it lacked capital, and in the long run was therefore unable to prevent the deterioration and death of its community.

The South Shore Bank shows the power that a financial institution can have to promote development in its community. No other community development banks in the United States, however, have been successful for a sufficiently long period to make a real impact. At the beginning of the 1990s, several banks in other poor areas of the country were trying to replicate South Shore's success,[6] but it was too early to evaluate them. Woodlawn is in some respects an extreme case, but it is more typical of poor communities, particularly in central cities: Woodlawn demonstrates that the absence of a financial institution that can collect and direct capital for economic development may go hand in hand with the social and economic deterioration of an area.

Home Mortgage Lending

A great deal is known about the home mortgage lending of banks and other financial institutions, far more than is known about other aspects of banking activity in poor neighborhoods. Mortgage lending patterns are well documented because of the passage in 1975 of the federal Home Mortgage Disclosure Act (HMDA), which required banks and other depository institutions to disclose publicly, by census tract, the dollar amount and number of their home mortgages and home improvement loans. In 1989, the HMDA reporting requirements were expanded significantly.[7] The patterns that are

---

[6] They included the Southern Development Bancorporation, a bank holding company founded in 1988 in Arkansas, sponsored by and modeled after South Shore Bank's holding company, Shorebank Corporation; Community Capital Bank, founded in 1990 in Brooklyn, New York; and Development Bank of Washington, D.C., which at the time of writing was being organized in the nation's capital.

[7] The most recent data are fully described in Glenn B. Canner and Dolores S. Smith, from which much of the information in this section is taken.

revealed by the HMDA data are disturbing, partly for what they show directly about mortgage lending and partly because they hint at the uneven distribution of the other bank services that are not so well documented. The pre-1990 HMDA data can be combined with information about personal income and racial composition from the census tracts. The resulting patterns are striking. Using rather reserved language, Glenn B. Canner and Dolores S. Smith of the Federal Reserve Board described the overall findings of a large number of studies of lending in individual cities and by individual banks:

> For the most part, one basic lending pattern has stood out: Considerable differences exist in the levels of home lending activity across neighborhoods within local communities when the neighborhoods are grouped by median family income or racial composition....Overall the HMDA data show that a smaller proportion of home purchase loans made by reporting lenders are for properties in low or moderate-income neighborhoods (those where median family income is less than 80 percent of the median family income of their MSA).[8]

In other words, banks lend significantly less to the poor than to the middle class. According to the 1980 census, low-income areas contained 16 percent of the owner-occupied housing units in MSAs, and yet in the latter part of the 1980s they received only between 10 and 12 percent of the number of home purchase loans. Upper-income neighborhoods, in contrast (those whose median family income exceeded 120 percent of the median family income of their MSA), contained 23 percent of the units, and received roughly 33 percent of the home purchase loans. These figures refer to the number of home purchase mortgage loans, not the dollar amount of lending. No one would be surprised to discover that a disproportionate share of the money went to high-income areas; what these data reveal is a disproportion in the number of loans.

When the racial composition of the different neighborhoods is taken into account, the picture becomes more skewed. In 1988, newspapers in Atlanta and Detroit conducted studies comparing mortgage lending in predominantly white and predominantly minority communities of roughly comparable average incomes.[9] The newspapers found the same pattern in both cities. Banks made three to four times more home purchase loans, per single family housing unit, in the predominantly white areas than in the

---

8   Ibid. MSA stands for metropolitan statistical area.

9   "The Color of Money," *Atlanta Journal-Constitution*, and "The Race for Money," *Detroit Free Press*.

predominantly minority areas. The principal conclusions of the Atlanta Journal Constitution were stated clearly:

> Whites receive five times as many home loans from Atlanta's banks and savings and loans as blacks of the same income—and that gap has been widening each year, an Atlanta Journal-Constitution study of $6.2 billion in lending shows.
>
> Race—not home value or household income—consistently determines the lending patterns of metro Atlanta's largest financial institutions, according to the study, which examined six years of lender reports to the federal government.
>
> Among stable neighborhoods of the same income, white neighborhoods always received the most bank loans per 1,000 single-family homes. Integrated neighborhoods always received fewer. Black neighborhoods—including the mayor's neighborhood—always received the fewest.

The same pattern was found in Atlanta area home mortgage loans purchased in the secondary market by the Federal National Mortgage Association (Fannie Mae) and other secondary market lenders.[10] These institutions purchased twice as many home mortgages per 100 homeowners in predominantly white neighborhoods as in predominantly minority neighborhoods. In the period July 1, 1987 through June 30, 1989, the figures were 13.9 loans per 100 homeowners in white areas, as against 7.0 in the minority areas. The pre-1990 data, therefore, showed significant differences in mortgage lending by income levels and racial composition of different areas of cities.

The 1989 expansion of the HMDA allows a more detailed examination of the patterns of mortgage lending. Under the new requirements, reporting was extended beyond depository institutions to include independent mortgage companies. This is an important addition, since non-depository mortgage companies are particularly active in low-income areas. All home mortgage lending institutions are now required to report the number of loan applications and their disposition, not just the loans actually made. They are also required to report the race or national origin, gender, and annual income of the applicants.

At the time of writing, results from the expanded HMDA are just beginning to come in; within a few years, there will doubtless be many detailed

---

[10] Ols, Jr.

Table 4.1
(Percentages by Applicant Income and Race)

Denial Rates for Applications for Mortgages to Purchase Homes
1990

Applicant Income and Race	Government-backed Mortgage	Conventional Mortgage
Less than 80% of median MSA income		
Native American	26.5	27.7
Asian/Pacific Islander	13.9	17.2
Black	29.4	40.1
Hispanic	22.4	31.1
White	14.7	23.1
Other	21.3	26.1
Joint (white/minority)	17.3	26.3
80% - 99% of median		
Native American	17.8	16.6
Asian/Pacific Islander	12.7	13.7
Black	24.8	29.3
Hispanic	17.0	21.5
White	10.6	13.7
Other	13.5	21.1
Joint (white/minority)	13.0	18.0
100% - 120% of median		
Native American	17.0	14.0
Asian/Pacific Islander	12.4	12.6
Black	23.1	26.3
Hispanic	14.7	19.1
White	9.5	11.2
Other	15.0	18.0
Joint (white/minority)	12.9	15.0
More than 120% of median		
Native American	15.6	12.8
Asian/Pacific Islander	11.2	11.2
Black	20.8	21.4
Hispanic	14.2	15.8
White	8.6	8.5
Other	17.1	15.8
Joint (white/minority)	10.6	10.5

Table 4.2
(Percentages by Census Tract Characteristics)

Denial Rates for Applications for Mortgages to Purchase Homes
1990

Census Tract Characteristic	Government-backed Mortgage	Conventional Mortgage
Racial composition (minorities as percentage of population)		
Less than 10	11.2	11.5
10-19	13.4	13.8
20-49	16.1	16.5
50-79	21.1	19.3
80-100	23.2	24.0
Income (median income as percentage of MSA median)		
Low (less than 80%)	17.8	20.2
Middle (80% - 120%)	13.0	13.9
Upper (more than 120%)	11.2	9.7
Income and racial composition (minorities as percentage of population)		
Low-income		
Less than 10	14.0	17.8
10-19	14.9	18.9
20-49	17.3	19.4
50-79	20.6	21.2
80-100	24.2	24.4
Middle-income		
Less than 10	11.3	12.7
10-19	13.5	14.5
20-49	15.8	16.3
50-79	22.2	18.1
80-100	21.5	23.7
Upper-income		
Less than 10	10.3	8.8
10-19	12.0	11.3
20-49	14.9	13.0
50-79	13.9	15.3
80-100	17.1	16.8

studies of mortgage lending in individual cities. The Board of Governors of the Federal Reserve System has published a few nationwide tabulations for 1990. While limited, they both confirm and extend the conclusions that were apparent in the earlier data.

In 1990, 6.4 million applications for mortgage loans were recorded. Since applications are included along with loans actually made, denial rates can be calculated. Tables 4.1 and 4.2 contain the denial rates for the country as a whole, 4.1 according to the income and race of the applicants, and 4.2 according to the average income and racial characteristics of the census tract.[11]

The new HMDA data are revealing. Table 4.1 shows that lenders refuse a higher than average proportion of mortgage applications from poor people and from minorities. Both factors are important. Starting with income, for each racial group, low-income people are more likely to be denied mortgages than middle-income people are, and middle-income people are more likely to be denied than upper-income. For example, a lower-income white person is almost three times as likely to be rejected for a conventional mortgage as an upper-income white. Turning to race, within each income category, Blacks, Hispanics and Native Americans suffer more denials than whites do; for example, a Black person is about twice as likely to be rejected as a white.

Looking at the characteristics of the census tracts in Table 4.2, the findings are similar. Denial rates are higher the greater the minority proportion of a community's population and the lower the typical incomes in the neighborhoods. The first panel of Table 4.2 shows the patterns by race: the more nonwhite, the greater the likelihood that a mortgage loan application will be denied. The second panel shows the patterns by income: the poorer the neighborhood, the greater the likelihood of denial. The last three panels show that the racial composition of a neighborhood influences the denial rates, even when income is held constant. For example, looking only at low-income neighborhoods, the denial rates in predominantly minority neighborhoods are much higher than in predominantly white neighborhoods: 24 percent versus 14 percent in the case of government-backed mortgages.

The differences in denial rates in these tables are almost surely an understatement of the true differences in the mortgage markets in different areas of the country. In many cases, potential applications that are likely to be rejected are simply not filed. Realtors who are familiar with the lending policies of local financial institutions will decline to work with people or properties that are unlikely to receive a mortgage, and thus the loan application is

---

[11] Canner and Smith.

never made.[12] Sometimes informal inquiries are made to a loan officer and rejected out of hand, the consequence being that no formal loan application is made and no record is kept under the HMDA.

A narrower study of mortgage lending in the San Francisco Bay Area, using the expanded HMDA data for 1990, comes to much the same conclusions.[13] For example, at the area's largest mortgage lender, Bank of America, an affluent African American was more likely to be denied a mortgage than a low-moderate income white: 31 percent denial rate versus 27 percent in Oakland, 45 percent versus 25 percent in San Francisco.

In an ambitious study sponsored by Ralph Nader's Essential Information, Inc., Jonathan Brown used computer techniques to map loans in 16 metropolitan areas made by both banks and mortgage companies in 1990 and 1991. He identified 49 lenders and 62 separate instances in which predominantly minority neighborhoods were either excluded or under-served.[14]

Thus the voluminous data on home mortgages that have been collected over the years show clear patterns. Fewer home purchase loans are made in poor and minority communities than elsewhere, in absolute terms and also per hundred units of owner-occupied housing. One of the explanations of this disparity is that mortgage applications from the poor and from minorities are disproportionately likely to be rejected.

Bank Services Besides Mortgage Lending

Home mortgage lending by financial institutions is exceptionally well documented; other aspects of bank activities in low- and moderate-income communities are hardly documented at all. Governments do not require reports on the geographic dispersion of other bank activities nor on the income and race of the people who engage in other types of business with the banks. No equivalent of the HMDA exists in such areas as consumer and small business lending, location of branches, services offered by branches, or deposits. A few state and local governments have passed commercial lending disclosure laws but the quality of the data that are generated is uneven.[15]

In order to assess the need for community development credit unions in

---

[12] See, for example, *Atlanta Journal-Constitution*, "The Color of Money," op. cit., for interviews with realtors in predominantly black areas who say that they generally steer their clients toward mortgage companies rather than banks or savings and loan associations because their experience is that the latter are unlikely to approve a loan in their neighborhood.

[13] California Council of Urban Leagues.

[14] Brown with Bennington.

[15] See Flax-Hatch for a discussion of the data generated by Chicago's ordinance on the disclosure of commercial lending.

poor areas, one would like to have comprehensive information on all financial services, not just home mortgages. Credit unions, after all, are not exclusively home mortgage lenders. They are largely consumer lenders, and some of them lend to small businesses as well. In the absence of systematic data, however, one must make do with scattered, unsystematic information and inferences.

Looking first at personal loans, what evidence exists seems to indicate that low-income people seldom get them from conventional financial institutions such as banks, savings and loan associations, and credit unions. The poor are unlikely to turn to such institutions when they need advances for a vacation, a car, education, health care, or the purchase of major appliances. This type of lending is the niche in which mainstream credit unions do a great deal of their business, but seldom with the poor. While comprehensive data on this point are lacking, studies and interviews from widely scattered neighborhoods show a consistent picture.

Organizers of new CDCUs frequently survey the state of financial services in their neighborhoods as a part of the chartering process. One such survey, conducted by the Woodstock Institute in Chicago's Austin area in preparation for the founding of the Austin/West Garfield Federal Credit Union, showed that people in the neighborhood experienced a severe lack of credit for their personal needs. Summarizing the findings, Kathryn Tholin wrote that local leaders

> *felt strongly that there was a lack of affordable financial services in the community, particularly for low-income residents. The local banks were widely perceived as not making an effort to make loans within the community. Furthermore, experience had demonstrated that the local banks were also not interested in serving the deposit needs of local residents or of local organizations. Because local banks charged high fees for small accounts, lower income residents in the community did not have access to either banking services or credit from banks. Even middle income residents could not get small loans from local banks. Respondents cited consumer loans, home improvement loans and loans for purchase or repair of used cars as particular needs they felt were unmet in the community.*[16]

It would not be surprising to find that financial institutions do an even less thorough job of lending in low-income neighborhoods for personal, consumer purposes than they do for home mortgages. In the case of mort-

---
[16] Tholin, 4.

gages, after all, the collateral is substantial and verifiable and it does not necessarily lose value over time. A used automobile, on the other hand, is of more uncertain value and is certain to depreciate. In the case of debt consolidation, vacation, medical, and other sorts of personal lending, there may be no collateral at all that can be repossessed if the borrower fails in his or her repayment obligations. Thus a lender falls back to a large extent on an assessment of the income and assets of the borrower, and perhaps character as well. By definition, income is lower in low-income areas and certainly assets are lower too, and thus lenders have reason to be cautious. If racism and other forms of discrimination play a role in lending decisions, they are more likely to do so in consumer than in mortgage loans because the importance of character, as judged by the lender, is more central.

The many CDCU loan officers with whom the author has talked have said that their institutions are not in competition with other conventional financial institution when it comes to making personal loans to their low-income members. This is not to say that the poor members are unable to get credit, but the sources for the poor are likely to be a pawnshop, a finance company, or a loan shark. For example, in the mountains of eastern Kentucky, the principal alternatives were thought to be pawnshops and finance companies. On the Navajo reservation in Arizona people usually turn to pawnshops, and in several central cities, in addition to pawnshops and finance companies, they deal frequently with individual loan sharks. Small business borrowers in poor neighborhoods sometimes get credit from their suppliers, at high implicit rates of interest. A study in South Central Los Angeles shows this type of non-conventional lending increasing three-fold in the 1980s.[17]

The non-conventional lenders who do business with poor people are quite different from banks and other standard financial institutions. Their interest rates are generally much higher. Annual rates as high as 50 to 100 percent are common, and the rates sometimes go higher. Borrowers are sometimes unaware of the real rates; for example, Rosenthal and Schoder found people on the Lower East Side of Manhattan who referred to 10 percent per week payments to a loan shark as "ten percent interest."[18] Non-conventional lenders sometimes use unscrupulous, even predatory, practices. The South Central Los Angeles study cited above shows, for example, that two of the largest finance companies in the area have been sued frequently for fraud and unfair business practices.[19]

---

[17] Haas.

[18] Rosenthal and Schoder.

[19] Haas.

On the other hand, non-conventional lenders sometimes provide services that are not possible in more bureaucratic institutions. In comparison to the latter, they reduce transactions costs, namely the time and money costs of doing business. The informal sector lenders frequently have a much less complicated application process and a shorter waiting period. Because they are located closer to the borrowers, the borrowers waste less time traveling to and from appointments and time saved is time during which a low-income person can be earning money.[20] What this indicates is not so much that the non-conventional sector serves poor people well as that conventional institutions often serve them badly, even when loans are available. It also indicates that CDCUs would be well advised to focus not only on the explicit costs of their loans but also on the hidden costs, and to do what they can to minimize delays and bureaucratic procedures.

What is true of mortgage and consumer loans is also true of small business loans; poor people and racial minorities find them very difficult to obtain. A study of commercial lending in Chicago, conducted by the Woodstock Institute, showed that in 1986 and 1987, the city's principal banks directed just one-third of their commercial lending to the city, compared to two-thirds to the suburbs. Of the one-third in the city, three-quarters went to the downtown Loop area, leaving only one-quarter of one-third for the neighborhoods. It was not possible to show how poor neighborhoods fared in comparison to middle-class and prosperous neighborhoods, but one would be surprised to find that they did very well.[21]

As part of its larger study on redlining, the *Atlanta Journal-Constitution* examined small business lending in its area, and especially loans guaranteed by the Small Business Administration.[22] The principal conclusion was summarized in an interview with a county planner: "Redlining is worse on the commercial side than in housing." The newspaper found that most banks would not consider a commercial loan for less than $100,000. Using their normal underwriting rules, this implies that an entrepreneur would have to have $25,000 to $50,000 in start-up equity capital, a sum far beyond the reach of most low-income people. As in the case of mortgages, income was not the only determinant of the dispersion of loans; race also mattered considerably. The newspaper found that the largest three banks in Atlanta had a much smaller share of SBA loans in predominantly black areas than their

---

[20] I am grateful to Ginger McNally for her M.A. thesis, which refers to a study demonstrating the high opportunity costs of conventional loans as compared to informal sector loans in Latin America: Christen; McNally.

[21] Flax-Hatch.

[22] Op. cit.

share of deposits in those areas. The owner of a minority small business investment corporation was quoted as saying, "The bank is making these loans to white establishments. You don't want to think it's out and out racism, but you wonder." Whatever the reason, it is clear that commercial capital is scarce in poor neighborhoods.

Not only do banks lend less in poor than in middle-class communities, they provide fewer financial services of all kinds. During the 1980s, many banks reduced the number of their branches, and they did so disproportionately in low-income areas. A study commissioned by the City of Los Angeles revealed branch openings and closings from 1987 through 1990. In this period there were 27 openings and 416 closings, the latter concentrated in low-income areas.[23] Gilda Haas of Communities for Accountable Reinvestment studied the branch closures of two major banks in the Los Angeles area, Bank of America and Security Pacific. She reported:

> During this period, Security Pacific closed 21 branches and Bank of America closed 30. 71 percent of Security Pacific closures and 67 percent of Bank of America's were in low and moderate income communities. None of Security Pacific's closures and only four of Bank of America's closures were in upper income neighborhoods. 52 percent of Security Pacific's branch closures and 30 percent of Bank of America's occurred in neighborhoods which are 80-100 percent minority, while only 10 percent and 7 percent respectively of Security Pacific and Bank of America's closures took place in communities that have less than 10 percent minority populations.[24]

This pattern of bank branch closures, particularly in low-income neighborhoods, seems to be common throughout the country. A number of community development credit unions were formed during the 1980s specifically in response to branch closings that left a neighborhood with no standard banking services. When Manufacturers Hanover Trust Company closed the last bank branch in a 100-square block area of Manhattan's Lower East Side, it inadvertently created a movement that led to the chartering, in 1986, of the Lower East Side People's Federal Credit Union.[25] In Philadelphia, Southwest Germantown Association Federal Credit Union moved its

---

[23] "Taking it to the Bank: Poverty, Race, and Credit in Los Angeles," a report to the City of Los Angeles prepared by the Western Center on Law and Poverty, June 1991, cited in Haas.

[24] Haas.

[25] The story of the credit union is told in Rosenthal and Schoder.

operations into a branch building that was closed by Fidelity Bank. As banks become scarcer in low-income communities, they are replaced by a variety of substitute institutions, including check cashing establishments or currency exchanges. The currency exchanges provide some essential financial services, but to a more limited degree and at a higher cost than do banks. Checks can be cashed, but at a discount that sometimes reaches as high as 10 percent. Money orders are sold, but for a higher fee than banks usually charge.[26] Furthermore, since the currency exchanges are not insured, poor people who buy money orders from them are at risk until the money orders clear. They are not depository institutions for poor people and they do not provide either interest or credit. So when currency exchanges replace banks, important financial services are lost. In South Central Los Angeles in 1991, a study found just 19 bank branches but 133 currency exchanges, a ratio of 1 to 7.[27]

The Drain of Capital

Evidence exists that banks and other financial institutions do not provide capital to poor communities but instead drain capital out of them. The evidence is not conclusive since so much of it is hidden in the files of the institutions, but it is at least suggestive.

In order to test this proposition conclusively, one would like to know the deposits in each neighborhood or branch in comparison to the loans made in that neighborhood or by that branch. The larger the latter in comparison to the former, the more the bank is helping a community use its own resources for its own use. Even the balance sheet figures on these subjects would not be conclusive because of the complications caused by the banks' selling of loans on the secondary market, but they would be helpful. In their absence, we are left with inferences and a few case studies.

In Philadelphia, the Southwest Germantown Association Federal Credit Union gained access to the books of the Fidelity Bank branch it was replacing, to discover that the branch had only $100,000 in loans on the books compared to $15 million in deposits. Clearly, that branch was functioning like a great pump, sucking up the community's financial resources and draining them out somewhere else.

The *Atlanta Journal-Constitution* used nationwide estimates of savings by

---

[26] A Woodstock Institute survey of 18 currency exchanges in Chicago's Austin community in 1986 found these fees: For check cashing, 90 cents plus 1.2 percent of the amount of the check (for example, the fee for a $125 check was $2.40). For money orders, 75 cents plus 1 percent of the amount of money (for example, the fee for a $120 money order was $1.40). For utility bills, 50 cents; for state plates, $3.50; for a book of stamps, 75 cents; and so forth. Tholin.

[27] Haas.

Black and white populations to estimate the bank deposits in predominantly Black and predominantly white areas of the city in 1986. Comparing these with the HMDA mortgage data for the same year, it calculated that Blacks received 9.1 cents in the form of mortgage loans on each dollar saved, while whites received 13.7 cents. The newspaper had no information on other types of lending, but if the same patterns exist in personal and commercial lending—as they probably do—then it is clear that the banks channel money out of Black areas at a much faster rate than they do out of white areas.

The most comprehensive study of the drain of capital from poor areas is by ACORN, the Association of Community Organizations for Reform Now, one of the principal groups lobbying for tighter controls on bank lending.[28] ACORN used information from the Federal Deposit Insurance Corporation on deposits by bank branch and compared it to HMDA information on mortgage lending by branch. The neighborhoods in which the branches were located were categorized by income level and by racial composition, using census tract data. Summarizing the study, the authors wrote:

> Nationally, the study revealed that, for every dollar on deposit in predominantly minority neighborhoods, about 4 cents was loaned for mortgages in those same neighborhoods in 1989. By contrast, for every dollar on deposit in predominantly white neighborhoods, nearly 8 cents are reinvested in those same neighborhoods....
>
> The discrepancies were not materially reduced when comparing neighborhoods of comparable income, but different racial and ethnic profiles. For example, middle-income, predominantly minority neighborhoods received only two cents in loans for every dollar on deposit in those areas, while middle-income, predominantly white neighborhoods received nearly seven cents in loans for every dollar on deposit in those areas.

These findings are shown in Tables 4.3 and 4.4.[29] Philadelphia is the one exception where, the authors say, banks may have responded to community pressure to increase lending in the central city. In all the other cities studied, the ratio of mortgage lending to deposits was considerably lower in minority than in white communities.

---

[28] Association of Community Organizations for Reform Now (ACORN).

[29] Data from ibid.

Table 4.3

Loan-to-Deposit Ratios by Racial Composition of Neighborhoods

City	up to 25% Minority	>25% Minority	>75% Minority
Brooklyn	17.3%		11.8%
Chicago	7.6		2.4
Dallas	7.5		1.3
Detroit	–		0.4
New Orleans	14.5		1.0
Philadelphia	3.6		5.0
St. Louis	4.2		2.7
Washington DC	10.2		7.8
Boston	12.3	8.8%	
Kansas City	5.9	0.5	
Little Rock	9.8	2.0	
Milwaukee	3.0	0.5	
Minn-St. Paul	6.0	0.8	
Phoenix	8.6	1.8	

Table 4.4

Loan-to-Deposit Ratios in Middle-Income Neighborhoods by Racial Composition of Neighborhood

City	up to 25% Minority	>25% Minority	>75% Minority
Brooklyn	7.0%		4.8%
Chicago	21.7		2.1
Dallas	8.0		0.6
Philadelphia	3.1		1.2
Washington DC	20.1		3.3
Boston	9.6	0.4	
Kansas City	7.8	0.6	
Milwaukee	3.7	0.4	
Phoenix	3.3	1.5	

Because of the limited information that is available, the ACORN study looks only at mortgage lending in comparison to deposits. One would like to have data on all lending. As noted above, however, every reason exists to think that personal and commercial lending is just as skewed, and probably more so, as mortgage lending. If Tables 4.3 and 4.4 could be compiled to include all lending, they would probably show that the proportion of a community's savings that is returned to it in the form of loans is significantly higher for whites than for non-whites. On the basis of what is known, therefore, it is very likely that banks act to drain capital out of poor and minority communities. This drain is both predictable and disturbing. It is predictable because, on the basis of all that is known about lending patterns in poor communities, it is clear that financial institutions do not regard such areas as good investment risks. They do not invest much money in them. The funds that are deposited by residents of poor communities become part of the resource base of the financial institution, and that institution is free to move those resources anywhere in the world that it deems prudent and profitable. Most financial institutions create no connection between the area that generates its resources and the area that absorbs those resources. One would be surprised to learn that the savings of poor communities are returned to those communities.

Yet the capital drain, if not surprising, is disturbing. Capital is a very important resource. A labor force, no matter how skilled, educated, and energetic, can make little progress in economic development without capital, without funds to make investments. The poorest areas of the country, both urban and rural, are the most needy, the areas where economic development could make the most impact on the lives of people. Ideally, at least some surplus funds from rich areas of the country would be redirected to the poor, to help repair some of the glaring gaps in living standards that mar the social landscape. At the very least, a poor community should be able to make use of its own financial resources to address its most pressing needs. But in fact what happens is that the financial resources of the poor are siphoned off into capital networks that for the most part benefit people who are better off than they are.

The need for community development credit unions is shown most dramatically by the outflow of funds from poor neighborhoods. Since a credit union is constrained to make loans only to its members, it provides a mechanism for a community to have access to its own resources. The mechanism is not airtight, since in some cases funds escape when the credit union is not fully loaned out and therefore makes investments with its surplus funds in financial institutions that lie outside its field of membership. But credit union managers always prefer to lend to members rather than make outside investments, if for no other reason than that the rate of interest on the former always exceeds the rate on the latter.[30] So while there may be some leakages of funds from the community, they are usually fairly small. In addition, the use of non-member deposits by a CDCU can promote a reverse flow of resources into the poor community.

The credit union structure is not essential to prevent the outflow of funds. The South Shore Bank in Chicago, by making loans only within its

---
[30] See, for example, Table 5.11, in the next chapter.

target community, and by accepting deposits from outside the community as well as from within, acts to create a positive flow of funds. It does this because of the social commitment it has undertaken, but it is almost unique in this respect. Most banks do not have this sort of commitment.

Legislation

For several decades, community groups and spokespeople for the poor have protested the actions of financial institutions, and have petitioned the government for redress. The focus has been largely, although not exclusively, on mortgage lending and the allegation of redlining. Among the protesters' allies in Congress was former Senator William Proxmire of Wisconsin, who wrote in 1976:

> *"Redlining" is a term that was scarcely known four years ago. But thanks to the painstaking efforts of community groups to preserve their neighborhoods, we now know that arbitrary refusal by lenders to invest in older urban neighborhoods dooms those neighborhoods to a premature death. That process, popularly called redlining, has been documented in scores of cities by community groups that labored in the basements of county court houses to produce statistics which show conclusively that many neighborhoods were not getting a fair share of mortgage money. And the community groups petitioned Congress for redress.*[31]

Congress responded with a series of acts intended to promote urban development and end discrimination of various sorts.[32]

The first major legislation was passed in 1968 as a part of President Johnson's Great Society program. Section 103 of the Housing and Urban Development Act specified certain older, poorer, and decaying sections of cities as worthy of special federal programs.

The first important anti-discrimination legislation in banking was the 1968 Civil Rights Act. Title VIII of that act is known as the Fair Housing Act. It prohibits discrimination in the sale, rental, financing, and marketing of housing on the basis of race, color, religion, national origin, or, after a 1988 amendment, handicapped or family status.

The prohibition against discrimination was extended beyond housing, to include all lending, by the Equal Credit Opportunity Act of 1974, which

---

[31] Quoted in Bentson, Horsky, and Weingartner.

[32] The highlights of the legislative history are reviewed in Calem.

specifically enjoined discrimination on the basis of race, color, religion, national origin, marital status, age, or welfare status.

The Home Mortgage Disclosure Act (HMDA) of 1975 required depository institutions to disclose by census tract the number and dollar amounts of their home mortgage and home improvement loans. As noted above, it was amended in 1989 to include all mortgage lenders, and to require disclosure of loan applications and of the race, gender, and annual income of the applicants. The HMDA was intended to open discriminatory practices to public view, to help enforcement of the Fair Housing Act, and to make redlining more difficult if not impossible.

Some legislation has been proposed at the state and local levels to expand HMDA reporting requirements. In California, for example, a bill that has been before the Assembly several times would require banks to report on all their lending, including commercial and consumer lending, not just on their mortgages. To date, none of this legislation has been adopted by states; a few cities, most notably Chicago, do have broader reporting requirements for financial institutions seeking deposits from the local government.

Finally, the Community Reinvestment Act (CRA) of 1977 called on all banks and savings and loan institutions to serve the credit needs of their entire communities, in particular low- and moderate-income areas and not just the wealthy areas. It requires the covered financial institutions to make a public record of their actions to comply with the Act, it invites the public to comment on that record, and it authorizes the government regulatory bodies to monitor compliance. In 1993, President Clinton called for a review of the CRA and its compliance regulations because of general dissatisfaction with the way it was working; this will be discussed in Chapter 7.

Taken together, these laws require that financial institutions be non-discriminatory in their provision of credit, and that they take affirmative steps to serve all parts of their communities. The HMDA is intended to provide the information by which outsiders can judge whether lenders are complying with the legislative requirements, at least in the area of mortgages.

In fact, however, the legislation has proven to be unsatisfactory to almost everyone concerned. Lending institutions generally regard it as a cumbersome intrusion on their business affairs, and completely unnecessary as well, since they claim to be not discriminatory in the first place. Community groups, on the other hand, say that they have seen little or no change in bank behavior as a consequence of the legislation.

To understand why the legislation of the last quarter century has had so little impact on the role of financial institutions in poor communities, one must consider the controversy over discrimination in lending.

Discrimination

There is no agreement as to whether financial institutions discriminate illegally against the poor and against racial minorities. The evidence presented in this chapter might seem to constitute overwhelming evidence of discrimination. The fact that non-whites receive fewer mortgage loans than whites, and that they are turned down more frequently than whites even when they have the same income, would seem definitive. Some people argue, however, that discrimination is not proven, that there may be perfectly equitable, rational, non-discriminatory reasons for these unequal results.

A sophisticated example of the latter sort of reasoning is contained in a statistical study of mortgage loans in Rochester in the mid 1970s by Benston, Horsky, and Weingartner.[33] They identified a central city area which community groups claimed was redlined and compared it to a suburban area. They found that mortgage loans were in fact made by banks in the central city; in other words, the most extreme form of the redlining hypothesis—that banks refused to lend in the central city—was transparently false. The authors explored a less extreme proposition, that banks set more stringent terms on the loans they make in the central city: higher interest rates, for example, or lower loan-to-value ratios or shorter terms. They found that some of the terms were less favorable in the central city, in particular that the number of months to maturity was smaller. Through a series of statistical tests, however, they demonstrated that most if not all of the difference in loan terms could be explained by the characteristics of the borrowers and of the property and were not associated with the area of the city.

A prudent lender must consider the creditworthiness of the applicants, and this can be divided into several dimensions. First, the lender must decide whether the applicant is likely to be able to make the payments on the loan. The main determinant is the applicant's income, but it is not the sole one; also relevant are the applicant's expenses, previous financial obligations, and credit history. Second, the lender must decide if the applicant has access to sufficient cash to cover all the immediate costs—in the case of a mortgage, these include the excess of the selling price over the loan, plus the various closing costs. And third, the lender must decide if the collateral on the loan is adequate, for example, if the house that is being bought with the loan has sufficient value, both currently and in the future, to cover the lender's exposure should the borrower default.

Bentson and his colleagues found that while the loan terms were somewhat less favorable in central Rochester than in the suburbs, this was a predictable consequence of the fact that the borrowers in the central city were

---
[33] Op. cit.

somewhat less creditworthy, according to the standard criteria of credit outlined in the last paragraph. There was almost no evidence that the lenders treated people in the two areas by unequal standards. The authors concluded that there was no evidence that redlining existed, that banks engaged in discrimination based on the area of the city in which the property or the borrower was located.

Some problems exist with the Rochester study, as with any study. While the authors chose two areas for comparison based upon community views about where redlining occurred, in fact the two areas chosen had almost exactly equal average family incomes, and the authors lacked information about the racial composition of the areas. It is not clear, therefore, that the study drew its data from an area that would be likely to show discrimination in lending, were it to exist.

At the very least, however, studies such as those of Bentson and his colleagues demonstrate that redlining and bias are complicated issues, not to be demonstrated by casual empiricism. The fact that banks lend less to the poor and to racial minorities does not by itself prove that they are violating the anti-discrimination laws.

A mountain of additional data has been generated by the HMDA since the time of the Rochester study, but they do not resolve the question of whether redlining exists and whether banks discriminate on the basis of race or geographical area.

One common complaint about the pre-1989 HMDA data is that they revealed nothing about the demand for mortgage loans. One reason why fewer mortgages are made in central cities, or to racial minorities, may be that there is less demand for loans. Perhaps suburban populations are more mobile, with more houses up for sale and consequently a higher demand for mortgages. It was because of concern about the issue of demand that applications as well as approved mortgages were covered in the most recent version of the HMDA, so that rejection rates could be calculated. As shown above, there are in fact significant differences in rejection rates, by race and income. It follows that differences in demand cannot be the sole explanation of differences in mortgage lending rates in different communities. Differences in demand may still, however, be part of the explanation.

In addition, since even the most recent version of the HMDA provides little information about the creditworthiness of the loan applicants, the data cannot be used to demonstrate illegal discrimination. The fact that fewer mortgages are extended to lower-income than to upper-income people—per unit of housing in a neighborhood or per number of applications—may indicate simply that lenders are doing a responsible job of weeding out people who lack the capacity to repay. Even the data showing lower lending rates and higher denial rates to racial minorities, when income is held constant, may be consistent with non-discriminatory lending practices because of a lower level of net worth among minorities.[34]

The strongest evidence that banks engage in mortgage lending practices that discriminate against minorities is contained in a 1992 study by the Federal Reserve Bank of Boston. It examined the economic characteristics of about 3,000 mortgage applicants in the Boston area in 1990. It found that for the most part banks used ordinary financial criteria in rejecting or accepting mortgage applications, but in addition that they discriminated against racial minorities. The study has been roundly criticized by economists at the University of Texas who have reexamined the Boston data, however. They assert that much of the reported information is obviously in error, and that even if it is not, the information does not support the study's conclusion of racial discrimination.[35]

One of the factors that makes a determination of discrimination in lending difficult is that there are different concepts, different definitions of discrimination. Discrimination based on intent is quite different from discrimination based on impact, and the latter can exist in the absence of the former.[36] Federal Civil Rights legislation helpfully distinguishes between "intentional discrimination" and "disparate impact."

Intentional discrimination is clearly forbidden in many areas of commerce. For example, the Equal Employment Opportunity Act (Title VII of the 1964 Civil Rights Act) states:

> *It shall be an unlawful employment practice for an employer (1) to fail or refuse to hire or to discharge any individual, or otherwise to discriminate against any individual with respect to his compensation, terms, conditions, or privileges of employment, because of such individual's race, color, religion, sex, or national origin. . . .*

The 1968 Fair Housing Act similarly states that:

> *. . . it shall be unlawful for any bank . . . to deny a loan or other financial assistance to a person applying therefore . . . or to discriminate against him in the fixing of the amount, interest rate, duration or other*

---

[34] A Federal Reserve survey in 1986 showed that Black families had on average 17 percent of the net worth and 9 percent of the financial assets of white families. See Canner and Smith.

[35] Liebowitz. For a rebuttal to the criticism, see the letter to the editor by Lynn Elaine Browne, Director of Research for the Federal Reserve Bank of Boston, *The Wall Street Journal* (September 21, 1993), A23.

[36] On intentional discrimination versus disparate impact, see Ayres.

terms or conditions of such loan . . . because of the race, color, religion or national origin of such person. . . .

In the area of employment discrimination, a series of court rulings established the doctrine of disparate impact, namely that unlawful discrimination could occur as a consequence of apparently neutral practices if those practices had the effect of disadvantaging a protected class of potential employees. In the late 1980s, however, several Supreme Court decisions, most notably *Wards Cove Packing Co. v. San Antonio*, weakened this basis for finding discrimination. As a consequence, the 1991 Civil Rights Act explicitly established disparate impact as a form of unlawful discrimination, in the area of employment, when:

a complaining party demonstrates that a respondent uses a particular employment practice that causes a disparate impact on the basis of race, color, religion, sex, or national origin and the respondent fails to demonstrate that the challenged practice is job related for the position in question and consistent with business necessity. . . .

Federal legislation does not formally establish disparate impact as a form of illegal discrimination in the areas of housing or lending, but only in employment. Nevertheless, the relevance of the concept extends well beyond employment. The question of discrimination by financial institutions, therefore, should be divided into two categories, relating to intention and impact.

The data are simply not sufficient to establish the existence of intentional discrimination in lending. Neither, however, are they sufficient to demonstrate that intentional discrimination does not exist.

A good argument can be made to reject the hypothesis of intentional discrimination but, on the other hand, a good argument can be made to embrace it. The argument supporting the view that there is little or no intentional discrimination is that there would be a financial cost to a lender of engaging in such discrimination. A lender faced with two equally attractive loan opportunities, one in a white suburb and one in a Black urban area, and who chose only the former, would be giving up on a perfectly sound business opportunity. Even if one supposes that the lender in question is prepared to forego this opportunity, the lender's competitor will likely see the missed opportunity and will fill the gap. Furthermore, in a competitive business environment, a firm that consistently passes up sound opportunities to make money is likely to be driven from the market, leaving only non-discriminatory firms in place.[37] It is a most logical, although not completely airtight, argument.[38]

The argument supporting the existence of intentional discrimination and redlining is rather more historical than logical. The United States is a country whose origins are steeped in slavery. Until recently, in some areas its laws not only permitted but required discrimination in many aspects of public, private, and commercial life. Until the last few decades, most of its white leaders and indeed most of its white people were explicitly and unashamedly racist. More recently, while racist language is generally (not always) viewed as unacceptable, race and racism are at the forefront of many people's emotions. Income and social gaps between the rich and the poor, and between the white and the non-white, have been growing in recent decades. In such a society, financial institutions cannot be expected to be immune to the general malaise. When confronted with the clear evidence that poor people and non-whites have much less than their share of access to financial services, one can draw the obvious conclusion that these are the fruits of discrimination and racism.

This conflict in interpretation goes straight to the heart of Americans' consciences, and it is obviously beyond the scope of the present study, or my ability, to resolve it. I can report that the great majority of the people in the community development credit union movement with whom I have discussed the issue believe that the people in their communities are the victims of racial discrimination by financial institutions.

Turning to the other form of discrimination, there is no question but that disparate impact in bank lending is a fact. Disparate impact is exactly what the data show. What is not so clear is whether the disparate impact in lending would be judged by a court to be illegal, if there were a law in lending similar to the law in employment specifying disparate impact as grounds for a suit. In the area of employment, disparate impact is unlawful only if "the respondent fails to demonstrate that the challenged practice is job related for the position in question and related to business necessity." In the area of lending, the Community Reinvestment Act calls on banks to serve the credit needs of low- and moderate-income communities, but it requires them to do so in a manner consistent with safe and sound banking practices.

---

[37] For the seminal statement of this type of argument, see Gary S. Becker, 1957.

[38] The argument depends upon the existence of what economists call "perfect competition," in particular the assumption that there are so many firms in competition with each other that they drive the rate of economic profit (as opposed to accounting or financial profit) down to zero, even for the most efficient firm. Consequently a firm which is less than optimally efficient—for example, one that discriminates— will suffer losses over the long run and will eventually disappear. If financial markets are not perfectly competitive, however, and they may not be, then room exists both for efficient firms to make excess profits and for inefficient (discriminatory) firms to make sufficient income to stay in business.

The obvious defense of financial institutions to the charge of discriminatory disparate impact is that to take greater lending risks in low-income neighborhoods would be to put their profits, assets, and continued existence in jeopardy.

Such a defense should not be taken as self-evident. For one thing, it is contradicted by the experience of the South Shore Bank in Chicago, noted above. South Shore showed that loans in a poor, African American, central city neighborhood could be successful and could generate a profit for the shareholders. Its success actually induced other lenders to enter the area.

On the other hand, South Shore initially took a great risk. In attempting something that had not been done before, its management could not be assured of success. Perhaps this is part of the problem in other urban, underfinanced areas of the country. Few banks are willing to make an initial commitment to an economically depressed area because they do not see immediate, sound business opportunities there. If other banks would take the initiative, they would follow. Or, if a group of lenders would enter the area together, so that the risk to any one was reduced, they would participate. In the absence of such actions, most banks decline to make loans which, on an individual basis, they regard as too risky—and as a consequence a whole neighborhood or a whole population is underserved.[39]

Either financial institutions discriminate inappropriately on the basis of neighborhood characteristics and race or they do not; it is extremely frustrating that decades of legislation, data gathering, and studies have not resolved the question definitively. In order to establish the importance of community development credit unions, however, it is not essential to show the existence of illegal discrimination.

What is very clear from the data, and from the experience of countless people and institutions, is that poor neighborhoods and poor people, non-white neighborhoods and non-white people, have less access to loans and to other financial services than do groups that are better off. It is also clear that this is not a small issue, that access to finance is critical to economic development, to the progress of individuals and groups. Finance is not everything, but without finance many doors are closed.

Inequitable outcomes need not be the consequence of purposeful discrimination, of the malfunctioning of markets and of the firms that operate within them. The search for illegal and unethical behavior may be a chi-

---

[39] In the language of economics, there may be external benefits to making apparently risky loans in depressed neighborhoods. The initial inflow of capital will improve the business and residential climate for subsequent homeowners, entrepreneurs, and lenders. Since the initial lender cannot capture these benefits, but bears the whole risk of the loan, it may not be willing to make the loan. Where social benefits exceed private benefits, there will be less than the socially optimal amount of activity.

mera. Inequality is a trademark of capitalism, not an aberration. The people of eastern Europe who abandoned Communism because of its constraints on freedom discovered, in some cases to their chagrin, that the free markets they adopted favored some of them at the expense of others. Communism had guaranteed a job for everyone, for example, but capitalism produced unemployment. So it should come as no surprise if ordinary capitalist banking firms, doing business to the best of their ability, trying to maximize returns to their shareholders and seeking the most profitable lending opportunities, produce a pattern of access to credit that is seriously unequal. In addition, of course, they may be acting in illegal, discriminatory, racist, and unethical ways, but such behavior is not proven, nor is it necessary in order to produce unequal results.

Proponents of community economic development have sometimes been quick to assume that the source of the problem faced by low-income areas is overt discrimination and racism. If discrimination were the source of the problem, it could be combated through legislation, through the courts, through education, and through concerted political action. The country has had a lot of experience in successfully fighting racism. But if the source of the problem is the ordinary, non-discriminatory functioning of impersonal, capitalist markets, then the solutions are harder to come by. Legislative requirements for non-discriminatory behavior will not work, no matter how carefully enforced. Non-discriminatory application of lending criteria to all applicants and all neighborhoods may be exactly what has produced the disparate impact. What low-income communities will need is local institutions, which they own and control, that can counter the forces of the market. To the extent that the free market rather than racism is the problem, community development credit unions and other community-based financial institutions are exactly what poor neighborhoods need.

Conclusion

Conventional financial institutions do not provide adequate services in many poor communities. They do not provide the loans that are needed for housing, business development, and consumer purposes, and they sometimes act to drain funds out of poor communities.

Whether they do this because of active, intentional, and discriminatory practices, or simply because of the logic of competitive capitalist markets is an interesting but not central question. More important is the simple fact of the dearth of financial services.

Community-based financial institutions, such as CDCUs, that are dedicated to serving the needs of poor communities are therefore needed.

They are not the only possible solution. The point of the Community Reinvestment Act is to pressure banks and thrifts into serving low-income communities more fully. In addition, larger, mainstream credit unions can expand into low-income communities and provide financial services. Most people in the community development credit union movement welcome other institutions that are genuinely responsive to their neighbors' needs. But they remain skeptical. Almost two decades of the CRA have not led banks to change their behavior markedly, and it is not clear whether large credit unions, whose membership base lies in middle-class communities, behave any differently from banks in poor areas.

Community development credit unions in low-income areas may be able to do what banks and other conventional institutions cannot, because of their cooperative, non-profit structure and because of their base in the community. A corporation's first responsibility has to be to its owners, its stockholders, and their interest is in profits. If banking in poor communities does not generate high profits, then the poor communities are not served by banks. Credit unions also serve their owners, but their owners are their members, their depositors, the people of the local community. Their owners' interest is not in profits but in service at reasonable rates. Therefore CDCUs may occupy a niche that other institutions reject.

CDCU organizers must be careful not to assume, however, that they can be successful just because they have a different organizational structure or just because the banks have rejected good business opportunities because of their inherent racism. Credit unions may not have to maximize profits, but they do have to stay solvent. As Chapter 5 shows, because they operate in poor neighborhoods, they face business problems that are more challenging than those confronting financial institutions serving the middle class.

Lillian Bent (standing), Manager of the Union Settlement Federal Credit Union in New York.

Photo: NFCDCU

Opening day (May 1988) at D. E. Wells Youth Credit Union in Springfield, Massachusetts, the first youth credit union in the country.

Photo: NFCDCU

Medicine man blessing the Casa Grande, Arizona branch of First American Credit Union, a CDCU serving Native Americans.

Central Brooklyn Partnership: pledge drive.

Photo: NFCDCU

Frontier Housing, Inc., in Morehead, Kentucky. It is a low-income housing builder and a branch of Central Appalachian People's FCU.

Photo: Tom Del Salvio

Joyce Rogers, assistant manager at Central Appalachian People's FCU since 1986. She began in 1981 as a credit union volunteer, the branch contact person at Redbird Mountain Medical Center.

Photo: Gienia Mikee

A Chinese herb and medicine store in the Tenderloin district of San Francisco. A start-up loan was made by Northeast Community Federal Credit Union to the son in order to enable the father, an herbalist in Vietnam, to begin life anew in San Francisco.

Photo: Northeast Community FCU

Santa Cruz Community Credit Union: Jeff Wells, Vice President; Mardi Wormhoudt, President; John Isbister, Board Member.

Photo: Trey Dunbar

Clifford Rosenthal, Executive Director of the National Federation of CDCUs, speaking at a meeting of the Lower East Side People's Federal Credit Union in New York.

Photo: NFCDCU

CHAPTER 5

THE OPERATIONS OF CDCUs

An emphasis on small deposits, small loans, technical assistance and member counseling can be very expensive.
—Linda Hoke[1]

Lending to low-income people can, indeed, be a risky business. But...that risk can be managed. And when it is managed successfully, the social rewards are great: economic opportunity, personal dignity, and community empowerment.
—Clifford N. Rosenthal[2]

Like all financial institutions, community development credit unions attract funds and they allocate funds. They accept deposits from their members (and in some cases from non-members), and in turn they lend and invest most of those deposits. They assume the risk inherent in lending. From their loans and investments they earn interest. They use the interest earnings to pay for their expenses, to compensate the members for their deposits, and to save in their reserve accounts.

---

[1] Hoke.

[2] Rosenthal and Schoder.

This chapter explores these basic operations of CDCUs, using information from their financial statements on December 31, 1991.[3]

Credit Unions' Financial Statements

The chapter begins with an overview of the sort of information that is included in credit unions' financial statements.

Every business entity has at least two types of financial statements, a balance sheet and an income statement. The balance sheet shows the condition of the institution—its assets, liabilities, and net worth—at a moment in time. The income statement shows the income, expenses, and profit of the business over a period of time. To use the language of economists, the balance sheet shows stocks, while the income statement shows flows. Or, to use a more familiar image, the balance sheet shows the level of water in the bathtub at a particular moment; the income statement shows the flow of water in, and the drain of water out, over a period of time, that produced the level of water in the tub. This chapter uses balance sheets as of December 31, 1991, and income statements covering the period January 1 to December 31, 1991.

Table 5.1 is an accurate, although simplified, balance sheet for the Santa Cruz Community Credit Union on December 31, 1991.

The largest asset of the credit union is its loans outstanding. These can be thought of as IOUs, held by the credit union, indicating the sums owed by the members to the cooperative. The "allowance for loan loss" is a fund held by the credit union as a negative asset, in anticipation of loans that may not be repaid and will have to be charged off. Net loans is the difference between loans outstanding to the members and the allowance for loan loss; it is an estimate of the true value of loans that will be recovered by the credit union. The next largest asset is the investments; these are funds placed in other financial institutions or financial instruments of some sort that earn interest for the credit union. Cash is held in the office to conduct transactions with the members. The fixed assets consist of the building that the credit union owns plus its furnishings and equipment, principally its computer.

On the Liabilities and Capital side of the balance sheet, the liabilities consist of notes payable and other obligations that the credit union owes. The deposits are included on the right hand side of the balance sheet because they are funds that the credit union owes to the people who have placed

---

[3] The tables in this chapter may be compared with statistics developed by the NCUA on credit unions identified by that agency as serving a low-income membership. As explained later in the text, the NCUA low-income list is somewhat different, and smaller, than the list of CDCUs used in this chapter. The NCUA has undertaken to produce an annual report on the performance of these credit unions.

them in the institution. It is here that the principal ambiguity lies in credit union accounting. If the credit union were a privately owned bank, then the deposits would be a liability; they would represent funds owed by the bank to its customers. A credit union is not a privately held corporation, however; it is a cooperative whose member-savers are its owners. It seems not quite proper to think of the members' deposits as a liability of the credit union, since they are funds "owed" by the credit union to its own owners. So member shares are usually counted as capital rather than liabilities. On the other hand, the rationale for counting shares as capital is less compelling than it was before 1970, when deposit insurance was introduced, since the shares are not at risk. If the credit union has deposits from non-members, they are unambiguous liabilities.

Table 5.1
($ in Thousands)

Balance Sheet
Santa Cruz Community Credit Union, December 31, 1991

Assets		Liabilities and Capital	
Cash	790	Liabilities	435
Investments	5,370	Deposits	17,288
		Shares	17,288
		Non-member deposits	0
Loans	11,586		
– Loan loss allowance	-296	Net capital	642
= Net Loans	11,290		
Fixed assets	647		
Other assets	268		
Assets	**18,365**	**Liabilities and Capital**	**18,365**

By definition, a balance sheet balances. The assets are always equal to the liabilities plus the capital. This occurs because the last item on the liabilities plus capital side is a residual. Different types of institutions give it different names; in credit unions the name of choice is reserves or net capital. There are actually different capital accounts in a credit union, including regular reserves, special reserves, and undivided earnings. For some purposes, the allowance for loan loss is taken away from the asset side and included as a positive reserve account. Together, however, these capital accounts total whatever sum is needed to make the two sides balance. The logic behind this is straightforward. The left hand side of the balance sheet shows what the credit union has. All but the last item on the right hand side show what the credit union owes, either to outsiders or to its own members. Whatever is left over, whatever the credit union has but does not owe, is the net capital, owned collectively by the members. The net capital can be, and in some cases unfortunately is, negative.

Table 5.2 is the income statement for the same credit union, for the calendar year 1991.

Table 5.2
($ in Thousands)

**Income Statement
Santa Cruz Community Credit Union
January 1 to December 31, 1991**

Income		Expenses and Surplus	
Loan interest	1,317	Operating expenses	1,299
Investment interest	375	Provision for loan loss	91
Other operating income	441	Dividends	595
		Net surplus	148
Total	**2,133**	**Total**	**2,133**

A credit union's income results mainly from the interest it earns on its assets. In Santa Cruz, as in most credit unions, the major part of this is in the form of interest earned on the loans that are made to the members. A smaller portion comes from the interest earned on the investments. In addition, some income results from fees and penalties that are assessed as people do business with the credit union.

On the right hand side of the income statement are the operating expenses, including salaries, insurance, and many other items. The provision for loan loss is the source of the funds that become the allowance for loan loss on the balance sheet. Once these two sets of payments are subtracted from income, the remaining revenues of the credit union constitute its surplus. The surplus is divided into two parts. Some is returned to the members individually in the form of a dividend on their savings (credit unions are also permitted to return surplus earnings to members in the form of an interest rebate on their loans). Some, called here the Net Surplus, is retained by the members collectively, and is transferred to one of the reserve accounts. The income statement balances because the surplus is calculated as a residual, the difference between income and expenses.

In some ways the dividend is analogous to the interest payment made by a bank to its depositors, but in other ways it is different. The interest payment made by a bank is an expense, a contractual obligation of the bank just as is the wage payment it makes to its employees. Once a bank has accepted a deposit from a customer, it is required to make interest payments on that deposit, at whatever level it has announced, until such time as it publicly changes its announced rate. In a cooperative credit union, on the other hand, because the depositors are the owners, they cannot guarantee a payment to themselves. The member-owner-savers can receive a dividend payment only to the extent that the credit union generates a surplus. Consequently, dividend payments are not guaranteed in advance but are declared by the board of directors of a credit union at the end of an accounting period. A member may be told in advance what dividend rate to expect, but that rate can never be guaranteed until the credit union generates the surplus funds.

In most institutions, the last item would be called "profit," and some credit unions do use this term. "Surplus" is a better word, however, because credit unions are non-profit institutions. Their net earnings do not belong to a small group of shareholders, as in a corporation, but to all of their members collectively. It is not a goal of a credit union to maximize its surplus, but simply to generate enough of it to keep a reasonable level of reserves (or net capital) to protect against losses.

The entries in the financial statements of the country's CDCUs can be used to develop a picture of how those institutions operate.

A Note on the Data

The data used in this chapter are derived from the "Call Reports" or "Reports of Condition" that federally insured credit unions file with the National Credit Union Administration semi-annually. From this set of over 13,000 credit unions, the author selected a small number of institutions for study as CDCUs. Since CDCU is not an official designation, a certain arbitrary judgment was required in making the selection. First, all 91 members of the National Federation of CDCUs in the spring of 1992 were included, on the grounds that if credit unions wished to participate in the CDCU movement at the national level they should be counted. Second, most of the credit unions designated by the NCUA as "low-income" were included. The two lists overlap considerably but not completely, and the NCUA list is longer. Not all NCUA low-income credit unions were included, however. The university student credit unions on the low-income list were excluded, as were all of the employee-based credit unions except those whose employer was an institution specifically serving low-income people. In the former case, while students may lack money, this is typically a temporary condition, and they do not need a social change agent to transform their community. In the latter case, most credit unions dealing with employees of a single company do not have a mission of outreach to low-income people or a purpose of social change. In addition, a small number of credit unions with assets numbering just a couple of thousand dollars, or even in the hundreds, were excluded, since they barely exist as institutions. One quite large church credit union was excluded because its reported data in some categories seemed to be wildly anomalous and therefore suspect, and would have skewed the averages seriously in some cases.[4]

The selection yields a set of 180 CDCUs for the reporting date of December 31, 1991. The balance sheet items in the reports refer to that date, and the income statement items to the calendar year 1991. For the purpose of deriving the tables in the spread analysis, some of the balance sheet items from December 31, 1990 were included. Some of the tables that follow are based on fewer than 180 CDCUs because of data limitations.

These data make possible quite complete analyses of the financial condition of the CDCUs. They also permit comparison between the CDCUs and all American credit unions. Data summaries for all credit unions are published semi-annually by CUNA.[5] Because of the form in which CUNA presents its data, however, the comparisons are tricky, and this requires some explanation.

Much of the data that are shown in the tables that follow are in the form of averages of ratios across all CDCUs or across CDCUs in a certain category. The method is to calculate the ratio in each credit union and then to average the ratios. This procedure gives each credit union, the small as well as the large, equal weight in the average. The average can be interpreted as a "typical" value for a CDCU. CUNA uses a different method in presenting its data for all American credit unions. It sums the numerator and denominator of each ratio separately, across all the credit unions in the category under consideration, and then takes the ratio of the two sums. This method weights the credit unions according to their size in the compilation of the final figure. Put differently, it treats all credit unions as if they were lumped together into a single institution.

Each method is "correct," but each takes a different perspective. Since much of the focus of this study is on the description and analysis of quite small institutions, the author decided it was important to retain a perspective that gives equal weight to all CDCUs. But when comparisons between CDCUs and the wider credit union industry are needed, the "summation" method has to be used. These latter cases are always clearly labeled. The aver-

---

[4] I am grateful to Bill Hampel, Chief Economist, and Marc Shafroth, Director of Data and Statistics, at CUNA, who culled the CDCU data from the larger sets of data for all credit unions in the country, and who supplied me with easily accessible disks. I would be happy to give copies of the disks and the associated documentation to other researchers. The disks are formatted for dBase III and IV on DOS.

[5] Credit Union National Association, *Credit Union Operating Ratios and Spreads*. Unless otherwise noted, all of the industry-wide credit union data in this chapter are taken from this source.

ages for all American credit unions (in contrast to just the CDCUs) are constructed in such a way as to represent credit unions of the same size as the CDCUs. Consequently, whatever differences exist between the two averages—the CDCU figure and the figure for all credit unions—reflect true differences in the character of the institutions, and not just differences in size.[6]

The Questions

The remainder of this chapter proceeds systematically through the operations of the country's CDCUs, asking the following questions:

- Where do CDCUs' resources come from? This section looks at the right hand side of the balance sheet, the liabilities and capital.

- What do CDCUs do with their resources? This section turns to the left hand side of the balance sheet, the assets.

- How do CDCUs earn their income? Next the focus turns to the income portion of the income statement.

- How do CDCUs allocate their income? This section looks at the use of income, for operating expenses, for dividend payments to the members, and for reserves.

- How do CDCUs create a spread between income and outgo? Next the chapter treats the gap between income and expenses, or the "spread."

- How are CDCUs rated by their examiners? Finally, the financial data are used to illuminate the ways in which federal and state

---

[6] The following method is used when comparing CDCUs with all credit unions. CUNA presents averages, using the summation method, for all credit unions and for ten asset size categories: (in millions of dollars) less than 0.5, 0.5-1, 1-2, 2-5, 5-10, 10-20, 20-50, 50-100, 100-200, 200 and over. For the most part, in this study two asset-size categories are used, less than 0.5, and over 0.5, since this division cuts the number of CDCUs roughly in half.

The smaller CDCU category is compared directly with the smallest CUNA category. The figures for CDCUs over a half million dollars, and for all CDCUs, are compared with CUNA figures for all credit unions, with the latter figures weighted according to the proportion of CDCU assets in each size category (not according to the proportion of assets in each category for all credit unions). In other words, the figures for all American credit unions are artificial composites, based on the assumption that those credit unions are distributed by size in the same manner that CDCUs are. Relatively small credit unions are thus given much more weight than they world have when compared to all other American credit unions. The proportional distribution of assets in CDCUs, by size, in December 1991, from smallest to largest category, was: .054, .085, .122, .211, .108, .233, .187, 0, 0, 0, summing to 1.0. These weights were multiplied by the CUNA figures in each size category, and results summed, to arrive at a comparative figure for all credit unions. When the comparison was for credit unions over a half million dollars in assets, the first proportion was eliminated, and the remaining ones adjusted to sum to 1.0. Note that this method completely excludes American Credit unions in the top three size categories, above $50 million, because no CDCUs are of this size. Using this method, the resulting comparison between CDCUs and all American credit unions are based on institutions of the same size.

examiners assess CDCUs, according to the "CAMEL" system.

Where Do CDCUs' Resources Come From?

Table 5.3 analyzes the liabilities and capital of 180 CDCUs, as of December 31, 1991. Each item is shown as a percentage of total assets (or, since the amount is the same, as a percentage of total liabilities plus capital). The table shows where the credit unions' resources come from.

Total liabilities plus capital consist of savings deposits, plus borrowings and other liabilities, plus reserves. The savings deposits are divided into two parts: member deposits or shares, and non-member deposits. So in Table 5.3, column 1 equals columns 2 + 3, and Total Liabilities plus Capital equals columns 1 + 4 + 5 + 6. Column 7 is a more expansive version of reserves than column 6, adding in the allowances for loan and investment losses which are normally carried as negative assets on the balance sheet.

Table 5.3 shows that the majority of the resources come from savings deposits, 86 percent for the average CDCU. The ratio of deposits to assets rises with the size of the credit union.

CDCUs receive on average almost seven percent of their resources from non-member deposits. NCUA forbids non-member deposits in most American credit unions, but allows them up to a level of 20 percent of assets in the credit unions it designates as serving low-income people. The 20 percent limit is sometimes relaxed upon petition by an individual credit union. CDCUs can sometimes obtain the support of outside organizations such as churches, foundations, corporations, and philanthropic groups, through their use of non-member deposits. The deposits are made either directly or, as explained in Chapter 3, through the intermediary of the National Federation of CDCUs. They are insured up to $100,000 just as are member deposits, and they receive a rate of interest that is negotiated at the time of deposit.

Table 5.3 shows the differences in the reliance of the various categories of CDCUs upon non-member deposits. The urban-rural distinction does not make much difference. Large CDCUs make proportionately more use of non-member deposits than do small CDCUs. Non-church credit unions rely much more heavily upon them than do church-affiliated credit unions and, not unexpectedly, members of the National Federation make a great deal more use of them than do non-members.

From the figures in Table 5.3, it would not seem that the NCUA's 20 percent limit represents a hardship, since even among NFCDCU members the average use of non-member deposits is only about half the limit. The table masks, however, the fact that most CDCUs do not use any non-member deposits, while those that do use them tend to depend quite heavily on them. Of the 180 credit unions in this set, only 58 (or 32 percent) had any non-member deposits at all at the end of 1991; for these 58, the average ratio of non-member deposits to assets was 20.8 percent.

Table 5.3
(As Percentages of Total Assets)

Distribution of Liabilities Plus Capital in 180 CDCUs, December 31, 1991

Credit Union Category	1 Total Deposits	2 Shares	3 Non-Member Deposits	4 Borrowing	5 Other Liabilities	6 Net Capital	7 Total Reserves
Assets up to $500K	82.7	77.2	5.5	0.2	2.4	14.7	17.2
Assets > $500K	89.3	81.4	7.9	1.1	1.3	8.2	10.2
Church	85.2	82.4	2.9	0.7	1.9	12.1	14.9
Non-Church	86.4	78.1	8.3	0.7	1.8	11.1	13.2
Urban	87.5	81.0	6.4	0.7	1.8	10.1	12.4
Rural	83.6	76.4	7.2	0.7	2.0	13.7	16.0
NFCDCU	88.9	77.8	11.1	1.3	1.3	8.4	10.6
Non-NFCDCU	83.1	80.9	2.2	0.0	2.4	14.5	16.9
All CDCUs	**86.0**	**79.3**	**6.7**	**0.7**	**1.9**	**11.4**	**13.7**
Summation Method							
CDCUs up to $500K	84.4			0.3	2.3	13.0	15.4
All CUs up to $500K	84.5			0.1	1.6	13.8	15.6
CDCUs $.51-50 Mil	91.2			0.7	0.9	7.1	8.7
All CUs $.51-50 Mil	90.0			0.1	0.9	9.0	9.8
CDCUs	90.9			0.7	1.0	7.5	9.1
All CUs	89.7			0.1	1.0	9.2	10.1

This is not to say that all 58 credit unions use non-member deposits right up to the 20 percent limit. Twenty-seven had less than 15 percent non-member deposits, 14 had between 15 and 25 percent, and 17 had over 25 percent. Most if not all of the latter group received special permission from the NCUA to exceed the limit. A significant number of CDCUs have succeeded, therefore, in attracting outside, socially responsible investments into their communities through the use of non-member deposits.

Column 6 of Table 5.3 is Net Capital as a percentage of assets; this represents the assets of the credit union that are not offset by the amounts that the credit union owes to either members or outsiders. It is one of the most important indicators of the financial strength of a credit union. A healthy level of capital indicates that a credit union has a cushion to withstand a period of negative earnings or some other kind of significant loss. Capital is somewhat stronger in the rural credit unions than in the urban, and in the church credit unions than in the non-church; it is considerably stronger in the small CDCUs than in the large ones and in the credit unions that are not affiliated with the National Federation.

The bottom panel of Table 5.3 compares the CDCUs to all American credit unions, using the summation method outlined above. Use of the summation method can make a considerable difference. Note, for example, that the net capital ratio in column 6 is 11.4 percent for all CDCUs when the ratio of each credit union is given equal weight, and just 7.5 percent when the weights are proportional to the assets in the summation method. This follows from the fact that the larger credit unions—which are weighted more heavily in the summation method—have lower capital ratios, as shown in the first two rows.

CDCUs derive roughly the same portion of their resources from deposits as do other credit unions. They use more borrowed funds, although the proportion is small in both cases. The net capital ratio of the CDCUs shown in column 6 is, however, somewhat lower, particularly for credit unions over a half million dollars in assets.

To get a full picture of capital adequacy, however, one should add the allowance for loan loss together with the reserve accounts, as is done in column 7. The allowance for loan loss is an account that is available to be drawn down should a loan default.

When all of the capital accounts are summed, the financial strength of CDCUs is seen to be almost comparable with that of all credit unions of the same sizes. The overall reserve ratios are almost exactly the same for the small credit unions, and just one percentage point different for the larger ones. Contrary to the opinion of some observers, poor people's credit unions do not tend to be financially weaker than other credit unions, at least in terms of their reserve accounts.

The reason CDCUs have almost comparable reserve ratios, however, is that their allowances for loan loss tend to be higher than in other credit unions. As will be shown, this is a prudent step on the part of CDCUs since their delinquency and default rates on loans to their members tend to be higher.

What Do CDCUs Do with Their Resources?

Table 5.4 shows the distribution of the various types of assets of CDCUs as percentages of total assets. The table begins to answer the question of what CDCUs do with their resources.

On the asset side of the balance sheet, the allowance for loan losses is carried as a negative item; total assets are equal to columns 1 - 2 + 3 + 4 + 5 in Table 5.4.

Table 5.4
(As Percentages of Total Assets)

Distribution of Assets in 180 CDCUs
December 31, 1991

Credit Union Category	1 Loans	2 Allowances for Loan and Investment Losses	3 Cash	4 Investments	5 Fixed and Other Assets
Assets up to $500K	42.6	2.5	11.3	47.7	0.8
Assets > $500K	59.2	2.1	5.7	34.9	2.1
Church	44.8	2.8	10.0	47.1	0.8
Non-Church	53.7	2.1	7.8	38.7	1.8
Urban	48.3	2.3	9.4	43.0	1.5
Rural	55.7	2.4	6.9	38.2	1.5
NFCDCU	53.2	2.2	8.2	39.0	1.8
Non-NFCDCU	48.8	2.4	8.8	43.5	1.2
All CDCUs	**51.0**	**2.3**	**8.5**	**41.2**	**1.5**
Summation Method					
CDCUs up to $500K	47.8	2.5	9.0	44.5	1.1
All CUs up to $500K	60.2	1.7	7.2	33.6	0.7
CDCUs $.51-50 Mil.	62.4	1.6	3.6	32.3	3.0
All CUs $.51-50 Mil.	59.9	0.9	3.1	36.0	1.9
CDCUs	61.6	1.6	3.9	32.9	2.9
All CUs	59.9	0.9	3.3	35.9	1.8

The largest single asset is loans to members. The loan-to-asset ratio is strongly and positively related to the size of the CDCU. Non-church CDCUs, rural CDCUs, and NFCDCU members have significantly higher loan-to-asset ratios, on average, than do their counterparts.

Most of the assets that are not loaned to members are invested or are held in cash. Consequently, the cash and investment ratios move roughly inversely to the loan ratio: when the latter is higher, the former are usually lower. The loan-to-asset ratio is therefore the clue to the overall structure of the assets.

It would be useful to establish whether the variation in loan-to-asset ratio by church, urban, and National Federation categories are independent phenomena or whether those categories are just proxies for size. After all, in each case the group with the lower loan-to-asset ratio is also the group with the smaller credit unions, and smaller CDCUs have lower loan-to-asset ratios. Table 5.5 breaks down the loan-to-asset ratio in the different categories of CDCUs.

Table 5.5
(Loans as Percentages of Total Assets)

Loan-to-Asset Ratios in Categories of CDCUs

	Assets		Total
	up to $500K	>$500K	
Church	39.1	55.2	44.8
Non-Church	44.8	60.3	53.7
Urban	37.8	57.1	48.3
Rural	49.3	63.9	55.7
NFCDCU	44.2	57.6	53.2
Non-NFCDCU	41.7	62.6	48.8
Total	**42.6**	**59.2**	**51.0**

Credit union size is not the sole variable associated with differences in the loan-to-asset ratios. Within each size group, church and urban CDCUs still have lower loan-to-asset ratios. National Federation affiliation largely disappears as an explanatory variable, however: among the small credit unions affiliation is associated with little difference in the ratios, and among the larger credit unions the ranking is actually reversed.

Size is still independently important as well. Within each of the six groupings in Table 5.5, the small credit unions have lower loan ratios than the large.

The difference in loan ratios by church affiliation is expected. Many church credit unions operate mostly as savings clubs rather than as borrowing clubs or community development agencies. Table 5.9 below shows that the ratio of number of loans to total membership is just 18 percent in the church CDCUs, compared to 28 percent in the others.[7] Informal evidence indicates that their members tend to be older than the members of other credit unions, and perhaps reluctant to borrow because of uncertainty about their ability to repay in the future. One of the purposes of the National Federation's organizing project among church credit unions has been to encourage them to become more aggressive lenders, in order to help meet the

---

[7] These figures are likely overestimates of the proportion of members who are borrowers since some members have more than one loan.

financial needs of their members as well as providing a safe place for their deposits.

The difference in loan ratios by urban-rural status is not expected. It is not immediately clear why loan ratios should be higher in rural areas. Nevertheless there is a significant gap, one which remains even after the credit unions are segregated by asset size.

The fact that smaller CDCUs have lower loan ratios than larger CDCUs is also unexpected. Such a relationship is not found among all U.S. credit unions. If the association had turned out to be the opposite—smaller credit unions with higher loan ratios—the obvious explanation would have been that the smaller credit unions were limited by their assets in meeting their loan demand while the larger credit unions had plenty of funds to go around.

A possible explanation of the actual relationship is that the smaller CDCUs have poorer members who have more difficulty establishing creditworthiness in order to qualify for a loan. The data provide only marginal support for this hypothesis, however: among the urban CDCUs, for example, the average median family income in the neighborhood was $12,026 for the small credit unions and $12,420 for the large in the 1980 census, hardly enough of a difference to create a major impact on loan demand.

It may be the case that the small credit unions are so small that their members simply do not think of them very often when they are in need of a loan. Or it may be that they are so small that they lack the resources to make informed judgments about loan requests and are therefore conservative in granting loans. They may lack a loan officer on the staff.

The ratio of loans to assets fluctuates in most credit unions, as the demand for loans responds to overall economic conditions. At the end of both 1981 and 1986, the average loan-to-asset ratio in community development credit unions in the United States was 59 percent. The significantly lower ratio in 1991 probably reflects the sustained recession of that year.

The bottom panel of Table 5.4 compares the allocation of assets in CDCUs and all credit unions. Compared to the industry as a whole, the loan ratio is much lower in the small CDCUs and slightly higher in the larger CDCUs. The larger CDCUs can be satisfied that they have done as well at getting loans out to their members during a serious recessionary period as have credit unions in general. But the comparison for the smaller credit unions indicates a serious difficulty.

Low loan ratios create two sorts of problems for credit unions. The first has to do with their mission of service. Credit unions are organized in large measure to provide a source of loans for their members, and this is particularly important in low-income neighborhoods that lack capital. To the extent that they are not recycling their members' savings in the form of loans back into their communities, they are failing to meet at least part of their goal. Of course credit unions cannot by themselves overcome an economic recession; they cannot stimulate a demand for loans which is lagging. Furthermore, they will not survive if they push loans onto people who cannot make good use of them and lack the capacity to repay. Nevertheless, the low loan ratios at the beginning of the 1990s were a source of concern.

The second problem created by the low loan ratios is the income that the credit union forgoes. Resources that are not lent to the members can be invested in financial institutions but, as Table 5.11 below shows, the interest on investments is typically much less than the interest a credit union obtains by lending to its members. Most CDCUs struggle to meet their expenses, and they can ill afford the income loss implied by a low loan ratio.

Table 5.4 reveals several other features of interest, besides the loan ratios. The allowance for loan loss accounts are consistently higher in the CDCUs than in all U.S. credit unions. This confirms what was seen in the previous section.

Finally, the CDCUs have consistently higher amounts of non-earning assets, that is to say, cash and fixed and other assets, than do mainstream credit unions in the U.S. The relatively high level of cash may be a consequence of people in poor communities using the CDCU as a check cashing office rather than as a savings and lending institution. Or, it may indicate a lack of investment expertise in CDCUs; certainly the CDCUs are in no position to waste the income that their assets could be earning.

Since loans are so important to CDCUs—they are the largest item among the assets, and they represent the most important purpose of the institution—they are examined next in greater detail. Table 5.6 shows the distribution of loans by type. A word of caution is due here. The loan types in Table 5.6 refer to the collateral that is used to secure the loan, not to the purpose for which the loan proceeds are directed. Chapter 6 contains an estimate of loan purposes for seven CDCUs. The relationship between the two concepts can be confusing. For example, a home equity line of credit is treated in Table 5.6 as a real estate loan since it is secured by a house, but the borrower may use the funds for any purpose at all, including business expansion or the purchase of a car.

CDCUs concentrate heavily upon unsecured, personal signature loans. These are loans in which the borrower simply pledges to repay; in some cases a co-signer also pledges to repay if the primary borrower defaults. But the credit union does not take an ownership right to property that can be repossessed in the event of nonpayment. Almost half of the loan money in the average CDCU is unsecured. The ratio is much higher, in fact greater than two thirds, in the smaller credit unions with assets of less than a half million dollars, while in the credit unions larger than a half million it is less than one third.

Table 5.6
Loan Types as a Percentage of Total Loans

Dollar Amounts of Outstanding Loans in CDCUs

Credit Union Category	Unsecured	New Auto	Used Auto	Real Estate	Other
Assets up to $500K	67.4	5.8	5.5	2.1	19.2
Assets > $500K	30.7	12.0	12.5	22.9	21.9
Church	59.9	11.1	7.7	6.0	15.3
Non-Church	43.9	8.1	9.7	15.6	22.7
Urban	48.4	9.2	8.2	12.4	21.8
Rural	49.3	8.6	10.6	13.3	18.2
Total	**48.7**	**9.0**	**9.1**	**12.7**	**20.5**
Summation Method					
CDCUs up to $500K	59.7	10.1	7.4	4.4	18.4
All CUs up to $500K	39.5	16.5	21.8	1.4	20.8
CDCUs $.51-50 Mil	28.1	9.3	8.0	37.4	17.2
All CUs $.51-50 Mil	24.0	26.9	16.7	18.4	14.1
CDCUs	29.4	9.3	8.0	36.0	17.3
All CUs	24.8	26.4	16.9	17.5	14.4

Compared to all American credit unions, the concentration on unsecured loans is significantly greater in the small CDCUs, and somewhat greater in the larger ones.

The size of the CDCU is strongly related to the concentration in other types of lending as well. The larger CDCUs, which do proportionately less unsecured lending, do more lending on automobiles and real estate. The difference is particularly striking in real estate.

The urban-rural distinction is not significant in terms of the type of lending. Church affiliation makes little difference in automobile lending, but church CDCUs tend to emphasize unsecured lending and correspondingly de-emphasize real estate lending.

Table 5.7 explores the question of whether church affiliation makes a difference in types of loans once credit union size has been corrected for. The table indicates that asset size is the most important variable associated with differences in unsecured and real estate lending. Within each size category, however, church affiliation continues to make a difference, with the church

CDCUs doing more unsecured lending and less real estate lending.

Table 5.7
(Percentage of Total Loans)

Loan Types by CDCU Size and Church Affiliation

	Unsecured Loans			Real Estate Loans		
	Assets		Total	Assets		Total
	up to $500K	>$500K		up to $500K	>$500K	
Church	74.8	32.5	59.9	1.0	15.4	6.0
Non-Church	62.5	30.2	43.9	2.9	24.9	15.6
Total	**67.4**	**30.7**	**48.7**	**2.1**	**22.9**	**12.7**

Table 5.8
($ in Thousands)

Average Loan Size for Credit Unions Making Each Type of Loan

Credit Union Category	Unsecured	New Auto	Used Auto	Real Estate	Other	All Loans
Assets up to $500K	1.3	7.0	3.2	5.8	1.8	1.6
Assets > $500K	1.6	7.4	3.7	21.4	3.5	4.2
Church	1.7	7.5	4.1	18.7	2.7	2.5
Non-Church	1.4	7.3	3.4	18.6	3.0	3.1
Urban	1.7	7.3	3.8	24.6	3.4	3.3
Rural	1.0	7.4	3.1	10.4	2.2	2.3
Total	**1.5**	**7.3**	**3.5**	**18.6**	**2.9**	**2.9**
Summation Method						
CDCUs up to $500K	1.2	6.5	3.3	6.5	1.3	1.5
All CUs up to $500K	1.3	6.1	3.3	6.0	2.0	2.0
CDCUs $.51-50 Mil	1.7	7.0	3.3	21.9	3.8	3.8
All CUs $.51-50 Mil	1.7	7.2	4.1	20.8	3.2	3.7
CDCUs	1.7	6.9	3.3	21.6	3.5	3.6
All CUs	1.7	7.2	4.1	20.4	3.1	3.6

The most likely explanation for the concentration of small and church CDCUs upon unsecured loans is that those credit unions have limited resources to lend and unsecured loans tend to be smaller than other loans. Not only are those credit unions smaller in terms of total assets, they are also smaller in terms of assets per member; that is to say, they have less to go around to satisfy the loan demand. The average assets per member in the small CDCUs below $500,000 are $666, while in the larger credit unions the figure is almost three times as large, $1,783. Church CDCUs have on average $997 per member, compared to non-church CDCUs with $1,317. The smaller CDCUs have fewer assets per member than do all American credit unions of the same size; using the summation method, the respective figures are $607 versus $984.

CDCUs do considerably less lending for automobiles than do other credit unions. For most middle-class Americans, an automobile is the largest personal investment they make aside from their house, and many American credit unions specialize in providing the financing for that investment. Low-income people spend less on cars than do the middle-class, however, and their credit unions consequently do less car lending.

Table 5.9

Loans Per Member, December 31, 1991

Assets up to $500K	0.20
Assets > $500K	0.27
Church	0.18
Non-Church	0.26
Urban	0.20
Rural	0.30
Total	**0.24**
Summation Method	
CDCUs up to $500K	0.18
All CUs up to $500K	0.30
CDCUs $.51-50 Mil	0.29
All CUs $.51-50 Mil	0.43
CDCUs	0.28
All CUs	0.42

Table 5.8 shows the average size of loans, by loan type and CDCU category. The table shows the balance outstanding on the loans on December 31, 1991, not the amount for which the loans were initially made (an amount which would, of course, be larger). It shows that the average size of unsecured loans is significantly less than the average size of all other types of loans. Because small credit unions concentrate on unsecured lending, their overall average loan size, in the last column, is much lower than in the larger

CDCUs, in spite of the fact that their loans are of fairly comparable size within each category (with the exception of real estate). Similarly, church credit unions make smaller loans on average than do the non-church credit unions, because of their concentration on unsecured lending, in spite of the fact that within almost every category of lending, church credit unions make slightly larger loans.

Not only do small and church CDCUs conserve their resources by concentrating on unsecured loans; they also make fewer loans overall than do other kinds of CDCUs. Table 5.9 shows that, in addition, urban CDCUs lend to fewer members than do rural ones. Consistent with this finding, the bottom panel of Table 5.9 shows that CDCUs lend to many fewer of their members than do typical American credit unions.

Returning to Table 5.8, the bottom panel shows that CDCUs do not typically make smaller loans than other credit unions in the same size range.

How Do CDCUs Earn Their Income?

Credit unions generate most of their income by charging interest on the assets which they lend and invest. Table 5.10 shows the different categories of income as percentages of gross income.

The two principal sources of income for the CDCUs are interest earned on loans to members and interest earned on investments. Table 5.10 can be usefully compared with Table 5.4, which shows the loan-to-asset ratios by credit union size and by other characteristics. In credit unions in which the loan-to-asset ratio is higher, the proportion of income generated from loans is higher and the proportion generated from investments is lower. Note, however, that the proportion of income generated from loans is consistently greater, in all categories, than the loan-to-asset ratio. This occurs because member loans are the most profitable use that a credit union can make of its assets. Interest rates are consistently higher on member loans than on investments, and they are certainly higher than on fixed, non-earning assets such as buildings and computers that do not generate an income (although they may save rental expenses).

The larger CDCUs derive about the same proportion of their income from loans as do all credit unions of the same size. The smaller credit unions earn significantly less from loans. Interestingly, in all American credit unions, the proportion of income deriving from loans falls with the size of credit union, while in CDCUs it rises. The issue was discussed above in connection with Table 5.4; small credit unions in poor communities have difficulty generating loans.

Finally, Table 5.10 shows that CDCUs earn a much higher proportion of their income from fees than do all American credit unions. This reveals something of the difficulty of conducting a financial business in a poor community. The leadership of CDCUs would prefer not to charge extensive fees since their members are all too familiar with the phenomenon that "the poor pay more," in both prices and extra fees, on many of their transactions. As will be shown below, however, CDCUs suffer systematically from higher expenses than do mainstream credit unions. To cover these expenses, they turn in part to fees.

Table 5.10
(Items as Percentages of Gross Income)

The Components of Income

Credit Union Category	Net Loan Interest	Investment Income	Fees	Other Operating Income
Assets up to $500K	56.6	36.7	2.9	3.9
Assets > $500K	71.0	20.8	4.9	3.3
Church	59.8	35.4	2.0	2.8
Non-church	65.7	25.7	4.7	3.9
Urban	61.0	32.3	3.3	3.4
Rural	68.9	22.3	4.9	3.9
Total	**63.9**	**28.6**	**3.9**	**3.6**
Summation Method				
CDCUs up to $500K	65.0	28.8	3.4	2.8
All CUs up to $500K	77.6	19.4	1.3	1.8
CDCUs $.51-50 Mil	72.5	17.8	7.1	2.5
All CUs $.51-50 Mil	73.4	21.8	2.9	1.9
CDCUs	72.2	18.4	7.0	2.5
All CUs	73.6	21.7	2.9	1.8

Table 5.11 shows the rates of interest that the CDCUs charged on different types of loans. Only credit unions which made each particular type of loan, and for which data are available, are included in the averages; the total in each category is shown in the row labeled N.

The first four columns of Table 5.11 show the rates that were charged by credit unions on four different types of loans at the end of 1991. The final column, showing the rate of return on investments, is not strictly comparable with the first four. Credit unions made countless different investments with many different rates. What the final column shows, therefore, is the actual income earned by the credit unions on their investments during the calendar year 1991, divided by the average of the beginning and ending investment levels in that year. In a later section this same kind of information will be presented for loans. The actual rate of return on loans generally tends to be somewhat lower than the stated interest rate because of delinquencies in repayments and defaults. Thus the contrast between the figures in the first four columns and those in the last is somewhat overstated. Nevertheless the gap is huge—with the investment figures being typically less than half of the loan figures—and the adjustment to the loan figures would only make up a small portion of that gap.

Table 5.11
Annual Percentage Rates for the Last Week of December, 1991

Average Interest Rates Charged on Loans

Credit Union Category	Unsecured 2-Year Maturity	New Auto 4-Year Maturity	Used Auto 3-Year Maturity	First Mortgage 30-Year Maturity	Return on Fixed Rate Investments
Assets up to $500K	14.7	12.5	13.9	12.8	6.4
Assets > $500K	15.5	11.6	13.5	11.5	6.2
Church	14.0	11.8	13.1	11.7	5.7
Non-Church	15.6	11.8	13.8	11.7	6.5
Urban	14.7	11.4	13.3	11.2	6.5
Rural	16.0	12.5	14.2	12.3	6.0
Total	**15.2**	**11.8**	**13.6**	**11.7**	**6.3**
N	**167**	**98**	**99**	**46**	**157**
Comparison with All CUs*					
CDCUs up to $500K					6.1
All CUs up to $500K	14.3	11.2	12.7	12.3	5.9
CDCUs $.51-50					6.4
All CUs $.51-50	14.6	10.0	11.7	10.5	6.4
CDCUs					6.4
All CUs	14.6	10.1	11.8	10.6	6.3

*Since the first four columns are based on rates reported directly by the credit union, and not on ratios calculated from reported values, the summation method is not used. The rates shown for all credit unions are comparable to those shown for CDCUs in the panels above. For the last column, the summation method is used.

Several interesting conclusions emerge from Table 5.11. First, interest rates vary considerably on different types of loans. They are highest on unsecured loans and lowest on new car loans and first mortgages. There are different reasons for this variation. To a certain extent it reflects the credit union's assessment of risk. The risk on a new car loan or a first mortgage is relatively low because even if the borrower defaults the collateral can be repossessed and sold, while the risk on an unsecured loan is correspondingly higher. The credit union attempts to compensate itself for the higher risk by charging a higher interest rate. To some extent, in addition, the variation in interest rates reflects general variations in the market. Those CDCUs that are in competition with other lenders for their members' business need to keep their rates in line with rates in the community.

Second, rural CDCUs charge consistently higher interest rates than do urban CDCUs. One can think of at least three different reasons why this might be the case. The rural credit unions might have higher delinquencies on loan repayments than the urban, and consequently have to charge higher interest rates to achieve an equal net rate of return. The rural credit unions might have higher expense ratios than the urban, and consequently charge higher interest rates in order to generate the income to meet their expenses. Or the rural credit unions might face less competition from other lenders and therefore be able to charge higher interest rates without driving their member-borrowers away. Table 5.12 below shows, however, that rural CDCUs have lower than average delinquency rates and only slightly higher default rates, so delinquency cannot be the explanation. Table 5.13 shows that rural CDCUs have about the same expense ratios, so expenses cannot be the answer. It is likely, therefore, that rural CDCUs charge higher interest rates because they face less competition from other lenders and their members have fewer options.

Third, interest on loans is much higher than interest on investments. Thus credit unions increase their profitability as well as serve their members better by keeping their loan ratio as high as possible and their investment ratio low.

While credit unions face a certain conflict in setting interest rates on loans—needing to balance the concern of the members as individuals in getting low rates against the concern of the members collectively in providing for a financially healthy credit union—they face no conflict in trying to secure as high a return on their investments as possible. That being the case, some of the differentials in the last column are quite interesting. It appears that church CDCUs and rural CDCUs are considerably less successful in maximizing the returns from their investment portfolios than are the nonchurch and urban CDCUs, respectively. One suspects that they take a rather more amateur attitude towards financial management. Both small and large CDCUs keep up well with the performance of other credit unions, however. Fourth, the interest rates charged by CDCUs are consistently higher than those charged by other American credit unions of the same size. This finding may be discouraging to people concerned that "the poor pay more." It is certainly a hope that CDCUs, established for the purpose of serving low- and moderate-income people, could offer loans at the same rates paid by middle-class Americans. Just as in the case of fees, however, the reality is that the poor pay more.

One cannot explain the higher interest rates by an intent to exploit the poor since the CDCUs are controlled by representatives of their own communities. As possible explanations of the gap, none of the factors listed under the second point above can be rejected. CDCUs tend to have both higher delinquency rates and higher expense ratios than mainstream credit unions. In addition, less competition from other lenders may account, at least partially, for the higher rates.

The finding that CDCU interest rates on loans are typically somewhat higher than those charged by other American credit unions needs to be put in context. First, the CDCU rates are generally the lowest that are available to people in low-income neighborhoods. The rates charged by pawnshops, finance companies, and other non-conventional lenders are almost always much higher than CDCU rates. So are rates on low-balance credit cards that are sometimes available to low- and moderate-income people. Second, the higher rates compensate at least in part for the higher costs of doing business in poor neighborhoods and the higher delinquency rates; it is because of these costs that many banks and savings and loan associations have left poor areas of the country. And third, any extra income that is earned by CDCUs stays in the local community; it is not siphoned away as is the case with some retail establishments that charge high prices and then export the profits.

A credit union's income is reduced to the extent that its borrowers fail to make the contractual payments on their loans. Table 5.12 shows the delinquency rates experienced by the CDCUs at the end of 1991, and the charge-off rates during 1991. A loan is considered to be in delinquent status if the repayments are two months or more in arrears. The first column shows the delinquency rate in dollar terms, that is to say, the average across the credit unions of the balance owing on the delinquent loans divided by the total balance outstanding on all loans. The second column shows the delinquency rate by number of loans, or the number of loans in delinquent status divided by the total number of loans.

Most loans that are in delinquent status are ultimately repaid, and since the credit union accrues interest on the outstanding balance it eventually earns its due income on the loan, even if somewhat delayed. Some loans go into default, however, and must be charged off by the credit union. The credit union does this by reducing the allowance for loan loss, which as will be recalled is a negative asset on the balance sheet, by the same amount as it reduces its loan asset. The final column of Table 5.12 shows the loans charged off in 1991 as a percentage of total loans outstanding at the end of the year.

Table 5.12
As Percentages of Total Loans Outstanding on December 31, 1991

Delinquency and Charge-off Rates

Credit Union Category	Delinquency Rate $	Delinquency Rate No.	Charge-off Rate
Assets up to $500K	9.0	12.5	2.7
Assets > $500K	8.1	9.8	2.1
Church	12.5	15.5	1.5
Non-Church	6.8	9.2	2.8
Urban	9.0	11.7	2.2
Rural	7.7	10.1	2.7
Total	**8.5**	**11.1**	**2.4**
Summation Method			
Assets up to $500K			
CDCUs	10.1	11.2	1.6
Church CDCUs	16.4	18.1	1.2
Non-Church CDCUs	6.4	8.7	1.8
All CUs	5.6	7.1	1.4
Assets $0.51 - $50 Mil			
CDCUs	5.4	7.5	1.8
Church CDCUs	9.0	10.3	1.7
Non-Church CDCUs	5.1	7.2	1.8
All CUs	2.4	3.0	1.0
All			
CDCUs	5.6	7.9	1.8
Church CDCUs	10.2	12.1	1.6
Non-Church CDCUs	5.1	7.4	1.9
All CUs	2.6	3.3	1.0

Table 5.12 shows that the charge-off rates are much less than the delinquency rates, indicating that most delinquent loans are eventually paid off. The delinquency rates are lower in terms of dollar balance than in terms of number of loans. This implies that the typical dollar balance on delinquent loans is smaller than the typical dollar balance on all loans outstanding.

The delinquency rate is somewhat higher in small CDCUs than in large, and somewhat higher in urban than in rural (although the charge-off rate in the urban credit unions is lower). The principal contrast comes in terms of church affiliation, with the church CDCUs having significantly higher delinquency rates (although, again, lower charge-off rates).

The average delinquency rates for the church credit unions conceal some extraordinarily high individual rates. The highest, 50 percent on the dollar balance of loans, is suffered by a small church credit union with just $35,000 in assets, located in a central city. Three other church credit unions had delinquency rates above 30 percent at the end of 1991.

Why the church delinquency rates are so high is a matter of conjecture. Church CDCUs have lower loan-to-asset ratios than do the other credit unions, and it may be that they have simply not developed the expertise to make good judgments about lending because they have less experience. It may be particularly difficult for credit committees in churches to turn down loan applications from parishioners since fellowship is valued highly in a church context. A report by the National Federation of CDCUs shows that some borrowers, apparently confused about the relationship between the church and the credit union, think that the church is rich enough that they should not have to pay back their loan. Some leaders of church CDCUs have cited interference from the pastor as a factor impeding sound lending policies.[8] In any case, it is clear that delinquency rates are disturbingly high in some church credit unions.

The bottom panel of Table 5.12 shows that delinquency and charge-off rates are much higher in CDCUs than in all credit unions, for both small and large institutions. The bottom panel is expanded, in order to explore the question of whether church CDCUs alone are responsible for the difference in delinquency rates between CDCUs and all credit unions. The figures show that they are not. While the church delinquency rates are particularly high, the non-church rates are also above the average delinquency rates for all credit unions. For small credit unions the difference is just marginal: 6.4 percent in the non-church CDCUs compared to 5.6 percent in all credit unions. For the larger credit unions the difference is more significant: 5.1 percent compared to 2.4 percent.

The conclusion is inescapable and unsurprising. CDCUs have higher than average delinquency rates on their loans, no doubt because their members are poorer than average Americans. CDCUs make loans to people many of whom would not be deemed creditworthy at a mainstream credit union or

---

[8] National Federation of Community Development Credit Unions, "Final Report: Church-Based Credit Union Study."

other conventional financial institution; that is their principal reason for existence. Since poor people live so close to the margin of existence, even relatively small economic reverses can put them in a position in which they are unable to meet their financial obligations.

Turning to the last column of Table 5.12, one sees that for the most part the charge-off rates are higher in the CDCUs than in all credit unions. This is consistent with the information on delinquency just reviewed. Institutions with higher delinquency rates on repayments are likely to have to declare a larger number of loans in default and write them off the books.

The interpretation of charge-off rates is somewhat ambiguous, however. On the one hand, a high charge-off rate would seem to follow naturally from a high delinquency rate. On the other hand, a charge-off is sometimes an alternative to a delinquency. Once a non-performing loan has been written off the books, it no longer appears as a delinquency. One way credit unions have of lowering their delinquency rate is simply to let the loans go into default, provided that the allowance for loan loss is sufficient to cover the write-off.

Examining a similar data set to the one used here, Lindsay Neunlist of the NCUA has pointed out that although low-income credit unions have higher charge-off rates, their ratio of charge-off to delinquency rates is lower.[9] Given the caveats expressed in the previous paragraph, this may indicate that while CDCU borrowers fall behind in their payments more frequently, they tend to stick with their loans and eventually make good on them.

How do CDCUs Allocate Their Income?

Credit unions' income is allocated completely to three categories of uses: (1) operating expenses, (2) dividend and interest payments, and (3) transfer to reserve accounts. Table 5.13 shows how the income of the country's CDCUs was divided among the three categories during 1991. On average, CDCUs allocated 47 percent of their income for operating expenses, 34 percent for dividend and interest payments, and 19 percent for transfer to the reserve accounts.

The portion of income transferred to the reserve accounts does not differ much between the various categories of CDCUs. Larger CDCUs and church CDCUs tend to have lower expense-to-income ratios, and they use the savings in expenses to increase their dividend payments to their members.

The fact that the expense-to-income ratio falls with asset size among the CDCUs (as it does also among all credit unions) may indicate that there are

---

[9] Neunlist.

some economies of scale in providing financial services. That is to say, not all expenses have to be increased at the same rate that the membership and the assets are growing, and consequently the larger credit unions are able to realize some savings, at least proportionately.

Table 5.13
(Percentages of Total Income)

Average Uses of Total Income by CDCUs, 1991

Credit Union Category	Operating Expenses	Dividends and Interest	Transfer to Reserve Accounts
Assets up to $500K	48.8	31.2	20.0
Assets > $500K	44.6	36.6	18.8
Church	43.2	37.6	19.2
Non-Church	48.1	32.4	19.5
Urban	46.3	34.0	19.7
Rural	47.2	33.8	19.0
Total	**46.7**	**34.0**	**19.4**
Summation Method			
CDCUs up to $500K	48.0	30.8	21.3
All CUs up to $500K	44.4	39.4	16.2
CDCUs $.51-50 Mil	42.7	41.4	15.8
All CUs $.51-50 Mil	36.5	50.2	13.3
CDCUs	43.0	40.9	16.1
All CUs	36.9	49.6	13.5

Table 5.14
(Operating Expenses as Percentages of Total Income)

Expense-to-Income Ratios by Church Affiliation and Size

	Assets		Total
	up to $500K	> $500K	
Church	43.6	42.6	43.2
Non-Church	52.2	45.1	48.1
Total	**48.8**	**44.6**	**46.7**

The anomaly in Table 5.13 is that the expense-to-income ratio in church CDCUs is comparatively low in spite of the fact that church credit unions are typically smaller than their non-church counterparts, and the first two lines of the table show that small CDCUs have on average higher expense-to-income ratios. Table 5.14 explores this by breaking out the church and non-church credit unions according to their size. It shows that the expense ratio in church CDCUs is quite consistent, whatever the asset size, while in non-church CDCUs the ratio falls considerably with size. The explanation may be that some of the more important fixed expenses in the non-church CDCUs—that is to say, expenses like rent which need to increase little if at all as the credit union grows—are paid for by the sponsoring church in the case of the church credit unions. In any case, the fact that small CDCUs have on average higher expense ratios is due entirely to the non-church credit unions.

Returning to Table 5.13, the bottom panel shows that CDCUs have consistently higher expense-to-income ratios than do other credit unions. This is the case whether the comparison is among small or large credit unions. It also shows that CDCUs allocate more of their income to reserves—probably in order to compensate for higher delinquencies and defaults in their loans. As a consequence, CDCUs have much less income (about ten percentage points less) to return to their members as dividends. To see the point in a different way, note that CDCUs allocate more of their income to operating expenses than to dividend and interest payments, while other credit unions typically allocate more to dividends and interest.

There are a number of reasons for the relatively high expense ratios of CDCUs. They normally have to spend more staff time dealing with members because fewer of their transactions occur in computerized payroll deduction form than in other credit unions. In some cases, CDCUs find it more expensive to determine the creditworthiness of their borrowers and to process their loans. The most fundamental reason, however, is that their members are poor, with relatively low savings balances.

To understand the consequence of low savings balances upon the expense ratio, one can envision the financial effect of a member upon a credit union. The member creates income for the credit union and also expenses. The income results from the member's savings deposits which the credit union lends or invests, thereby earning interest. The larger the savings deposit, the larger the interest income. The expenses come largely from the transactions the member engages in: each deposit, each withdrawal, each inquiry, each loan payment, requires the use of staff time, computer time, and supplies. Unfortunately, the level of transactions appears unrelated to the level of a member's savings. Members with $100 in their account engage in roughly as many deposits and withdrawals as do members with $10,000. If all members impose roughly the same expenses on the credit union, but only members with high deposits generate high income, then credit unions with a preponderance of poor members will suffer from a relatively high ratio of expenses to income. This is the systematic and inescapable reason for the comparatively high expense ratios of CDCUs in Table 5.13.[10] More generally, any financial institution has difficulty thriving among a low-income clientele, and therefore banks are scarce in poor neighborhoods while pawnshops and loan sharks charge such high interest rates.

Table 5.15
(Percentages of Total Income)

Compensation and Fringes

Credit Union Category	Compensation	Other Expenses	Total Expenses
Assets up to $500K	10.0	38.8	48.8
Assets > $500K	20.1	24.5	44.6
Church	9.3	33.9	43.2
Non-Church	17.6	30.5	48.1
Urban	15.4	30.9	46.3
Rural	14.6	32.6	47.2
Total	**15.1**	**31.6**	**46.7**
Summation Method			
Assets up to $500K			
CDCUs	14.3	33.7	48.0
Church CDCUs	7.9	33.2	41.1
Non-Church CDCUs	18.3	33.9	52.2
All CUs	16.3	28.1	44.4
Assets $0.51 - $50 Mil			
CDCUs	21.1	21.5	42.7
Church CDCUs	18.4	27.3	45.7
Non-Church CDCUs	21.3	21.2	42.5
All CUs	17.2	19.3	36.5
All			
CDCUs	20.8	22.2	43.0
Church CDCUs	16.4	28.4	44.8
Non-Church CDCUs	21.2	21.6	42.8
All CUs	17.1	19.8	36.9

Another reason for the relatively high expense ratios in CDCUs may be that they offer more services to their members than do other credit unions,

---

[10] It is also why non-member deposits can be so important to a low-income credit union. Non-member deposits tend to be relatively large and they require few transactions (sometimes as few as one a year), so they can effectively cross-subsidize the small depositors who account for the bulk of CDCU funds.

but cover the cost by charging fees for the services. In 1993 the NCUA acknowledged this possibility by instructing its examiners to rate credit unions not on their overall expense ratio but on their net expense ratio, where net expenses are equal to total expenses minus fees. Table 5.15 permits a closer look at the expense-to-income ratio by dividing out the component of expenses that represents compensation and fringe benefits paid to employees. This is the largest single item among the expenses.[11]

The higher expense ratio for small CDCUs is not associated with higher levels of compensation to employees. To the contrary, small CDCUs spend only 10 percent of their income on staff compensation, while larger credit unions spend 20 percent. Church CDCUs spend much less on employees than do non-church CDCUs.

The bottom panel of Table 5.15 shows that the compensation ratio is actually less in the small CDCUs than in small credit unions generally, while it is greater in the larger CDCUs. The comparatively low compensation ratio for small credit unions can be seen, however, to be entirely due to the small church CDCUs. Once the church CDCUs are factored out, the remaining small non-church CDCUs devote a higher proportion of their income to compensation than do credit unions generally.

Table 5.16

Staffing in CDCUs

Credit Union Category	Credit Union	Full-time-equivalent Employees Per:		
		1,000 Members	$100,000 Income	$1,000,000 Assets
Assets up to $500K	0.6	2.5	6.5	5.6
Assets > $500K	3.2	2.0	1.5	1.5
Church	0.9	1.7	3.2	2.7
Non-Church	2.3	2.5	4.3	3.9
Urban	1.9	2.2	3.5	2.8
Rural	1.8	2.4	4.8	4.8
Total	**1.9**	**2.2**	**4.0**	**3.5**
Summation Method				
CDCUs up to $500K	0.6	1.9	3.3	3.0
All CUs up to $500K	0.8	3.3	3.4	3.4
CDCUs $.51-50 Mil	3.2	1.8	1.0	1.0
All CUs $.51-50 Mil	7.2	2.0	0.8	0.8
CDCUs	1.9	1.8	1.1	1.1
All CUs	6.9	2.1	0.9	0.9

[11] The other expense categories reported in the call data are travel and conference, office occupancy, office operations, educational and promotional, loan servicing, professional and outside services, member insurance, operating fees, and others.

Salary expenses reflect a combination of staffing levels and wage rates. Something about these can be inferred from the call reports but the inferences are imprecise. Credit unions report the number of full-time and part-time staff separately. They do not, unfortunately, report the hours for the part-time staff. Consequently the total number of hours—or, alternatively, the number of full-time-equivalent employees—is not known. In the tables that follow, the intermediate assumption is made that a part-time employee works half-time, and is equivalent to half a full-time employee. Using that assumption, Table 5.16 shows the average ratios of staff per CDCU, per 1,000 members, per $100,000 in income and per $1,000,000 in assets.

The typical CDCU has just less than two staff members. Naturally, the number is lower for the smaller credit unions and for the church-affiliated credit unions. CDCUs have fewer employees per credit union than is the case in the industry generally. They have somewhat fewer employees per member and somewhat more per dollar of income and assets.

Two features of Table 5.16 merit further exploration. First, church CDCUs have fewer employees per member, and per dollar of income and assets, than do non-church CDCUs, in spite of the fact that they are smaller. Second, small CDCUs have more employees per dollar of income than do larger CDCUs, in spite of the fact that the portion of income they spend on employees is considerably smaller (see Table 5.15).

Table 5.17
(Number of Credit Unions in Parentheses)

Employees Per Hundred Thousand Dollars in Income by Credit Union Size and Church Affiliation

	Assets		Total
	up to $500K	> $500K	
Church	3.9 (35)	1.9 (19)	3.2 (54)
Non-Church	8.2 (54)	1.4 (72)	4.3 (126)
Total	**6.5 (89)**	**1.5 (91)**	**4.0 (180)**

Table 5.17 explores the first issue by looking more closely at employees per $100,000 of income in church and non-church CDCUs. It shows that the staffing gap between the two types of credit unions is huge at the smaller size, and this compensates for the fact that most church credit unions are small and that smaller credit unions have higher proportionate staffing levels. Among the larger credit unions, the church staffing ratio actually exceeds the non-church ratio, but since there are so few church credit unions in this category, it does not pull the overall church ratio above the non-

church. Put simply, small church credit unions make do with many fewer employees than do non-church credit unions of a similar size. The explanation is likely that they rely more heavily on volunteers, and also that they take on fewer tasks, including less lending.

The second issue is that while small credit unions have more staff per $100,000 of income, they spend a smaller proportion of their income on staff. There are two possible explanations of this, both of which likely have some validity. The first is that many staff members in small CDCUs are paid by a sponsoring agency and not from the earned income of the credit union. The second is that wages are lower in the small credit unions.

The second explanation, that wages are lower in the small credit unions, is no doubt true, but a simple calculation shows that it cannot be the sole explanation. If all employees are paid from the credit unions' own income, then the wage rate, or compensation per employee, is equal to the ratio of compensation to income (in Table 5.15) divided by the ratio of employees to income (in Table 5.16). Performing the division, one sees that the implied annual wage rate is $13,224 in the large credit unions and $1,536 in the small. Even if the assumption about part-time employees is changed so that part-time is counted as one quarter rather than one half of full-time, the implied wages are $16,891 and $2,538 respectively. Under either assumption, the calculated wages in the large credit unions are quite low, and this probably indicates that they get some supplementary help from sponsoring agencies. The calculated wage in the small credit unions is impossibly low, indicating that they get the majority of their staff support dollars from sponsoring agencies, grants, or other outside sources.

How Do CDCUs Create a Spread Between Income and Outgo?

One way to understand the financial condition of a credit union is to identify the spread, that is to say, the gap between the income generated by its assets, on the one hand, and the cost of those assets, on the other hand. From this spread, the credit union must pay its operating expenses. Any surplus that is left over after the operating expenses can be transferred to the reserve accounts. This section analyzes the spread.

Almost all of the components of the spread have been looked at already. This section adds little new data, but it looks at the data from a different perspective.

The spread analysis is conducted in relationship to the assets of the credit union. The income, expenses, and surplus are all stated as ratios to assets. For example, the interest return on loans is the income derived from loans during 1991 as a percentage of loans outstanding. The gross income return on assets is the total of all the credit union's income as a percentage of its total assets. So far in this chapter, the assets used in calculations have been the figures as of December 31, 1991. This sole date is not adequate for rate-of-return studies, however. The loan interest income during 1991 was generated by the loans outstanding throughout the entire year, not just at the end of the year. As an estimate of this quantity, the asset amounts for December 31, 1990 and December 31, 1991 are averaged throughout this section.

During 1991, the typical CDCU achieved a rate of return on all assets of 10 percent. This is shown in column 4 of Table 5.18. Compared to all American credit unions of the same size, the CDCUs' rate of return was one percentage point higher.

Looking at the CDCUs by category, the larger CDCUs, the non-church CDCUs, and the rural CDCUs all had higher rates of return on assets than did the smaller, church, and urban CDCUs, respectively. Some of the reasons for these differences are revealing.

Table 5.18
(Percentages)

Rates of Return

Credit Union Category	1 Net Return on Loans	2 Return on Investments	3 Interest Return on Earning Assets	4 Total Return on All Assets
Assets up to $500K	12.7	6.4	9.5	9.4
Assets > $500K	12.6	6.2	10.4	10.9
Church	12.2	5.7	9.1	9.1
Non-Church	12.9	6.5	10.2	10.5
Urban	12.3	6.5	9.7	9.7
Rural	13.2	6.0	10.3	10.7
Total	**12.7**	**6.3**	**9.9**	**10.1**
Summation Method				
CDCUs up to $500K	12.9	6.1	9.6	9.6
All CUs < $500K	12.6	5.9	10.3	9.9
CDCUs $.51-50 Mil	12.5	6.4	10.5	11.1
All CUs $.51-50 Mil	11.9	6.4	9.9	10.0
CDCUs	12.5	6.4	10.5	11.0
All CUs	11.9	6.3	9.9	10.0

Looking first at the rate of return on loans in column 1—the interest earned by the CDCUs on their loans divided by the loans outstanding—the non-church and the rural credit unions both did better because they charged higher interest rates on loans (as was seen in Table 5.11), and because they enjoyed lower delinquency rates on loans (Table 5.12). There was almost no differential in rate of return on loans by size of credit union since, although the smaller CDCUs charged higher interest rates on some categories of loans, they suffered from somewhat higher delinquency rates.

The rates of return on investments were previously seen in Table 5.11. The small differences in column 2 are probably due to differences in skills in financial management.

Column 3, interest return on earning assets, is a weighted average of the first two columns, showing total interest earnings divided by both loans and investments outstanding. The final column adds fees and other income to the numerator of column 3, and fixed and other non-earning assets to the denominator. For the most part, these additions cancel out, leaving few differences between the third and fourth columns.

An interesting feature of Table 5.18 is that the differences in overall rate of return, shown for example in column 4, are generally greater than the differences in the rates of return on either loans or investments. The reason for this is that a very important determinant of the overall rate of return is the proportion of assets that are devoted to loans. Note, for example, the difference between small and large credit unions. On loans and on investments, looked at separately, the rates of return are very similar, marginally higher for the small CDCUs in one case, marginally lower in the other. Yet the overall rate of return on assets is much lower for the small CDCUs. The clue is back in Table 5.4, showing that the loan-to-asset ratio was 43 percent in the small CDCUs and 59 percent in the large ones. Since the return on loans is so much higher, this puts the large CDCUs in a stronger financial position. In terms of the church and non-church distinction, while a gap exists in columns 1 and 2, the greater gap in columns 3 and 4 is due to the lower loan-to-asset ratio in the church CDCUs shown in Table 5.4. Similarly in the urban-rural contrast, the lower loan-to-asset ratio in the urban CDCUs has the effect of lowering the overall rate of return.

The fact that the rate of return on assets was higher for CDCUs than for all credit unions of comparable size is due primarily to the higher interest rates that they charged on loans, as shown in Table 5.11. CDCUs had a slightly higher loan-to-asset ratio (Table 5.4), but not enough to cause much difference in the overall rate of return. Their return on investments was just barely higher and their delinquency rates were actually significantly worse. So the CDCUs' policy of charging higher interest rates on loans resulted in a higher overall rate of return.

When the CDCUs are segmented by size, however, it can be seen that the overall rate of return on the smaller CDCUs was below that of small credit unions generally. In this case, the culprit is the low loan-to-asset ratio shown in Table 5.4, which far more than compensated for the higher interest rates that the small CDCUs charged.

The second component of the spread analysis is the cost of funds. Column 1 of Table 5.19 shows the cost of member savings: the dividend payments divided by the shares outstanding during 1991. Column 2 is a more comprehensive estimate of the cost of funds. To the numerator of column 1 is added the interest cost of borrowed funds, and the denominator in column 2 is the credit union's total assets.

The most interesting feature of Table 5.19 is how much lower the cost of funds is for CDCUs than for credit unions generally of the same size. In 1991, small CDCUs paid only about three quarters as much for their funds as did all small credit unions; larger CDCUs, over a half million dollars in assets, paid about 90 percent of what all larger credit unions paid.

Table 5.19
(Percentages)

Cost of Funds

Credit Union Category	1 Cost of Shares	2 Dividend and Interest Cost of Total Assets
Assets up to $500K	3.3	2.7
Assets > $500K	4.3	3.9
Church	3.7	3.2
Non-Church	3.8	3.3
Urban	3.6	3.2
Rural	4.1	3.5
Total	**3.8**	**3.3**
Summation Method		
CDCUs up to $500K	3.4	2.9
All CUs up to $500K	4.6	3.9
CDCUs $.51-50 Mil	5.0	4.6
All CUs $.51-50 Mil	5.6	5.0
CDCUs	4.9	4.5
All CUs	5.5	5.0

The relatively low cost of funds is a mixed blessing for the CDCUs. Table 5.13 above showed that CDCUs have relatively high operating expenses and that they devote a high proportion of their income to reserves in order to compensate for loan defaults, leaving them with significantly less to return to their members in dividends. Now Table 5.19 shows the consequence of this squeeze; CDCU members in fact earn less on their savings than do members of other credit unions.

This may help to explain why many CDCUs have stayed so small; potential members prefer to deposit their funds elsewhere to get a higher return. Still, the CDCUs retain a deposit base, and this requires an explanation, too, in view of the relatively low returns on savings that they offer. Part of the explanation may be loyalty. Members often feel a connection to an institution that has been established by their neighbors and for their benefit, and they are willing to forego a little income on their savings in order to support it. They may stick with the CDCU in order to qualify for loans themselves. Another part of the explanation is that in at least some poor neighborhoods few financial institutions are competing for people's deposits, and consequently savers may not be able to obtain higher rates of return than the CDCU offers, at least not very easily. Sometimes they cannot meet the minimum deposit requirements at other institutions.

Among the CDCUs themselves there are some differences in the cost of funds. Small CDCUs and urban CDCUs pay less for their funds than large and rural CDCUs do, respectively.

Table 5.20
(Percentages of Average Assets During 1991)

Net Spread

Credit Union Category	1 Gross Return on Assets	−	2 Cost of Funds	=	3 Gross Spread	−	4 Operating Expenses	=	5 Net Spread
Assets up to $500K	9.4		2.7		6.7		4.8		1.9
Assets > $500K	10.9		3.9		7.0		5.1		1.9
Church	9.1		3.2		5.9		4.1		1.8
Non-Church	10.5		3.3		7.2		5.2		1.9
Urban	9.7		3.2		6.6		4.8		1.7
Rural	10.7		3.5		7.2		5.1		2.2
Total	**10.1**		**3.3**		**6.8**		**4.9**		**1.9**
Summation Method									
CDCUs up to $500K	9.6		2.9		6.7		4.7		1.9
All CUs up to $500K	9.9		3.9		6.0		4.4		1.6
CDCUs $.51-50 Mil	11.1		4.6		6.5		4.7		1.8
All CUs $.51-50 Mil	10.0		5.0		5.0		3.6		1.3
CDCUs	11.0		4.5		6.5		4.7		1.8
All CUs	10.0		5.0		5.0		3.7		1.4

Church affiliation makes no difference to the cost of funds, in spite of the fact that church CDCUs devote a significantly higher portion of their income to dividends than do non-church CDCUs (see Table 5.13). The answer to the puzzle lies in Table 5.18, which shows church CDCUs doing significantly worse in terms of overall return on assets; the result of this is that they must devote more of their income to dividends just to stay even in terms of dividend payments on shares. The gross spread is equal to the gross return on assets, from Table 5.18, minus the total cost of assets, from Table 5.19. The net spread is equal to the gross spread minus the ratio of operating expenses to assets, as shown in Table 5.20.[12]

Remarkably, there is very little variation in the net spread among the different categories of CDCUs. The differences in gross return in column 1 are partially compensated for by differences in cost of funds in column 2. For example, the gross return in small CDCUs is 1.5 percentage points less than in larger CDCUs, but the cost of funds is 1.2 percentage points less, leaving a difference in gross spread of just 0.3 points. Nevertheless, some significant differences in gross spread remain, with non-church doing better than church CDCUs, and rural doing better than urban. The gross spread in column 3 is correlated with the expense-to-asset ratio in column 4, however, categories with high gross spreads having high expense ratios. Consequently the net spreads come out quite close together around the overall average of 1.9 percentage points.

A substantial difference exists between the net spreads of the CDCUs and all American credit unions of the same size, with the CDCU spread being higher by about half a percentage point. The higher net spread is required because the demands on the CDCUs' net income are greater, as shown in Table 5.21.

The loans in default are charged off from the net spread (column 2), leaving the net income which is retained by the credit union (column 3). Part of the net income is allocated to the allowance for loan loss (column 4), which is held as a negative asset, and the remainder (column 5) is transferred to one of the reserve or capital accounts.

The amount to be transferred to the allowance for loan loss is stipulated by the federal or state examiners; it depends upon the amount currently in the allowance for loan loss, as well as the examiner's assessment of the quality of the loans that are on the books.

In CDCUs, the required provision for loan loss is frequently greater than net income, leaving a negative balance for transfer to other reserve accounts. Table 5.21 shows that on the average in 1991 the reserve accounts actually

---

[12] Because of rounding, some of the figures in Tables 5.20 and 5.21 appear to be subtracted incorrectly.

shrank in CDCUs because transfers to the allowance for loan loss exceeded net income. Further examination shows, however, that only a minority of the CDCUs experienced this shrinkage. Of the 157 CDCUs on which the rate of return tables are based, 58 lost reserves in 1991 after the provision for loan loss was transferred.

Table 5.21
(Percentages of Average Assets During 1991)

Allocation to Capital

Credit Union Category	1 Net Spread	–	2 Net Loans Charged Off	=	3 Net Income	=	4 Provision for Loan Loss	+	5 Other Transfers to Capital
Assets up to $500K	1.9		0.7		1.2		1.1		0.1
Assets > $500K	1.9		1.1		0.8		1.3		-0.5
Church	1.8		0.6		1.2		1.2		0
Non-Church	1.9		1.0		1.0		1.2		-0.3
Urban	1.7		1.0		0.8		1.4		-0.7
Rural	2.2		0.7		1.4		1.0		0.5
Total	**1.9**		**0.9**		**1.0**		**1.2**		**-0.2**
Summation Method									
CDCUs up to $500K	1.9		0.6		1.4		1.1		0.3
All CUs up to $500K	1.6		0.7		1.0		0.7		0.2
CDCUs $.51-50 Mil	1.8		1.1		0.7		1.2		-0.5
All CUs $.51-50 Mil	1.3		0.5		0.8		0.5		0.3
CDCUs	1.8		1.0		0.7		1.2		-0.5
All CUs	1.4		0.5		0.9		0.5		0.3

In summary, the spread analysis shows that CDCUs enjoyed a higher return on assets than did all American credit unions, and paid less for their funds. Consequently, their gross spread was substantially larger—by one measure, one and a half percentage points. Their expenses were substantially higher, however, as was the dollar amount of loans charged off, and as a result their net income was roughly on a par with other credit unions. Because the required provisions for loan loss were higher in CDCUs than in other credit unions, the amounts left over for transfer to the other reserve accounts were substantially less, and in many cases actually negative. Consequently, one of the most important tasks facing many CDCUs is to build their capital base.

How are CDCUs Rated by Their Examiners?

Each credit union in the country is rated by its federal or state examiners using the CAMEL system, where CAMEL stands for:

Capital Adequacy
Asset Quality
Management
Earnings
Liquidity Management

Each component is rated on a 1 to 5 scale, with 1 being the strongest and 5 being well below the minimal acceptable standard. In addition, the credit union as a whole is given a numerical rating. The CAMEL ratings are intended as a measurement of the risk that each credit union presents to the National Credit Union Share Insurance Fund.

Table 5.22
Percentages, Using the Summation Method

CAMEL Ratios*

Ratio	Assets up to $500K		Assets > $500K		Total	
	CDCU	All CU	CDCU	All CU	CDCU	All CU
Capital Adequacy:						
Net capital/assets	13.0	13.8	7.1	9.0	7.5	9.2
Reserves/assets	15.4	15.6	8.7	9.8	9.1	10.1
Asset Quality:						
Loan delinquency ratio ($)	10.1	5.6	5.4	2.4	5.6	2.6
Loan charge-off ratio	1.6	1.4	1.8	1.0	1.8	1.0
Non-earning assets/assets	1.1	0.7	3.0	1.9	2.9	1.8
Earnings:						
Net income/assets (before prov. for loss)	1.4	1.0	0.7	0.8	0.7	0.9
Net income/assets (after prov. for loss)	0.3	0.2	-0.5	0.3	-0.5	0.3
Op. expenses/assets	4.7	4.4	4.7	3.6	4.7	3.7

* The first two rows of figures are from Table 5.3, the third and fourth from Table 5.12, the fifth from Table 5.4, the sixth and seventh from Table 5.21 and the eighth from Table 5.20.

The ratings are communicated in confidence to the management and board of directors of the credit unions and are not available to the public.

The information on which many of the assessments are made is, however, available. The Capital, Asset, and Earnings ratings are based largely on ratios that have been shown in the tables in this chapter. The Management and Liquidity ratings are heavily influenced by more subjective criteria.

Table 5.22 brings together the most important figures for the CAMEL ratings, displaying them by asset size of the credit union and comparing them to all American credit unions of the same size.

Table 5.22 shows that, according to at least some of the criteria generally used to assess the health of credit unions, CDCUs are typically weaker than other credit unions. In terms of capital adequacy, CDCUs usually have lower ratios of net capital to assets (first row). When the allowance for loan loss is added to the reserves, the gap between the two groups is reduced but not eliminated.

In terms of asset quality, the CDCUs have much higher levels of loan delinquency and somewhat higher levels of loan charge-offs (third and fourth rows). In addition, more of their assets are in non-earning form (fifth row).

In considering earnings, the CDCUs do just about as well as credit unions generally, except in the case of larger credit unions, when the provision for loan loss is deducted. They do, however, have higher expense ratios.

While the actual CAMEL ratings are not available, Table 5.22 makes it clear that CDCUs are typically rated lower than other credit unions. In view of the difficulties of doing business in poor communities, this is hardly surprising.

Conclusions

Some of the interesting findings of this analysis of financial data lie in the details and need not be repeated. Lest the reader be lost in the details, however, some of the central points bear highlighting.

Taken as a whole, CDCUs do nearly as well financially as do mainstream credit unions of the same size; they are capable of managing the risk inherent in their business, generating income, keeping expenses under control, and accumulating reserves. But they do not do quite as well, and for predictable reasons. Working as they do in poor neighborhoods, CDCUs find that their expenses are higher, that their net profitability is lower, that more of their loans must be written off, and that as a consequence they are forced to charge more for their services.

Among the most striking findings are the following:
- Loan delinquency rates are substantially higher in CDCUs than in mainstream credit unions, but charge-off rates are only

slightly higher (Table 5.12). It follows that the proportion of delinquent loans ending up in default is relatively low in CDCUs. This may indicate that the high delinquency rates are a consequence of economic distress, not irresponsibility, and that when CDCU members are capable of it, most eventually make good on their loans.

- CDCUs devote a higher proportion of their income to operating expenses than do other credit unions (Table 5.13).

- CDCUs charge somewhat higher interest rates on their loans than do other credit unions (Table 5.11), probably in order to compensate for the greater loan losses and the higher expenses.

- The consequence of the relatively high expenses in CDCUs is that less is available to be paid to the members as dividends on their savings (Table 5.19). CDCUs reduce the dividend rates, but they do not skimp on transfers to the reserve accounts (Table 5.13). On the other hand they sustain greater losses from their reserves, and therefore the ratio of reserves to assets in CDCUs is close to, but not quite as high, as in other credit unions of comparable size (Table 5.3).

- CDCUs generate a greater spread between income and cost of funds than do other credit unions. The demands on that spread are greater, however, as a consequence of higher operating expenses, higher loan charge-offs, and higher required provisions for loan loss, the consequence being that the income available for transfer to the reserve accounts is lower in the CDCUs, and sometimes negative (Tables 5.20 and 5.21).

- CDCUs have higher staffing levels, relative to assets, than do other credit unions (Table 5.16) and devote a higher proportion of their income to employee compensation (Table 5.15).

- Compared to other credit unions, CDCUs make more unsecured loans and fewer automobile loans (Table 5.6). Within each category of loans, the size of loans is about the same (Table 5.8). CDCUs lend to a relatively small proportion of their members (Table 5.9).

- The facts that CDCUs suffer higher defaults on their loans, incur higher expenses, charge higher interest rates on loans, and pay lower dividend rates on savings make it difficult for them to attract middle- and high-income members, who have the option of doing business with financial institutions that offer them better rates. While it is not impossible to develop a credit union membership that is a mixture of low- and higher-income people, it is difficult.[13] It follows that CDCUs need to reach out to socially responsible investors and institutions.

- In some respects, small CDCUs face more difficult problems than do large ones. A smaller proportion of their assets are lent to their members (Table 5.4), and their operating expenses are a higher proportion of their income (Table 5.13). Still, they compensate for this, in part by paying lower dividends to their members (Table 5.20), and, as a consequence, they are able to keep up with their transfers to reserves (Table 5.21) and are able to maintain a ratio of reserves to assets that is actually higher than in the larger CDCUs (Table 5.3).

- Church-affiliated CDCUs are as strong financially as other CDCUs as measured by their reserve ratios (Table 5.3). They lend fewer of their assets (Table 5.4) and as a consequence generate less income (Table 5.20), but they compensate for this by incurring lower expenses (Table 5.13) and, in particular, lower wage payments (Table 5.15).

- The most important single indicator of the financial health, stability, and expected longevity of a credit union is its reserve ratio. Table 5.3 shows that CDCUs' reserve ratios are close to, although not quite as high as, the reserve ratios in mainstream credit unions of comparable size. In spite of the many difficulties they face, CDCUs are typically doing reasonably well.

- These data lead one to conclude, therefore, that financial institutions can be successful operating in low-income communities. They just cannot be quite as profitable as those operating in richer neighborhoods. Although this study does not deal with banks, it is likely that the flight of banks from poor neighborhoods is caused by a search for higher profits, and is not a consequence of actual losses. Or, at the very least, losses need not be sustained by a financial institution that takes seriously the mission of serving the financial needs of low-income people.

---

[13] This point is made in Neunlist.

CHAPTER 6

THE LENDING PRACTICES OF CDCUs

There's not many who are willing to give the small operator a chance, and at the credit union everybody has been willing to take a chance on me.

—James (Moose) Morgan[1]

The banks around here are just keepers of black folks' money. Just like everyone else, we need a lender and that is why the credit union was started.

—James Gilliam, St.Luke
Credit Union, North Carolina[2]

The most important impact of community development credit unions results from their lending. This chapter explores the lending practices of seven diverse CDCUs in order to illustrate the sorts of loans that they make and the sorts of people who borrow from them. [3]

Seven Credit Unions

The seven credit unions are
- Central Appalachian People's Federal Credit Union, in Berea, Kentucky. Its field of membership includes people associated

---

[1] Quoted in Central Appalachian People's Federal Credit Union, Annual Report, 1990 (Berea, Kentucky: 1991).

[2] Quoted in Tholin and Pogge, 2.

[3] This chapter is largely based on a previously published report, Isbister with the assistance of Thompson. It extends the study by Rosenthal and Schoder. Thanks to Joy Agcongay, Christina Cavazos, and Javier Tapia for help in collecting the data.

with 35 community organizations in the southern Appalachian mountains. Each of the 35 organizations functions as a branch of the credit union.

- First American Credit Union, whose head office is in Window Rock, Arizona, on the Navajo Reservation. It is the largest Indian credit union in the country. While its field of membership includes all Indians whose tribal headquarters are in Arizona, the files examined in this chapter come only from the Window Rock office where the majority of the members are Navajo.

- Mission Area Federal Credit Union, in a predominantly Latino neighborhood of San Francisco. It grew out of the political struggles of local community organizations in the 1970s. After a difficult early period, it rescued itself and grew slowly into a stable institution focusing on the needs of people living in a poor, central area of the city.

- Northeast Community Federal Credit Union, in the Chinatown area of San Francisco. It serves Asian immigrants who move into the center of the city. It was chartered in 1970 and initially served an almost exclusively Chinese population, but with changing immigration patterns significant numbers of Vietnamese have joined.

- North East Jackson Area Federal Credit Union, serving an African American rural community in the Florida panhandle. It was founded in 1965 with the assistance of the federal Office of Economic Opportunity as part of the War on Poverty. Many of its members are independent farmers.

- Santa Cruz Community Credit Union, serving a mixed-income population in Santa Cruz, California. It was founded by political activists concerned both with the environmental preservation of their coastal community and with social services for the poor. It has a particular commitment to community economic development.

- Watts United Credit Union in the Watts area of Los Angeles, a predominantly African American community. Founded just after the Watts riots of 1965, as a response to the terrible economic and social conditions in the area, it has been one of the few commercial successes in a neighborhood that remains devastated.

For each of the seven CDCUs, Table 6.1 shows the membership, assets, and outstanding loans, plus two ratios: assets per member and reserves to assets. Assets per member is an indicator, albeit imperfect, of the relative wealth of the credit union and its members, while the ratio of reserves to assets is an indicator of the credit union's financial condition.

Table 6.1

**Seven Credit Unions: Basic Comparisons
As of December 31, 1991**

Credit Union	Members	Assets ($000)	Loans ($000)	Assets/Member ($)	Reserves/Assets* (%)
Appalachian	1,682	2,306	1,232	1,371	3.5
First American	9,999	26,024	16,061	2,603	7.3
Mission Area	950	2,093	1,744	2,203	4.0
Northeast Community	834	3,209	1,947	3,847	10.6
NEJA	819	658	437	803	8.5
Santa Cruz	6,233	18,365	11,586	2,946	5.1
Watts United	2,185	1,454	1,258	665	13.6

*Includes the allowance for loan loss

Data were collected from loan files in each of the seven credit unions. An attempt was made to look at approximately 200 loans in each credit union, disbursed during 1990. The data are described more fully in the appendix.

Table 6.2

Median Values of Loans and Borrower Characteristics

	Appal.	First Amer.	Mission Area	North East	NEJA	Santa Cruz	Watts United
Amount ($)	504	300	5,000	5,500	1,500	3,108	2,600
Interest (%)	15.0	16.0	15.5	13.0	15.0	15.9	18.0
Term (months)	9	—	48	24	12	36	36
Purpose*	used auto	used auto	debt consol.	business	farm	credit card	used auto
Age	31	36	39	38	43	36	41
Sex	F	F	F	M	M	M	F
Income/Month	1,000	1,260	1,920	2,500	1,096	2,349	1,577

* The loan purpose shown is not the median, but rather the most frequently cited purpose.

Table 6.2 selects the median value for each of seven variables in the loan files of the credit unions. The first four rows are characteristics of the loans, while the last three are characteristics of the borrowers. The table allows a quick overview of some of the findings.

The Loans

Tables 6.3 and 6.4 analyze the loans in each credit union according to their purpose.[4] Table 6.3 shows the percentage distribution of the dollar amount of loans, while Table 6.4 shows the average size of loans, by purpose.

Table 6.3
(Percentage Distribution)

Dollar Amount of Loans by Loan Purpose

Purpose	Appal.	First Amer.	Mission Area	North East	NEJA	Santa Cruz	Watts United
New auto	3.5	—	13.7	3.9	—	15.8	27.2
Used auto	50.0	22.9	13.5	2.1	20.9	7.1	25.7
Home improvement	6.1	13.2	2.2	8.8	8.2	10.2	6.2
Debt consolidation	11.4	11.4	31.4	5.5	1.3	3.5	6.6
Medical	0.1	1.2	0.3	—	1.4	1.7	0.6
Travel	2.5	7.3	3.0	0.8	—	0.3	8.4
Furniture	2.6	2.3	0.2	0.0	0.6	0.1	4.2
Christmas	4.9	3.2	0.5		—	0.4	—
Business	0.4	1.6	16.8	48.0	44.2	28.1	—
Real estate	5.3	6.3	6.4	14.4	14.9	0.2	—
Taxes	1.8	2.5	2.4	2.3	0.2	0.3	—
School	4.6	14.6	0.4	—	4.1	—	3.6
Credit card	—	—	—	—	—	30.7	—
Other	6.7	13.5	9.3	14.1	3.9	2.0	17.5

Table 6.3 demonstrates that most CDCUs do a substantial amount of lending for automobiles, with CAPFCU and Watts United directing over half of their money to this purpose. The category "used auto" in these tables includes repairs as well as purchases. Other fairly large categories in some credit

---

[4] These tables are not directly comparable with the data on loan purpose compiled by NCUA and CUNA. The latter classify loans by collateral type, not by the real purpose for which the proceeds will be used. Thus, for example, an unsecured, personal loan which a borrower expects to use to purchase or repair an automobile will be classified by the NCUA as "unsecured" but in Tables 6.3 and 6.4 as "automobile." Note also that the loan purpose is stated in the borrower's own words on each application. Construction of Tables 6.3 and 6.4, therefore, required some interpretation in borderline cases, particularly when more than one purpose was given.

unions are business loans, debt consolidation, and, in one case, credit cards.

Table 6.4

Average Size of Loan by Loan Purpose

Purpose	Appal.	First Amer.	Mission Area	North East	NEJA	Santa Cruz	Watts United
New auto	7,977	—	10,401	12,783	—	10,995	12,145
Used auto	1,738	483	5,333	4,229	2,328	5,535	3,695
Home impr.	938	683	15,400	24,938	1,564	28,539	2,790
Debt cons.	1,191	336	6,533	7,844	820	5,685	3,547
Medical	250	400	1,648	—	1,513	13,247	808
Travel	562	577	1,936	2,250	—	2,215	2,690
Furniture	542	394	950	1,000	900	2,654	2,429
Christmas	414	370	3,000	—	1,198	—	—
Business	502	538	4,969	19,782	6,213	22,669	—
Real estate	2,448	651	4,577	29,760	5,337	6,076	—
Taxes	682	527	3,587	12,875	300	2,723	—
School	889	522	2,450	—	3,275	—	2,870
Credit card	—	—	—	—	—	1,819	—
Other	1,027	423	3,885	7,132	841	4,911	2,343
Average size	1,189	481	5,568	13,486	2,936	7,992	3,623
Median size	504	300	5,000	5,500	1,500	—	2,600
Industry							
Av. size	3,581	4,214	3,164	3,581	2,618	4,054	3,164
Av. term (mo)	15	—	43	44	17	48	40
Median term	9	—	48	24	12	36	36

Table 6.4 shows that in two of the credit unions, Central Appalachian and First American, the average size of a loan is considerably smaller than in typical United States credit unions of the same asset size.[5] In five of the credit unions, including the four that devote significant resources to business loans, the loans are on average larger than in other credit unions.

The lending experience of each credit union is considered in order.

Central Appalachian People's Federal Credit Union

At CAPFCU the typical loan size is very small. Only First American has smaller loans, and this is because of specific constraints that the latter's board of directors has placed on the lending policies in that credit union. At

---

[5] The data on industry-wide averages, calculated by asset size of the credit unions, come from Credit Union National Association, *Operating Ratios and Spreads, Year-End 1991*.

CAPFCU, the loans are small in most cases because the borrowers are poor and cannot afford to go deeply into debt. Signature loans, without collateral, were available in 1990 for amounts up to $500 (plus loan fees), and the median loan was in fact for that amount.

Not only is the typical loan size small, but the term, or length of time for repayment, is short; the usual loan is paid back in less than a year.

The loans are so small (and the borrowers so poor), that few if any of them would be attractive to commercial banks. And few of the members, the author was told, qualify for credit cards at other financial institutions. So the only alternatives that CAPFCU members have for this sort of loan are non-conventional lenders, all of whom charge much higher real interest rates than the credit union does.

The small size and short term of most loans impose a burden on the credit union. Each loan, no matter how small, requires staff time and attention, and those are not free. A $500 loan for nine months at 15 percent annual interest generates about $25 income for the credit union, and that $25 may barely cover the staff time used to evaluate the loan, to say nothing of the credit union's other financial costs such as insurance, supplies, rent, reserves, etc. The CAPFCU board and manager are aware of this problem and understand that since the credit union makes so many small loans it must find other ways to generate the income it needs to stay solvent.[6]

Over one-third of the loans and one-half of the loan money at CAPFCU are used for the purchase and repair of automobiles, and these are among the largest of the loans. This reflects the rural and isolated geography in the southern Appalachian mountains. Mountain people depend upon their vehicles for access to work and for much of their social interaction as well; for many people a working automobile is a necessity. The poverty of the area is reflected in the facts that almost none of the vehicles is new, and that the size of the auto loans, while large in comparison to most of the CAPFCU loans, is quite small when compared to the other credit unions.

Over 10 percent of the loans at CAPFCU are made for debt consolidation. As is the case at most of the other CDCUs, members find that they can turn to the credit union to organize and rationalize their debts when they get in over their heads.

CAPFCU makes more Christmas loans than the other credit unions. These are normally small signature loans to pay for Christmas presents and celebrations. The board of directors has debated whether this is a proper use of credit union loan funds. There is a high demand for loans for this purpose;

---

[6] In 1992, the CAPFCU board of directors instituted a $15 loan application fee, to help recover some of the costs of making small loans.

in December 1990, Christmas loans represented more than half of the loan requests. The fact that so many people need to borrow several hundred dollars to get through the Christmas season is another indicator of the marginal economic conditions in the area and of the personal way that the credit union can help people.

CAPFCU makes almost no business loans. As discussed below, however, an affiliated community development loan fund finances small businesses in the southern Appalachian mountain region.

First American Credit Union

First American is the largest of the credit unions in this study, and yet the striking feature of its loans is how small they are. The average loan at First American in 1990 was just $481, and the median $300. This is a consequence of policy decisions made by the board of directors.

All loans at First American are "line-of-credit" loans. A member is allocated a loan limit, after which he or she is able to borrow as often as desired, up to that limit. There is no set term on the loans; rather there is a minimum payment requirement of 3 percent of the loan balance each month, remitted through payroll deduction.

The loan limits are kept quite low. In no case do they exceed $2,500, and in the great majority of cases they are lower. Some members have loan balances higher than this, but only if the excess over the loan limit is secured by their own savings in the credit union.

For the initial loan, and to establish the credit limit, a member at First American fills out a standard loan application form, much the same as is found at other credit unions. Thereafter the member can request extensions over the phone or by dropping in at the office, and a staff person will fill out a very short, supplementary form. The funds are usually available the next day, if not immediately. In some respects, therefore, First American's lending procedure is similar to a credit card program.

The credit union lends this way for two principal reasons. First is a decision made many years ago by the board that, since funds were limited, it should try to spread them to as many members as possible, rather than concentrate them in just a few hands. The policy has been successful; approximately sixty percent of the members are borrowers, a very high proportion for any credit union. The board thought that, if the loan limits were kept quite low, members would use the money only for their most pressing needs, and would not be tempted to waste it or use it for low priority needs.

Secondly, the credit union has difficulty taking collateral, and therefore judges it prudent to keep the loan limit to any one member low. Real estate is not privately owned on Indian reservations, and therefore the credit union cannot establish liens against real property.

Automobiles are privately owned, but the laws governing repossession on the Navajo reservation make it almost impossible for the credit union to lend against automobiles. Under the standard laws of most states, lenders can engage in what is sometimes called "self-help repossession." If a borrower is in arrears on payments, the lender can simply collect the vehicle, provided that such collection does not provoke violence. On the reservation, in contrast, a lender can repossess only after a court hearing. Since the court process typically takes half a year, lenders understandably fear that not much will be left of the vehicle once they have authorization to collect it. As a consequence, First American seldom lends to Navajos using automobiles as security.[7]

For these reasons, First American makes almost exclusively small, signature, line-of-credit loans. It does, however, make a large number of such loans. In June of 1991, for example, 2,500 new loans or extensions were made.

For First American, Tables 6.3 and 6.4 refer to extensions of existing loans as well as to completely new loans. When a member requests $150 to be added on to an existing loan balance of $900, the transaction is treated in the tables as a $150 loan.

The largest single category of loans at First American is for used autos. These are exclusively for auto repairs; as just explained, the credit union does not lend for the purchase of autos. Significant amounts are lent for home improvements and for debt consolidation. Included in the category of "other" is a large number of loans for religious ceremonial purposes.

School loans occupy a more important part of the loan portfolio at First American than at the other credit unions. These loans are for tuition and supplies, school clothes, and graduation expenses.

Mission Area Federal Credit Union

Of the five lowest income credit unions in the study—CAPFCU, First American, Mission Area, NEJA, and Watts United—Mission Area makes the largest loans, and for the longest term.

---

[7] The author was told that Navajos usually finance their vehicles from dealers and finance companies that are located off the reservation, for example, in nearby Gallup, New Mexico. These dealers are, of course, subject to Navajo law when they come onto the reservation. In order to repossess, they typically wait until the borrower drives off the reservation, for example, to go to a grocery store in Gallup, and repossess the car there. There are stories of Indian women walking out of a store to find their car vanished. It was because First American was unwilling to engage in this sort of practice that it decided not to lend against vehicles on the Navajo reservation. In 1992, it did begin making a few automobile-secured loans to members living on other reservations in Arizona where the Navajo repossession law does not apply.

Table 6.4 shows that the typical loan amount is relatively high in almost all of the loan categories. An additional reason for the relatively high average size of loans at Mission Area is that lending is concentrated in several categories that tend to have high amounts, in particular, automobiles and debt consolidation.

Over a quarter of the funds are lent for the purchase of automobiles. Of these loans, half of the money goes for the purchase of new cars which are, of course, more expensive than used cars.

The largest single category of lending at Mission Area is debt consolidation, and the average loan in this category is relatively high, $6,533. The credit union also does substantial lending for business development.

Mission Area prides itself on its financial counseling and advocacy services. These services are concentrated in the loan categories of debt consolidation and automobiles, the categories in which most of the loans are made. When the manager, Raquel Castillo, provides a debt consolidation loan, she is often able to spend time talking with the member about how better to manage his or her affairs.

In the area of automobile loans, the manager frequently works with members to help them understand the market better and make more informed choices. She also works with automobile dealers in the neighborhood to get favorable deals for members, and is willing to go to bat for them when she thinks they have been cheated. One story she tells is of a member who requested a loan for a car she had agreed to purchase from a neighborhood lot. When Ms. Castillo looked at the papers, she discovered that the price exceeded the published Blue Book price by $3,000. She called the lot manager to complain, and he in turn explained, in some embarrassment, that the deal had been made by a new salesman who had not realized that this customer was a Mission Area member. The lot manager agreed immediately to a $3,000 rebate and the deal went through. Poor people are susceptible to being cheated, Ms. Castillo believes, and through this sort of advocacy work, she tries to provide them some protection.

Northeast Community Federal Credit Union

Northeast Community has the highest borrower incomes of the credit unions in the study, and it makes the largest loans.

Northeast Community concentrates on business lending, directing almost half of its money to this purpose. Again, this is considered more fully below.

An interesting feature of the Northeast Community loans is how little of the money, just 6 percent, is lent for automobiles. The reason for this is not that the members cannot afford autos, since credit unions that have much poorer borrowers concentrate more heavily on auto loans. The reason may be that the credit union's geographical area is such a highly congested urban neighborhood that members would find automobiles to be an expensive bother, not an asset.

A considerable amount of the loan money at Northeast Community is invested in homes. Table 6.3 shows that home improvement and real estate loans together account for almost one-quarter of the funds lent. These are typically quite large loans; Table 6.4 shows the average home improvement loan to be almost $25,000, and the average real estate loan to be almost $30,000. For the most part, the real estate loans are not first mortgages; rather they are second mortgages or supplementary loans of some other kind to help a member buy real estate. Home improvement loans are also typically quite large in Santa Cruz, but note in contrast how small they tend to be in the three rural credit unions, CAPFCU, First American, and NEJA. This difference is reflective of the large difference in housing costs between rural America and urban California, and it is also reflective of differences in member incomes.

North East Jackson Area Federal Credit Union

NEJA is the smallest of the credit unions in the study and, with the exception of CAPFCU, the one with the poorest borrowers.

The most distinctive feature of the lending at NEJA is the heavy concentration on business loans: 29 percent of the loans, amounting to 44 percent of the funds. These are crop loans to independent, African American farmers.

The emphasis on crop loans helps to raise the typical loan size above that found in the other rural credit unions. It keeps the loan term fairly short, however, since crop loans are almost never extended for more than one year.

Aside from the farm loans, the largest single category of loans is for automobiles. These loans are exclusively for used cars. There appear to be two reasons for this: the low-income status of the members effectively precludes them from the market for new cars, and the limited size of the credit union, together with its commitment to relatively large agricultural loans, reduces its ability to lend in the amounts necessary to finance new cars.

Santa Cruz Community Credit Union

Santa Cruz is the only CDCU in the study that has a credit card program, and Tables 6.3 and 6.4 give an indication of how important it is. Almost a third of the money was lent on credit cards. These tables count as a credit card loan not an individual purchase made with a VISA card, but rather the authorization of a new card or an increase in the credit limit on an existing card. The amount of the loan is taken to be the credit limit; since many members do not use their cards to the limit, this means that the tables somewhat overstate the amount of credit card lending in Santa Cruz.

While a credit card program might seem, at first glance, to be a kind of "upscale" feature, appealing to higher income, professional members, in fact the function of the credit card program at Santa Cruz Community has been the opposite. The VISA card has been the vehicle by which the credit union has been able to make smaller loans, to lower income members, including a higher proportion of women. Table 6.5 compares conventional personal loans in Santa Cruz to VISA loans (business loans are excluded from this comparison).

The role of the credit card program in Santa Cruz, of permitting smaller loans to lower income people, did not occur by happenstance; it was an explicit goal of the credit union management when the program was instituted. The fact that credit cards do not necessarily perform this function in typical financial institutions is shown by comparing Table 6.5 with Table 6.6. Table 6.6 shows the relative incomes, and the gender ratio, of VISA and conventional loan borrowers at an occupational credit union in central California that is given the pseudonym "Mainstream Credit Union." At Mainstream, the incomes of the VISA borrowers are no lower, and in terms of the median, are actually higher, than the incomes of the conventional borrowers. The VISA credit limits are somewhat less than the typical conventional loans, but not remarkably so. And the proportion of female borrowers is significantly smaller in the VISA program than in the conventional loans. By comparison, Santa Cruz has used its credit card program to target a lower-income stratum of its membership, including a higher proportion of women, and to make smaller-sized loans.

Table 6.5

**Comparison of Conventional and VISA Loans
Santa Cruz Community Credit Union**

	Conventional Loans	VISA Loans	Ratio of VISA to Conventional
Average borrower income	$3,199	2,370	.74
Median borrower income	2,520	2,076	.82
Average loan size	8,989	1,767	.20
Median loan size	5,906	1,500	.25
Ratio of female to total borrowers	.40	.51	

Table 6.6

**Comparison of Conventional and VISA Loans
Mainstream Credit Union**

	Conventional Loans	VISA Loans	Ratio of VISA to Conventional
Average borrower income	$2,791	2,787	1.00
Median borrower income	2,100	2,400	1.14
Average loan size	7,106	5,493	.77
Median loan size	5,824	5,000	.86
Ratio of female to total borrowers	.54	.44	

Santa Cruz does a lot of small business lending. Approximately 20 percent of the lending is for automobiles and 10 percent is for home improvement. The average amount of a home improvement loan is quite large, again reflecting the high value of housing in urban, coastal California.

Watts United Credit Union

The typical size of a loan at Watts United falls roughly in the middle of the credit unions studied. The loan size is the lowest, however, of the urban credit unions, and this doubtless reflects the poverty of the area and the relatively low incomes of the members.

The most notable feature of the lending at Watts United is that over half of the money is used for automobiles (including repairs). This is consistent with the freeway culture of Los Angeles and the notoriously poor quality of public transportation in that city. Without a car, residents of Watts are almost as isolated as the mountain people of eastern Kentucky (the other area where automobile loans exceed 50 percent of the loan portfolio). By far the largest loans at Watts United are made for new autos.

Business Loans

Four of the seven CDCUs make a substantial commitment to business loans, and a fifth is associated with a business lending institution.

As Chapter 7 will discuss in more detail, the NCUA discourages business lending, regarding it as "speculative" and responsible for most of the financial problems of credit unions. Its member business loan regulations are quite restrictive. Nevertheless, a number of CDCUs concentrate fairly heavily upon business lending.

Table 6.7 outlines the business lending programs of Mission Area, NEJA, North East Community, and Santa Cruz Community credit unions. The first two lines show the proportion of business to total loans in the four credit unions, both by number of loans and by dollar volume. The latter proportion always exceeds the former, reflecting the fact that the typical business loan is greater in size than the typical consumer loan.

Table 6.7

Business Loans in Four Credit Unions

	Mission Area	North East	NEJA	Santa Cruz
Proportion of business loans to total loans				
by number of loans	.11	.33	.21	.11
by dollar amount	.17	.48	.44	.28
Average loan amount	$4,969	19,782	6,213	22,668
Median loan amount	$5,000	20,000	6,870	10,000
Average term (months)	14	54	16	25
Average interest rate	14.2	12.8	15.3	13.4
Average borrower income	1,939	3,685	1,788	—
Average borrower age	50	40	50	39
Proportion female	.54	.25	.26	.31

Of these four credit unions, the smallest commitment to business loans is made by Mission Area. Among the sample of loans studied were several to buy equipment or merchandise for a small business. Most of the business loans in this credit union, however, went to non-profit organizations, for purposes such as covering the time gap between grants or purchasing merchandise for a fund-raising sale.

North East Jackson Area FCU in Florida is organized principally for the purpose of making business loans to independent African American farmers. Twenty-one percent of the loans, amounting to 44 percent of the dollar volume, are for this purpose. The loans range in size from several hundred dollars to $10,000.

By the nature of their business, farmers are debtors. They incur costs at the beginning of the growing season, and must then wait a number of months to sell their product. They borrow to cover their costs of production, and not infrequently they also borrow to cover their living expenses in the period before they sell their crops.

Almost all of the agricultural loans at NEJA are made to peanut farmers. Usually they are used for purchasing fertilizer, seeds, and chemicals at the beginning of the growing season. They are sometimes also used to buy equipment, to repair equipment, or to cover living expenses. The loans are usually quite short-term: sometimes less than a year, and seldom more than a year and a half; they are intended to carry the farmer over until the revenue accrues from the next crop. The payment schedules are generally unconventional. Rather than make monthly payments of equal amounts, the farmers undertake to make just one or two payments during the harvesting season.

In some cases the credit union takes farm machinery or vehicles as collateral. In most cases, however, it takes a lien on both the crop contract and the farmer's crop insurance. Thus the credit union has double protection, with security that is valuable whether or not the crop is successful.

North East Community FCU and Santa Cruz Community CU both specialize in loans to small, primarily urban, locally-owned businesses. Table 6.7 shows a higher concentration, in terms of both number of loans and dollar amount, at North East Community. This is in part a statistical artifact, however, resulting from the fact that Santa Cruz has a large credit card program while North East Community does not. If credit cards are omitted from the Santa Cruz loans, then Santa Cruz makes 26 percent of its loans for business purposes and it devotes 41 percent of its loan dollars to businesses. When this adjustment is made, the two credit unions are fairly comparable in terms of concentration on businesses.

The typical business loan at North East Community is relatively large, about $20,000, and it is made for a much longer term than is found at any of the other CDCUs, over four years. The sorts of businesses that the credit union deals with are mostly small retail establishments in the Chinatown and nearby downtown areas. They include a number of restaurants, laundries, bakeries, grocery stores, and print shops. Some of the loans are for start-ups, but most are for working capital, equipment, and expansion of already existing firms.

While Santa Cruz directs a slightly smaller proportion of its loans to business borrowers than does Northeast Community, still the actual volume of business lending is considerably larger in Santa Cruz because the credit union is larger.

Business lending, or more broadly, community development lending, is the principal purpose of the Santa Cruz credit union. It was founded in 1977 by a group of people who were dedicated to progressive social change in their community. Two years after opening their doors, they adopted what became the main identity of the credit union, the "60-40" policy. Under this policy, the goal was to allocate 60 percent of the loan money for community development purposes and just 40 percent for personal loans. Community development loans included loans to consumer and worker cooperatives, nonprofit organizations, and small and locally-owned businesses that were making a positive contribution to the life of the community. The thinking of the credit union leaders was that loans to encourage the creation and expansion of locally-owned businesses, especially businesses that provided decent working conditions for employees, would make a more permanent contribution to the community than would strictly personal consumer loans. Personal loans were not to be excluded, but they were given a lower priority.

The credit union tried to adhere to the 60-40 policy throughout most of the 1980s, although not always successfully. By the 1990s the policy had to be abandoned. Business and community development loans were actually at an all time high in terms of dollar volume. The credit union had grown so fast that community development lending could not keep up, however, particularly in view of increased regulatory constraints on business lending which took effect in 1987.

The variety of business loans is considerably broader at Santa Cruz Community than at the other credit unions. As at Northeast Community, there are restaurants, grocery stores, and print shops. Loans are also made to retail stores (toys, clothing, musical instruments, and others), to professionals (attorneys, chiropractors, and therapists), to small construction and trucking firms, and to farmers. Among the less conventional borrowers are alternative weekly newspapers and non-profit associations in such fields as food and nutrition, public radio, nursing, women's health, and peace. The credit union has put special emphasis on loans to low-income cooperative housing projects.

The three other CDCUs in this study—Central Appalachian People's, First American, and Watts United—do not engage in business lending except very occasionally. In the case of First American, the reason is that the credit union has decided to restrict itself to small, personal, signature, line-of-credit loans. In the case of Watts United, the credit union manager told the author that he does not believe the institution has the expertise to evaluate potential business borrowers adequately, and that its cash flow is still too small to embark upon such a program. He is interested, however, in exploring the possibility of working with a state loan guarantee program as a way of starting into the business loan field.

Central Appalachian People's stays away from business loans for quite a different reason. It works in partnership with an institution that is devoted solely to small business lending in the southern Appalachian mountains. The two groups divide the lending tasks, one specializing in business loans and the other in personal loans.

The cooperating business lender in Appalachia is the Human Economic Appalachian Development Corporation Community Loan Fund. The HEAD Corporation was created by a task force on poverty in 1974. Since its founding, it has sponsored a variety of community development activities, including the credit union. In 1987, it began the Community Loan Fund. The Fund accepts deposits from socially responsible investors throughout the United States. These investors include individuals, corporations, churches, community organizations, and foundations that have an interest in contributing to economic development in Appalachia. The deposits are made for a specific term and they receive interest; both the term and the interest rate are negotiated separately with each investor. Unlike deposits at a credit union, the deposits at the Community Loan Fund are not insured. As of mid-1991, the assets of the Fund stood at about $400,000.

Between 1987 and 1991, the Community Loan Fund provided technical assistance to 75 entrepreneurs and made loans to 45 individuals or businesses, totalling over $600,000. These included loans aimed at revitalizing Appalachian culture, for example, Shaker crafts, pottery, quilting, rugs, and homemade specialty foods. The Fund has lent to small businesses in monuments, printing, motor repair, landscaping, video, and T- shirt design. Loans have also been made to non-profit organizations in housing, childcare, and other social services.

The HEAD Community Loan Fund works closely with the credit union. Until recently, the HEAD Corporation was the nominal sponsor of the credit union; in 1993 the positions were reversed, and the credit union took over supervision of the loan fund. While in a formal sense the Appalachian credit union does not make business loans, it is part of an organization that puts considerable emphasis on economic development in the area.

In short, while community development credit unions are by no means uniform in this respect, many of them devote a considerable portion of their resources to business loans. They are rightfully concerned, therefore, that the NCUA's business loan regulation may restrict them unduly from achieving some of their principal goals.

Borrower Ages

Table 6.2 shows that the typical age of the borrowers varies considerably from credit union to credit union. The age differences are not related to differences in the age composition of the different ethnic groups in the United States. In 1989, the median ages of African Americans, Hispanics, and whites were 27.7, 26.1 and 33.6 years, respectively,[8] the differences being caused largely by the higher proportion of children in the non-white groups. In this study, in contrast, the highest borrower ages were found in the predomi-

---

[8] U.S. Department of Commerce, *Statistical Abstract of the United States, 1991* (Washington: 1992), Table 12.

nantly African American and Hispanic credit unions.

The oldest borrowers are found in the NEJA Federal Credit Union where the median is 43. This is probably a reflection of the social conditions of this area of the Black South; there is a reasonable living to be made by farmers who make a commitment to the area, but young people typically choose to leave because rural employment opportunities are so limited. The next oldest borrowers are found in the other African American credit union, Watts United. Here the likely explanation is not that the young people leave the area, since the average age of the entire Watts area is actually quite young. It is more apt to be that young African American men and women have so few economic opportunities that they cannot qualify for loans.

The high age of borrowers in the two predominantly African American credit unions, when taken together, is a reflection of the desperate conditions in which many young Black people find themselves today. Because of the absence of opportunities, they are leaving the rural South, as they have for generations. In the cities to which they migrate, however, they typically do not find much in the way of employment opportunities.

The youngest borrowers are found in the Central Appalachian People's Federal Credit Union. Although Appalachia is also an area of the country that loses many of its young people, the relative youth of the borrowers in this credit union is probably a consequence of the membership of the particular organizations that make up the field of membership.

Borrower Incomes

One of the purposes of gathering the data was to discover the extent to which CDCUs succeed in directing their lending to low- and moderate-income people. In this section, the information on the borrowers' incomes is presented, and then adjusted for differences in the borrowers' ages and the local cost of living in order to make more accurate comparisons.

Table 6.8 displays the percentage of borrowers in different income categories in each credit union, as well as the overall median and average incomes of the borrowers. The table shows significant contrasts between the credit unions.

The lowest borrower incomes were found in the three rural credit unions. Of these, the lowest was the Central Appalachian People's Federal Credit Union, with a median income of $1,000 per month and an average of $1,165 (the gap between the two measures indicates the extent to which the range of incomes above the median is greater than the range of incomes below). Half of the borrowers at CAPFCU earned less than $1,000 a month, and a significant portion actually earned less than $500. Only 4 percent of the borrowers earned more than $2,500.

Table 6.8
(Percentage Distribution)

Income of Borrowers

Gross Monthly Income	Appal.	First Amer.	Mission Area	North East	NEJA	Santa Cruz	Watts United
$ 0–499	8	3	1	1	8	0	1
500–999	42	23	7	2	33	5	13
1,000–1,499	29	37	16	13	26	9	30
1,500–1,999	10	21	27	22	18	19	24
2,000–2,499	8	9	16	8	5	20	13
2,500–2,999	2	3	17	16	5	13	6
3,0006–3,499	1	1	7	8	0	12	8
3,5006–3,999	0	1	2	11	3	7	1
4,000+	0	1	7	19	2	15	4
Total	**100**	**100**	**100**	**100**	**100**	**100**	**100**
Median Income	$1,000	1,260	1,920	2,500	1,096	2,349	1,577
Average Income	1,165	1,426	2,149	3,084	1,318	2,842	1,850

At NEJA the typical borrower incomes were just slightly above the CAPFCU incomes, and at First American, on the Navajo Reservation, the incomes were a bit higher still.

The four urban credit unions had higher borrower incomes. Watts United stood lowest, while Mission Area came next; Santa Cruz Community and Northeast Area had significantly higher borrower incomes.

Table 6.9 shows the median incomes of full-time workers in the United States in 1989, by ethnic group.[9] While these data are not directly comparable with the figures in Table 6.8, they show roughly how the incomes of the credit union borrowers compare with those of Americans generally. In five of the credit unions, the borrowers are poorer than workers in the country as a whole, while in Santa Cruz they are about the same and in Northeast Community they are somewhat better off. When compared to their respective ethnic groups, the borrowers at Appalachia, NEJA, and Watts are worse off, at Santa Cruz they are about the same, and at Mission Area they are better off.

Table 6.10 shows that in each of the seven credit unions, the median income of the male borrowers significantly exceeds the median income of the female borrowers. Taking all seven credit unions together, males' incomes are 31 percent above females'.

[9] Ibid., Table 736.

Table 6.9

**Median Monthly Income of Full-Time Workers
United States, 1989**

Ethnicity	Female	Male
White	$1,656	$2,487
Black	1,492	1,726
Hispanic	1,334	1,548
Total	**1,637**	**2,384**

The income difference by gender is consistent with the situation in the country as a whole. Table 6.9, for example, showed that among full-time workers in the United States in 1989, males' earnings exceeded females' by 45 percent. The economic literature on this phenomenon concludes that the male-female income gap is caused in part by the fact that women are more likely than men to move in and out of the labor force, in part by discrimination and in part by the lower educational attainment and hence the lower level of "human capital" on the part of women.

Table 6.10

Median Monthly Income by Gender

	Women	Men
Appalachian	$ 860	$1,170
First American	1,150	1,400
Mission Area	1,510	2,000
Northeast Comm.	2,000	2,745
NEJA	850	1,300
Santa Cruz	2,020	2,630
Watts United	1,490	1,710

The comparison in Table 6.8 between the incomes of the borrowers in the different credit unions may be distorted somewhat by the factors of borrower age and regional cost of living. Elsewhere, in a more complete presentation of these data, the author has shown that the borrowers' incomes tend to rise with age (except at the very highest ages) in most although not all of the seven CDCUs.[10] Some of the variation in median incomes may therefore be due not so much to fundamental differences in the social conditions of the borrowers as to differences in their ages. When a correction is made in the data for age differences, the principal adjustment is that the incomes at Central Appalachian People's credit union rise to about the level of the other two rural credit unions.

---

[10] Isbister.

A second adjustment is needed because of differences in the cost of living. According to data on regional price differences in 1990, it appears that the cost of living in a California city was about 40 percent higher than in Southern rural areas.[11]

Table 6.11 shows the average incomes of the borrowers in the seven credit unions, adjusted for both factors, age and cost of living. First, it is assumed that the age distribution of borrowers at all the credit unions is the same as at First American. Second, the incomes of borrowers at the three rural credit unions are raised by 40 percent, because of the cost of living differential, to make them comparable with the urban populations.

Table 6.11

Average Borrower Incomes Adjusted for Differences in Age and Cost of Living

Credit Union	Total	Female	Male
Appalachian	$1,730	$1,488	$2,034
First American	1,996	1,834	2,223
Mission Area	1,822	1,685	2,047
Northeast Comm.	3,125	2,485	3,437
NEJA	1,798	1,564	1,994
Santa Cruz	2,846	2,434	3,209
Watts United	1,842	1,718	2,071

When adjustments are made for the cost of living and for differences in the ages of the borrowers, the credit unions fall neatly into two income categories. Five of the credit unions are low-income, the three rural credit unions plus Mission Area and Watts United. In this group, average adjusted monthly borrower incomes range from $1,730 to $1,996, a difference of 15 percent. The second group consists of two more moderate-income credit unions, Santa Cruz Community and Northeast Community. In this group the average income range is $2,846 to $3,125, or 10 percent. The overall gap between the bottom of the first group and the top of the second is $1,395, or 81 percent.

The Importance of the Non-Poor

The data show clearly that five of the seven credit unions make most of their loans to poor people. A question arises about the other two credit unions, Northeast Community and Santa Cruz Community, where the me-

---

[11] American Chamber of Commerce Researchers Association, *Cost of Living Index: Comparative Data for 246 Urban Areas* (Louisville: Fourth Quarter, 1990), 23.

dian borrower is better off. Do those institutions serve low-income people? Are they really community development credit unions?

They do serve low-income people and they are community development credit unions. Table 6.8 shows that about a third of the borrowers at each credit union earn less than $2,000 a month which, if not the poverty level, is a low income on the California coast. The two credit unions use a strategy that is different from the strategy of the other five.

Every financial institution that does business with low-income people faces difficulties. Chapter 4 showed that banks and other conventional lenders encounter such problems making a profit off the poor that they increasingly avoid the business, choosing not to make loans or to withdraw from poor neighborhoods altogether. Chapter 5 showed that community development credit unions, while viable, are less successful financially than mainstream credit unions operating with predominantly middle-class memberships.

In fact, while exceptions exist, most CDCUs need to find away of bringing outside resources into a partnership with the savings of poor people if they are to be successful in the long run. At least three ways exist of doing this: non-member deposits, grants, and a broad field of membership that includes middle-income people. Most of the credit unions studied in this chapter have pursued one or more of these strategies.

The Appalachian credit union has attracted both non-member deposits and grant money from the outside. In 1991, about half of its deposits, or $900,000, came from outside its field of membership. Depositors included the Campaign for Human Development and the National Federation of CDCUs. The credit union qualified for a $200,000 loan from the NCUA Revolving Loan Program.[12] It has experienced no difficulty in attracting non-member deposits. The only limit is the cap imposed by the NCUA; while the agency has relaxed its usual 20 percent limit, it has not been willing to allow the credit union to increase these funds beyond the current level.

First American is less dependent upon outside resources. It has often sought non-member deposits, but the reason has been not so much to generate the income needed for survival as to permit continued lending when loan demand has outstripped savings.

Mission Area has made heavy use of both non-member deposits and grants. It was virtually rescued, early in 1981, by an NCUA $200,000 loan. At that time, its assets stood at just $100,000, so the outside loan tripled the

---

[12] According to federal regulations, a loan from the NCUA does not technically count as a "non-member deposit" when calculating the 20 percent limit, nor do deposits from outside the field of membership that are solicited to match the NCUA loan.

size of the credit union and transformed it. It has secured grants from the Vanguard Foundation and the San Francisco Foundation, and outside deposits from many foundations and other socially responsible investors.

NEJA has had little help from the outside, and perhaps for this reason it remains small. It has, however, received deposits from Presbyterian churches and from the National Federation of CDCUs, and in 1991 it received an NCUA loan.

Watts United was founded after the 1965 uprising with outside money, and many of its expenses were covered in the early years by a community agency, the Westminster Association. It has been largely on its own in more recent years, but it has qualified for an NCUA loan. Watts United has addressed the problem of solvency, in the absence of much outside help, by its pricing strategy; of the credit unions studied in this chapter, it charges the highest interest on loans and pays the lowest dividend on savings.

All of the five unambiguously low-income credit unions have found ways of bringing outside resources into their communities, to a greater or lesser extent. The other two credit unions, Northeast Community and Santa Cruz Community, have also made use of both grants and non-member deposits, and in addition they have attracted higher-income people into their membership.

Northeast Community has received a waiver from the NCUA to exceed the 20 percent limit on non-member deposits. In addition to such deposits, it participates in a guarantee program for business loans to Southeast Asian refugees, and it has received several grants. Santa Cruz Community does not currently have non-member deposits, but it has had a few of them in the past, in addition to an NCUA loan and a major grant in its early years from the John Hay Whitney Foundation. It also participates in a guarantee program for business loans to low-income people and minorities.

Both Northeast Community and Santa Cruz Community are fortunate to have a mixed-income membership. The reasons for their fortune are interesting. They are located in areas with both middle-class and low-income people, but geography alone is not enough to explain the mixture. Both credit unions began with a clear mission of social change from which they have not wavered: Northeast Community to help the Asian immigrant community, and Santa Cruz Community to help low-income people in the county of Santa Cruz. That mission proved attractive enough to many middle-income people that they were willing to join. In San Francisco it was largely ethnic loyalty that pulled the more prosperous people in. In Santa Cruz there was a strong progressive political movement, which came to see the credit union as its financial institution.

The middle-income people who joined these two credit unions did so at a certain cost to themselves. Chapter 5 showed that the rates offered by CDCUs are not quite competitive with those offered by other credit unions, and the same is true at Northeast Community and Santa Cruz Community. In many cases, middle-income people would be unwilling to accept the sacrifice, however small, that is involved in belonging to an institution that focuses on the needs of the poor, and therefore this model cannot be replicated everywhere.

It is not a coincidence that Northeast Community and Santa Cruz Community concentrate on business lending more than the other CDCUs do. Many of the business loans go to people who are not themselves poor, but who provide employment for people who otherwise would be. For example, Santa Cruz Community has provided agricultural loans for many years to a Chicano farming couple who are successful and have a comfortable income, and who each year provide stable employment, at an average annual wage of $14,800, to 70 Mexican and Mexican-American farmworkers who previously were low-income migrants. Hundreds of other employees of businesses that borrow from the credit union—motels, grocery stores, print shops, flower stalls, restaurants, etc.—are people who have been poor but who now have decent, moderately-paid jobs.

The strategy of bringing people who are better off into the membership of the credit union, along with low-income people, would not work in Watts, since the neighborhood is almost exclusively low-income, or at NEJA, because of the cultural divide between the African Americans and the whites, or in many other areas. But where it is feasible, it works. The middle-class people treat the institution as their own, as it in fact is. They deposit their savings, conduct transactions, and borrow from the credit union. In so doing, they effectively subsidize the credit union's dealings with its low-income members.

Conclusion

The typical loan purpose varies considerably between CDCUs. Some CDCUs concentrate on personal lending, including auto and debt consolidation loans, while others emphasize small business lending.

In spite of skepticism from regulators about the appropriateness of credit unions' lending to businesses, many CDCUs find ways to contribute to local economic development by making a significant number of business and community development loans.

Leaders in the CDCU movement have sometimes indulged themselves in a bit of a dispute about whether personal lending or business lending was the most appropriate use of their institutions' resources. Different credit unions have made different choices. Many do no business lending at all. At least one, Self-Help Credit Union in North Carolina, does only business and housing lending. Some do a mixture of both. The case studies in this chapter show, in the author's opinion, the importance of both kinds of lending. Business loans can help to transform a community by providing decent jobs to low-income people and by giving people an ownership stake. But it would be a mistake to regard the personal loans as somehow less important. When a CDCU allows an Appalachian family to celebrate Christmas, or a Navajo family to send their daughter to school, or an African American family in Watts to buy a used car, it is performing a very important function.

The ethnic composition of the credit unions' membership varies widely, including concentrations among Hispanics, African Americans, Native Americans and whites.

Five of the seven CDCUs studied in this chapter operate in communities that are marked by relatively low incomes and high poverty rates. Their borrowers are on average quite poor. Two operate in mixed-income communities, where low-income borrowers are balanced by middle-income; this mixture is part of a strategy that allows the credit unions to remain commercially successful while at the same time serving poor people.

The borrowers' incomes are much lower in the rural CDCUs than in the urban. When adjustments are made for differences in the cost of living and the age distribution of the borrowers, however, the typical borrower incomes in the rural CDCUs are roughly equivalent to the incomes in the poorer urban CDCUs. The incomes of male borrowers are significantly higher than those of female borrowers in each CDCU.

Appendix: The Data

The data were gathered by the author and several research assistants. A random selection was made of approximately 200 loans in each credit union, disbursed during 1990. Because NEJA is a small credit union, with few loans each month, the period was extended from 1989 through mid-1991, and even so only 103 files were available. At Santa Cruz the sample consisted of about 400 files, which provides a sufficient number of credit card and business loans, as well as personal loans.

The material in the loan files is not uniform from credit union to credit union, and even within a single credit union's files pieces of information are sometimes missing. In the comparisons between credit unions, therefore, the usable variables were restricted, and not all of the files could be used.

The information comes from different documents in the loan files. A loan file always contains an application, filled out by the member, and a promissory note, filled out by the credit union and signed by the member. Some, but not all, credit unions also have a worksheet containing relevant information and calculations, filled out by a loan officer.

Some arbitrary decisions were necessary. The first had to do with the income of the borrower. Wherever possible, the figure used was the gross monthly income of the principal borrower. Taxes and other paycheck deductions were not subtracted. In the case of the self-employed, the attempt was made to deduct expenses related to the generation of income, although this was not always possible. Note that individual income, not household income, was used, even when several incomes in a household were required to make the borrowers eligible for a loan. There were two reasons for using individual rather than household income: because the study was attempting to discover the characteristics of the borrowers, not to assess the decision-making process of the credit union, and because in some of the communities the concept of "household" was ambiguous. In the great majority of cases, the borrower's income was by a large margin the highest income in the household.

Each loan was assigned to a single borrower, even when the loan was legally made to a couple. In these cases, an attempt was made to decide, from looking at the complete file, who the principal borrower was, and to gather information about that person. This seemed the wisest choice, since otherwise the information would not be comparable between loans.

Some of the information in the files is certainly inaccurate. A person seeking a loan may have an incentive either to overrepresent or to underrepresent his or her income. The tendency to overrepresent comes from a desire to appear more creditworthy than the person actually is, while the tendency to underrepresent may come from people on public assistance who wish to conceal some of their income from the authorities. In some files, figures are confirmed by employers or by tax returns, but this does not happen in every case. Some credit union loan officers have said that they are particularly suspicious of income reported from self-employment, since the figures they are shown may not be net of income-related expenses. Errors such as these are unfortunate, but since they affect all of the credit unions, they are unlikely (with one exception) to influence the comparison between the credit unions. The one exception is NEJA Federal Credit Union in Florida, where many of the members are self-employed farmers, and where the overstatement of income may therefore be somewhat greater than in the other credit unions.

174 THIN CATS

CHAPTER 7

POLICY

> Mr. Chairperson, I understand the political climate existing here in Washington, D.C. following the savings and loan and bank crises. I know that laws were passed giving regulators expanded supervisory powers and that Congress clearly signaled the federal regulators to step up their enforcement activities and to look under every rock for threats to the insurance fund. Despite the fact that credit unions were doing very well, the NCUA apparently felt it was also given the signal to dramatically increase its regulatory pressure. In my judgment, they may have gone too far. I agree that we need a top priority of safety and soundness, but at what expense? Certainly not at the expense of curtailing the fundamental mission of providing credit to those who desperately need it.
>
> —Jeff Wells, Board member of the National Federation of CDCUs[1]

> A public-purpose banking system cannot be created by an act of Congress. It must grow from a network of well-organized citizens capable of articulating a vision for community renewal.
>
> —Martin Paul Trimble, National Association of Community Development Loan Funds[2]

---

[1] Testimony before the Subcommittee on Policy Research and Insurance and the Subcommittee on Economic Stabilization of the U.S. House of Representatives Committee on Banking, Finance and Urban Affairs (July 22, 1992).

[2] Trimble.

> Today I am sending to Congress an innovative program that will bring new life and new opportunity and new directions to communities all over America that lack capital and credit.
> —President Bill Clinton[3]

This chapter considers public policy towards community development credit unions. It concentrates on legislation and regulation at the level of the federal government.

CDCUs, like all credit unions and like almost all financial institutions, are private, non-governmental entities. Their success or failure is determined primarily by the extent to which they meet a market test, the extent to which they provide services that individuals are willing to use and support. They are not public agencies.

Nevertheless, governments have a great deal of influence over them. Credit unions are chartered, regulated, and examined by agencies of either the federal or a state government. They are required to carry deposit insurance which is provided by a federal agency, and they therefore have to meet the performance standards of the public insurer. To a certain extent they serve a public purpose, and consequently public bodies frequently show an interest in them.

The Regulation of Financial Institutions

In the United States in the late twentieth century, and in all other industrialized countries, governments regulate and constrain the activities of virtually all private businesses. They tax them, establish accounting standards, restrict their environmental impact, impose fair labor standards—including minimum wages, health and safety regulations, and collective bargaining rights—and in some cases test and regulate the goods and services that the businesses offer on the market. No sector of the private economy is regulated more closely, however, than the financial sector, the country's banks, thrift institutions, and credit unions. Financial institutions are subject to all of the regulations imposed on other businesses. In addition, they must subject their business practices to detailed examination and often control by public agencies. Public agencies have the authority to tell financial institutions how to allocate their assets, to forbid them from making certain loans, to require them to reserve funds to back up risky loans, and much more. They have the authority to liquidate or merge them.

This level of public control occurs because of a peculiar distinction be-

---
[3] Statement introducing the Community Development Banking and Financial Institutions Act of 1993 (July 15, 1993).

tween financial institutions and other businesses. All businesses have liabilities, but the liabilities of financial institutions are unique in that they constitute the largest part of the country's money supply. Most money that people have is held not in the form of paper notes or coins, but of deposits at a financial institution.[4] In the nineteenth and early twentieth centuries, when banks were largely unregulated, they grew rapidly during boom periods, but often went bankrupt during a downturn of the business cycle. When banks failed, their liabilities disappeared, and consequently the country's money supply fell, and thousands of people were ruined by the loss of their life savings. Both consequences were important. On the macroeconomic level, research has shown that the money supply, the amount of money in circulation in a society, is a principal determinant of the level of business activity; when the money supply falls, businesses fail and people are thrown out of work. On the individual level, the disappearance of a person's savings can be a tragedy.

The twentieth century response to this problem has been for the government to regulate financial institutions closely, in order to increase the chances that they will be operated prudently, and to insure their deposits. The two responses fit together. The federal government's deposit insurance means that a person's savings are protected, even if the financial institution should fail. By itself, deposit insurance helps to protect the institutions against failure because, since they have insurance, depositors are less likely to withdraw their funds when they suspect their institution is in trouble and thus less likely to provoke the very crisis they fear by starting a bank run. In addition, federal insurance brings government regulation to bear in a new way. As the insurer, the government has a strong interest in seeing that the financial institutions are operated safely, so that the insurance funds will not have to be paid out. Thus, for the financial institutions to get insurance for their deposits, they must meet the rigorous standards of the insurer. In return for providing the insurance, the government has the authority to examine the business practices of the financial institutions in detail, and to require many policies and behaviors in order to reduce risk.

None of this regulation and insurance eliminates risk or guarantees that the financial institutions will survive. In the 1980s, a large number of thrift institutions went bankrupt, principally because of imprudent business practices that the regulators did not prevent. While fewer banks failed, many of them too found themselves in grave difficulty, often because of unwise loans

---

[4] There are different definitions of the money supply. The narrowest one, called M1, is restricted to coins, notes, and checking deposits at commercial banks and a few other items, and it excludes deposits at credit unions entirely. But broader definitions of the money supply include many other types of deposits, including deposits at credit unions.

made to foreign countries. The credit unions were actually the soundest of the three types of financial institutions during this period.

Government regulation and insurance cannot eliminate risk, nor should they. Risk is the essence of banking. If there were no risk there would be no need for financial intermediaries like banks and credit unions. Individual savers would simply lend their funds to individual and business borrowers, secure in the knowledge that their assets were safe. But the risk that loans will not be paid back exists, and individual savers would like to avoid that risk to the maximum extent possible. They therefore pool their savings in financial institutions. The institutions in turn make many loans, and in a sense "manage" the risk. They place their loans in such a way that while they expect a few of them to go into default, they are reasonably sure that these few mistakes will be balanced by a much larger number of performing loans. The principal purpose of government regulation, therefore, is not to eliminate the risk, but to require financial institutions to manage it prudently.

At some times and in some circumstances, governments regulate financial institutions for a second purpose, namely, in order to direct credit in particular ways. They decide that the private market is not supplying sufficient loans to specific sectors of the economy, and they intervene to increase the flow of funds in those directions. They do this sometimes in response to perceived discrimination in lending. At other times no discrimination is alleged, but the government takes the position that the public would nevertheless benefit from more funds going to an area than the private sector is likely to provide on its own. Sometimes constraints are placed on private financial institutions to increase the loans to a sector of the economy; in other cases the government establishes publicly controlled banks to perform the task.

Many examples exist of this latter sort of government intervention. The Community Reinvestment Act requires banks to show that they are meeting the credit needs of their local communities. The Home Mortgage Disclosure Act requires financial institutions to report their mortgage lending performance in detail. Both pieces of legislation were passed in response to allegations of redlining, or discrimination in lending against minorities and poor communities. An example of a public bank that directs credit to a particular sector is the National Consumer Cooperative Bank, which lends only to cooperatives. It was established in response not so much to charges of discrimination as to the recognition that the ownership structure of a cooperative tends to make it relatively unattractive to a private-sector lender.

The Regulation of Credit Unions

Federally chartered credit unions are regulated by the National Credit

Union Administration (NCUA), an independent federal agency whose three board members are appointed by the President for six-year terms. State chartered credit unions are regulated by a variety of state agencies. The deposits of the great majority of credit unions are insured by a branch of NCUA, the National Credit Union Share Insurance Fund (NCUSIF). Members' deposits in a credit union are now insured to a level of $100,000, the same insurance level as is provided by the government to depositors in banks and thrift institutions.

The provision of share insurance gives NCUA the right to examine and regulate not only the federal credit unions but also the federally insured state chartered credit unions in order to protect the soundness of the insurance fund. As a consequence, virtually all of the country's almost 14,000 credit unions, whether or not they are federally chartered, are subject to the rules and regulations established by NCUA.

Federal supervision of credit unions was begun in 1934, with the passage of the Federal Credit Union Act.[5] Initially, the Credit Union Division was located in the Farm Credit Administration. Over the years it was moved around, first to the Federal Deposit Insurance Corporation and then to the Federal Security Administration. From 1952 through 1970, the Bureau of Federal Credit Unions was a section of the Department of Health, Education and Welfare; it was this bureau that was responsible for chartering the OEO credit unions. In 1970, NCUA was established as an independent agency.

The purpose of federal regulation has undergone fundamental changes since 1934. The Federal Credit Union Act was a part of President Roosevelt's New Deal legislation. Its explicit purpose was to encourage the growth of credit unions in order to promote both personal savings and also loans for "provident and productive purposes." During the later years of the Great Depression, the principal activity of the Credit Union Division was to organize new credit unions. The government organized many more credit unions than did the newly formed Credit Union National Association (CUNA), the private trade association of the credit unions. The Credit Union Division did not provide share insurance, nor did it impose strenuous restrictions on the activities of credit unions.

Again in the 1960s, the federal government took the lead in promoting credit union development, this time specifically in poor communities. As described in Chapter 3, the Office of Economic Opportunity helped to charter about 400 CDCUs in both rural and urban areas.

In later years, however, the federal government took the position that it was an inappropriate conflict of interest for it both to promote credit unions

---

5 For the history of federal credit union regulation, see Moody and Fite.

and to regulate them. It ceased to be a promoter of credit unions, and gradually adopted the more orthodox regulatory stance of protecting the public against possible abuses by credit unions.

An important milestone in this evolution was the establishment of NCUA in 1970. The new agency took over all the functions of the Bureau of Federal Credit Unions, and within a few months it added the task of insuring the share deposits of the country's credit unions. Since it now had the responsibility of protecting the assets of the insurance fund, it began to take a much more aggressive stance in regulation, holding credit unions to strict financial standards, forcing the closure of many small and financially weak credit unions, and tightening the requirements for new charters. Regulations were further tightened in the late 1980s as a response to the fiasco in the savings and loan industry and to the weaknesses that were revealed in the banks. NCUA took the almost explicit position that new credit unions should not be chartered, and that existing large credit unions should instead expand to incorporate wider fields of membership.

Community development credit unions were particularly vulnerable to this tightening of regulatory standards. While in some cases the tightening helped CDCUs by encouraging them to adopt sounder business practices, in many other cases it was their downfall. A CDCU with high delinquencies on loan repayments, with low levels of reserves relative to its deposits, or with losses on its income statement was vulnerable to the recommendations of the federal examiners to close it. Even CDCUs with fairly acceptable financial ratios were sometimes at risk when the examiners did not want to incur what they regarded as the expense and inefficiency of regulating small institutions.

No doubt some of the liquidations were inevitable; some credit unions had been formed without sufficient community support or expertise and they could not sustain themselves on an ongoing basis. But experienced observers in the CDCU movement believed that many of the liquidations could have been avoided had the NCUA examiners taken the trouble to understand the importance and the unique circumstances of the low-income credit unions. Clifford Rosenthal, Executive Director of the National Federation of CDCUs, told the author that he believed the federal examiners were often insensitive to the special features of minority communities and low-income institutions, and that had they chosen to work more positively with the CDCUs, many more of the institutions could have been turned around and saved. Ernest Johnson, of the Federation of Southern Cooperatives, spoke sadly of the credit unions he had advised, nurtured, and almost, but not quite, rescued.

In some respects, NCUA did recognize the special needs of poor communities and their CDCUs. In response to a directive from Congress in 1974, the agency recognized certain "limited income credit unions," which it permitted to accept non-member deposits and to participate in a revolving loan fund. The Democratic board member, Robert H. Swann (appointed in 1990), and his assistant, Christopher Kerecman, took a fresh look at CDCUs and attempted to redesign the regulations with an eye to their impact on the CDCUs. With the coming of the Clinton administration, the agency accelerated some of its attempts to be helpful to CDCUs. These most recent regulatory changes of the 1990s are described in the next section.

But in other respects, the NCUA regulators did not acknowledge that poor communities were different from middle-class communities, that their financial institutions faced problems that were systematically different, and that the application of rules and regulations should be appropriately modified for them. CDCUs, as generally the smallest and most vulnerable of the country's credit unions, frequently experienced federal examination and regulation as hostile. In 1990, Robert Loftus, director of public and congressional affairs for NCUA, told an interviewer:

> *In our testimony to Congress [throughout the savings and loan crisis] we made the point several times that, in some instances we try to be extra helpful or bend over backward for a CDCU because of the type of institution it is. Our comments didn't get a very favorable response from senators and members of Congress. As a result, I would have to say we've become less lenient with CDCUs.*[6]

The Changing Response of NCUA to CDCUs

In the 1990s, and especially with the election of President Clinton in 1992, the regulatory hostility began to dissipate. For the first time since the OEO period of the 1960s, the federal government began to assert that it was a policy goal to promote banking services for economic development in poor communities. The President introduced the Community Development Banking and Financial Institutions Act of 1993. NCUA took a number of new initiatives to support CDCUs. The government was returning to the dual view of its proper role: on the one hand, regulate and examine in order to increase the safety and soundness of the credit unions and their share insurance fund, but, on the other hand, encourage the flow of finance towards poor communities in order to promote economic development.

---

6 "Low Income Credit Unions Survive Amid Turmoil." *Credit Union Magazine* (Madison: Credit Union National Association, October 1990), 50.

In July of 1992 NCUA undertook a major reconsideration of its regulatory stance towards low-income credit unions—thanks, in considerable degree, to advocacy by the National Federation of CDCUs. It established a committee charged to consider all aspects of its regulation, including the limited-income designation, non-member deposits, participation in the Revolving Loan Program, chartering policies, and the examination and supervision of CDCUs. It undertook to prepare a detailed information base in order to analyze key factors among CDCUs.[7] The committee went on the road, holding hearings in Newark, New York, Philadelphia, Washington, Atlanta, and Chicago. As a consequence of this reconsideration, it changed a number of its policies.

To begin, it changed the criteria that it uses for identifying credit unions working within low-income communities. These credit unions, first recognized in response to federal legislation in 1974, are eligible to accept non-member deposits, to participate in the low-interest Community Development Revolving Loan Program, and to receive federally funded technical assistance.[8] It is likely that federal financial assistance to credit unions under President Clinton's community development banking initiative will be restricted to this group.

At the end of 1992, 139 credit unions were certified by NCUA as falling within this category. The number is low in comparison to the 180 CDCUs whose financial statements were analyzed in Chapter 5, or in comparison with the figures the National Federation of CDCUs sometimes uses of be-

---

[7] The terms of what the NCUA called its "Pilot Program - Community Development Credit Unions" are outlined in a memorandum to the NCUA board dated July 7, 1992. For the information base, see the two papers by Neunlist.

[8] In this era of enhanced sensitivity to verbal labels, NCUA has dealt with the nomenclature of these credit unions is a way so charming as to be worth quoting in its entirety. In the Federal Register 58 (April 23, 1993), in which the agency promulgates the final rules for the Community Development Revolving Loan Program, it reviews the question:

NCUA requested comment on whether the term "low income credit union" found in Section 705.3 should be changed to either "economic development credit union" or "community development union." Two of these commenters believe this wording is more accurate than the alternatives. One commenter believes confusion will result if the name is changed to "community development credit union." Three commenters suggest the use of "economic development credit union" to avoid negative connotations and possible confusion. Six commenters recommend using the term "community development credit union." Those commenters believe this term avoids the negative connotation some associate with the term "low-income credit union." NCUA believes that the term "low-income credit union" may have negative connotations in the credit union community. Furthermore, NCUA believes the term "community development credit union" may cause confusion due to the fact that many credit unions that have not participated in the Program are members of a trade association called the National Federation of Community Development Credit Unions. The term "economic development credit union" may be misleading since the purpose of the Program is to assist credit unions serving low-income members. Therefore the final rule deletes the reference to "low-income credit unions" in Section 705.3 without replacing it with any of the suggested terms. Instead credit unions taking part in the Program will simply be referred to in the final regulation as "participating credit unions" as defined in Section 705.3(b).

tween 300 and 400 CDCUs. When NCUA took over the administration of the Revolving Loan Program in 1987, it inherited a list of over 300 designated low-income credit unions, which it cut drastically. Some of the cuts were appropriate, but some seemed arbitrary. After reconsideration, the NCUA board agreed that the current criteria were excessively restrictive, and therefore it expanded them in April of 1993.[9]

Under the new rules, participating credit unions are ones that serve a "predominantly" "low-income membership." "Predominantly" means at least 50 percent, and "low-income" means below 80 percent of the country's average personal income, with some allowance for regional differences in the cost of living. The principal change in the new rules is the 80 percent standard, which was raised from a much more restrictive 70 percent. Credit unions can demonstrate that they qualify for inclusion by surveying the incomes of their members or, if that is too onerous a task, they can now do so by showing that they operate in a neighborhood which is predominantly low-income. NCUA states that a credit union can use this latter method, even if its field of membership is not geographical. As another new possibility, credit unions that do not meet the 80 percent test exactly, but which "serve and benefit low-income residents of a community and whose mission and goals are identical to those set out in the purpose section of the regulation"[10] can petition the NCUA board for inclusion. As in the previous regulations, student credit unions may meet these criteria, but they are not eligible to participate in the programs for low-income credit unions.

NCUA estimates that an additional 100 credit unions will qualify for participation under these more relaxed criteria. The actual number may well be greater. The changes are welcome ones. They will permit more poor communities to be helped by government assistance, while still insuring that the assistance is actually targeted to the poor, and not dissipated among higher income groups whose credit unions are capable of flourishing on their own.

At the same time that it relaxed its criteria for participation in programs relating to low-income members, NCUA expanded its Community Development Revolving Loan Program. The program was first begun in 1979 with a Congressional appropriation of $6 million. The funds were lent to community development credit unions in amounts of $200,000, at 2 percent annual interest, for a term of 5 years. The recipient credit unions were required to match the loan by raising their share deposits, from either members or nonmembers, during the loan period. After one round of funding, the program was cancelled by the new Reagan administration as a part of its reduction of

---

[9] See the Federal Register, op. cit.

[10] Ibid. Santa Cruz Community Credit Union, among others, is hoping to qualify under this provision.

domestic spending. The funds were not confiscated by the administration, however, and consequently they were available for a new round of lending in 1985. This time, though, the interest rate was set at 7.5 percent, a rate that put it out of reach of most CDCUs.

The program was turned over to NCUA in 1986, but not activated again until 1990. In three annual rounds, NCUA lent out $6.6 million (the original appropriation plus the accrued interest), in amounts up to $200,000. After the first round, most of the CDCUs that applied for the loans were approved. While the program was received positively by the CDCUs, there were a few negative notes. In some cases, the agency descended into a curiously detailed level of micromanagement by placing what seemed to be unnecessary restrictions on the use of the borrowed funds, by ruling that a CDCU could not use the federal money, or the matching funds that came from non-members, for loans but only for investments in other financial institutions. In other cases, it also ruled that the net income on those investments could not be used to meet the credit union's expenses, but had to be put straight into reserves. One credit union, PA FCU in Louisiana, actually declined the loan after learning of NCUA's conditions.[11] While the agency was no doubt wise to place restrictions on some credit unions, the actual restrictions were onerous and unnecessary in a number of credit unions that were completely capable of making responsible decisions themselves.

In 1993, NCUA announced new rules for the Revolving Loan Fund. Henceforth, loan requests of up to $300,000 would be entertained, the paperwork and bureaucratic requirements involved in applying for the loans would be reduced, and the availability of technical assistance from NCUA would be separated from participation in the loan program.

In spite of its erratic history, the Revolving Loan Program has been a useful tool for moving CDCUs towards self-sufficiency. In some cases, the recipient CDCUs used the borrowed funds to lend to their members, thereby increasing their impact on their communities, while at the same time improving their financial status by virtue of the spread between the interest paid by their members and the interest owed to the government. When the funds were not lent out, either because of NCUA restrictions or because of the credit union's choice, they nevertheless have been invested in such a way as to improve the financial standing of the credit union. The quantitative impact of the loans has often been substantial. Some of the CDCUs that received the loans in 1979—for example, Santa Cruz Community and Near Eastside Community in Indianapolis—used them as springboards to develop into multi-million dollar institutions. More recently, NEJA Federal

---

[11] National Federation of Community Development Credit Unions, *CDCU Report* (New York, Fall, 1991), 3.

Credit Union, the rural African American credit union in the Florida panhandle whose lending was analyzed in Chapter 6, received a $200,000 loan in 1991, thereby raising its assets by almost 50 percent, from $450,000 to $650,000. The changes made by NCUA in expanding and streamlining the program are likely to be quite positive.

Nevertheless, a number of people in the CDCU movement came to believe that an expanded low-interest loan program was not the most effective way in which the federal government could stimulate the growth of credit in low-income areas in the future. As was shown in Chapter 5, in the early 1990s, the typical CDCU, like the typical American credit union, was only 50 to 60 percent loaned out. It had plenty of funds to lend, and did not face a liquidity problem. Moreover, a prospective increase in the size of its asset basis was a mixed blessing, at least in the short run, because such an increase made its reserves-to-assets ratio goal more difficult to reach. What the CDCUs really needed was an increase in their reserves, their equity capital, and to achieve this they needed grants from the federal government, not loans. They began to advocate, therefore, for what became President Clinton's 1993 initiative on community development banking, to be described later in this chapter.

A third change made by NCUA in 1993 was that it began to deal with the attitudes and training of its staff who examine low-income credit unions. A common complaint from CDCUs over the years has been that the NCUA examiners treat them rudely, in a manner insensitive to cultural and class differences, and lack sufficient understanding of the problems that they face. Since the examiners are predominantly white, and the CDCU staff predominantly non-white, the question of racism, whether subconscious or overt, is frequently present. Federal examiners have a great deal of power over credit unions, including the power to liquidate them or to dictate their business practices in detail. Under these circumstances, the encounter between a small credit union in a poor, non-white neighborhood and its examiner is often fraught with tension, and it has considerable potential for miscommunication. Regional directors of NCUA have sometimes exacerbated the problem by using the examination of a small CDCU essentially as a training exercise, assigning the least experienced people to do the job.

The National Federation of CDCUs has asked NCUA to revise its Examiner's Guide in order to remove some offensive language relating to low-income credit unions and also to add a section on CDCUs in its training program for examiners. Without accepting all of the Federation's requests, NCUA has at least recognized the problem. It has set up a training session to help its examiners deal more sensitively and professionally with the CDCUs, and it is making attempts to recruit more people of color into the ranks of its examiners. It has agreed to review the Examiner's Guide. Whether any of this will make a difference to the quality of the examinations is still an open question.

While welcome, these improvements in the regulatory stance of NCUA do not exhaust the areas in which CDCUs have concerns. One of the most important areas of contention between the CDCUs and their regulators is the question of non-member deposits.

Chapter 2 discussed the use of the equivalent of non-member deposits in the early German cooperative banks, and Chapter 5 showed their quantitative importance in today's CDCUs. Non-member deposits (except deposits from the public sector) are forbidden in most credit unions, but allowed in those credit unions identified by NCUA as serving low-income people. They are an important mechanism in some CDCUs for promoting growth and financial self-sufficiency by attracting the participation of socially responsible investors such as churches and foundations.

The exception for low-income credit unions to accept non-member deposits is critical. For example, Tholin and Pogge describe how the Austin-West Garfield Community Credit Union, a CDCU in Chicago, opened for business with two $100,000 non-member deposits from local banks; without that start-off boost, the credit union might never have gotten going.[12] Another example is the Central Appalachian People's Federal Credit Union in eastern Kentucky, described earlier, where non-member deposits account for roughly 50 percent of the $2 million asset base.

Consequently, the CDCU movement suffered a major blow when NCUA decided in December 1988 to restrict non-member deposits to 20 percent of total shares. The decision was taken in response to serious fraud and the subsequent liquidation of the Franklin Community Credit Union in Omaha, Nebraska, a credit union which had made heavy use of non-member deposits. The decision to limit non-member deposits represented a curious response to the problem, however. The cause of the problem was fraud, not non-member deposits. One would have thought the proper response was to rethink the examination procedures which had allowed the fraud to go undetected until it was too late to save the credit union. Instead, NCUA decided to restrict the amount of non-member deposits. Faced with numerous protests from credit unions, it did relax the new rule somewhat, to allow regional NCUA directors to make exceptions in some cases if they deemed fit. Currently, therefore, most CDCUs are restricted to 20 percent non-member deposits, and even those which have exceptions must negotiate them separately, with no guarantee of success, for each new deposit.

---

[12] Tholin and Pogge.

Non-member deposits can represent a risk to CDCUs. Ordinary member share deposits are usually so numerous, and so small, that a credit union can count on the probability that withdrawals over a short period will be balanced, more or less, by new deposits, and that therefore while there may be a lot of in-and-out movement of funds, the overall size of the deposit base will not collapse. Non-member deposits, on the other hand, tend to be few and large. A decision by one or two non-member depositors to withdraw their funds on short notice could cause a liquidity problem for a credit union, that is to say, a shortage of cash that could threaten the solvency of the institution.

Still, the seriousness of the potential liquidity problem should not be overstated. Just as the Federal Reserve System functions as a "lender of last resort" for the nation's banks, so too NCUA operates a Central Liquidity Facility which is available to meet short-term liquidity crises faced by credit unions. Furthermore, liquidity was not the problem in Omaha; the problem there was fraud. Nor have non-member deposits caused liquidity problems for any CDCU of which the author is aware.

If NCUA is genuinely worried about the instability of non-member deposits, it could establish some regulations to increase stability. For example, it could rule that beyond some level, such as 20 percent, non-member deposits would have to be made for a specific term, so that the credit union could plan well in advance for their disappearance. It could require that non-members give notice of their intent to withdraw, the length of the notice depending upon the size of the deposit. Or it could require that non-member deposits, beyond a certain level, be matched to loans of the same maturity as the deposit. Regulations such as these would go a long way towards reducing the possible threat to CDCUs caused by non-member deposits without killing them off. NCUA's stance should be to encourage non-member deposits in order to increase the flow of funds into poor neighborhoods, while at the same structuring them to control the risk. In late 1992, in response to criticism from CDCUs and from the National Federation of CDCUs, NCUA agreed to reconsider its policy on non-member deposits and the process for requesting waivers from the 20 percent rule, but there has been no indication that the agency is willing to change the policy in any fundamental way.

A second area in which NCUA regulation has been harmful has been its member business loan regulations. The root of the problem in this case is that most American credit unions view themselves as consumer lenders, not business lenders, and so does NCUA. While the nineteenth-century German cooperative peoples' banks lent only for business purposes, most of their modern American counterparts do no business lending. In 1991, only 1,360 of 13,007 federally insured credit unions, or about 10 percent, held any member business loans at all.[13] At the end of that year, member business loans accounted for only 1.2 percent of the dollar volume of all credit union loans outstanding.[14] Consequently the regulators of credit unions tend to view business lending suspiciously, as being outside the normal and safe sphere of credit union activity. Since business loans carry particular risks of non-repayment, they would prefer that credit unions not make them, or at least restrict them severely.

NCUA has taken a strong stance against business lending. In its 1991 Annual Report, it referred to business lending as "speculative" and blamed most of the financial problems of credit unions upon an over-dependence on business loans. "Although less than 2 percent of all lending," the Report stated, "business lending accounted for 81 percent of insurance losses in 1991, almost twice the 1990 ratio. Although only 10 percent of federally insured credit unions make business loans, poorly reserved and problem credit unions hold a disproportionate share of business loans."[15]

What worried NCUA were some spectacular failures of credit unions in the late 1980s and early 1990s where there was evidence of reckless speculation in commercial ventures. The agency has not, however, presented evidence that business lending, properly carried out, is necessarily excessively risky. The President of the Credit Union National Association (CUNA), Ralph Swoboda, has criticized NCUA's position, questioning why a third automobile or a vacation is regarded by the regulators as a provident purpose, while capital for a small business is seen as speculative.[16]

NCUA's attitude on business loans runs into conflict with the basic purpose of at least some CDCUs. These credit unions view their principal impact upon their communities as being the encouragement of business and housing development for the benefit of low-income residents. While they offer personal loans in most cases, they tend to see those loans as making a shorter run, less permanent contribution to their communities. Among the CDCUs studied in Chapter 6, NEJA, Northeast Community, and Santa Cruz Community have a major commitment to business lending, and they are not alone.

---

[13] Federal Register 56 (September 25, 1991). A definitional problem exists here. For several years, loans made for a business purpose were not classified by NCUA as "member business loans" if the sum of such loans to a single borrower did not exceed $25,000. In 1993, the cutoff was raised to $50,000. Therefore, the number of credit unions doing business lending, broadly conceived, and the proportion of business lending, is probably somewhat greater than these figures indicate.

[14] Credit Union National Association. *Operating Ratios and Spreads, Year-End 1991*, Table 3.

[15] National Credit Union Administration, 1991 Annual Report (Washington: 1992), 7.

[16] Speech at the annual meeting of the National Federation of Community Development Credit Unions (Chicago: May 8, 1992).

Member business loan regulations were first adopted by the NCUA board in 1987 and then tightened at the end of 1991. NCUA's intention at the beginning of 1991 was to impose even more restrictive rules, but an overwhelmingly negative response in the public comment period persuaded it to back off somewhat. The new regulations are lengthy and complex. The most constraining rule is that no one member may receive a business loan exceeding 15 percent of the credit union's reserves, or $75,000, whichever is greater. NCUA had originally intended to restrict total business lending of a credit union to 100 percent of reserves; while in the end it did not impose this rule, it did require credit unions with business loans exceeding reserves to report all business loans to the examiner in considerable detail.

The effect of the member business loan regulations can be seen in a credit union such as Santa Cruz Community which emphasizes business lending. The size of its reserves restrict it to a maximum business loan to any one member of about $100,000. This limit does not represent much of a problem in the case of start-up loans. The failure rate in start-ups is relatively high, and the credit union therefore prefers to begin with a fairly small loan that is well-protected by collateral. The problem arises with continuing loans to successful businesses. These loans tend to be safer because the businesses have a proven track record. But as they grow, the businesses have larger needs for capital, often exceeding the $100,000 limit. One of the most successful businesses started by Santa Cruz Community, a producer of natural fruit juices, wanted to continue to borrow from the credit union but needed more than $100,000. Since the credit union was prevented from making the loan, the business approached a local bank which was happy to provide the funds. In this case, it is hard to see how NCUA's member business loan regulation improved the financial condition of the credit union, protected its members, or promoted the safety and soundness of the Share Insurance Fund.

As in the case of non-member deposits, NCUA has identified a legitimate area of concern but has used the wrong tools to deal with it. There is no doubt that business lending can be risky. Some businesses fail and are unable to pay back their loans. But this does not mean that financial institutions in general turn their backs on business lending. On the contrary, banks and other institutions lend enormous sums to businesses. Rather than reject business lending, they learn how to do it prudently. They require business plans, they insist upon the personal experience and qualifications of the borrowers, they are careful to take liens on collateral that are adequate to protect the loans, and they compensate for risk by charging higher interest rates. Of course, credit unions should not stumble into business lending blindly, but if they take these sorts of precautions there is every reason to think that they can be successful. The delinquency and default rates on business loans at NEJA, Northeast Community, and Santa Cruz Community are low, indicating that credit unions wanting to do business lending can be successful. Rather than restrict the size of a member business loan so severely, NCUA would have been better advised to instruct its examiners to pay particular attention to the quality of business loans and to insist that the sorts of precautions noted above be taken. With this sort of policy, the agency could have helped CDCUs respond to the most pressing needs in their communities—the lack of employment and economic development—while also helping them to increase the safety of their assets.

One of the consequences of NCUA's restrictions on business lending by credit unions has been to increase the importance of another kind of lending institution in poor neighborhoods, community development loan funds. The loan funds accept below-market-rate, uninsured deposits from socially responsible investors, and in turn make loans for affordable housing and also for small businesses and non-profits. Because the deposits are not insured, the funds are not closely regulated by the government and few restrictions are placed on the lending. The principal restrictions are imposed by the loan funds themselves since they need to stay solvent.

Some CDCUs have developed working relationships with loan funds, or have even sponsored loan funds, as a way of doing business lending without falling under NCUA restrictions. The most successful example of this is the Center for Community Self-Help in North Carolina which sponsors two institutions, a credit union and a loan fund. The same staff operates both institutions and can decide easily whether to make a loan from the credit union or from the loan fund, depending upon whether it fits within NCUA's regulations.[17] In 1993, the Central Appalachian People's Federal Credit Union took control of the loan fund that had previously been its sponsor. And in Santa Cruz, the credit union sponsors a non-profit institution which accepts grants and in turn deposits those funds in the credit union to secure business loans made by the credit union. This procedure has a result that is similar to a community loan fund, since share-secured loans in a credit union are exempt from NCUA's member business regulations.

The community development loan funds represent a way to get around NCUA's restrictions on business lending and also its restrictions on non-

---

[17] The NCUA business loan regulations have proven to be so restrictive that, at least in early 1993, almost all the business lending was done through the loan fund. In the first four months of 1993, Self-Help made only $86,000 in member business loans through the credit union, while channeling $1.5 million in business loans through the loan fund, because of the restrictions on credit union lending. Private communication from Davis McGrady of Self-Help to Jeff Wells, May, 1993.

member deposits. It is not an optimal solution, however, since deposits in the loan funds are not insured. The absence of insurance places a burden on the depositors, and it results in less money being available for lending than would be the case if insurance were provided. The use of a loan fund makes community development lending completely dependent on loans from outsiders. Furthermore, most CDCUs neither sponsor nor have a working relationship with a loan fund. Consequently, the NCUA member business loan regulations impose serious burdens on poor communities.

A third way in which NCUA has stifled CDCU development is its policy on new charters. Table 7.1 shows the number of charters issued and cancelled, and total outstanding, for federal credit unions in selected years.[18]

Table 7.1

Federal Credit Unions, Selected Years, 1935-1992

Year	Charters Issued	Charters Canceled	Net Change	Total
1935	828	—	828	906
1940	666	76	590	3,855
1945	96	185	-89	3,959
1950	565	83	482	5,128
1955	777	188	589	8,175
1960	685	274	411	10,374
1965	584	270	324	11,978
1970	653	412	151	13,555
1975	373	334	39	13,011
1980	170	368	-198	12,802
1985	55	575	-520	10,247
1990	3	3410	-377	8,629
1991	14	291	-277	8,352
1992	33	341	-308	8,044

The table shows that new charters exceeded cancellations of charters, and the number of federal credit unions grew, until the 1970s. Thereafter, new charters fell dramatically, cancellations increased (although irregularly), and as a result the number of federal credit unions fell. Similar data are not available for state chartered credit unions, but in the period since 1980 the number of federally insured state credit unions fell slightly.[19]

---

[18] National Credit Union Administration, 1992 Annual Report (Washington: 1993), 30-31.
[19] Ibid., 33.

These figures do not imply that credit union activity fell; credit union members, assets, and loans continued to grow. But the number of credit unions fell as small credit unions were liquidated or merged with larger institutions.

It is difficult to assign responsibility for the decline in the number of credit unions, how much of it has been due to market forces and how much to regulation. To a large extent, the cause must be economies of scale as shown in Table 5.13, the fact that costs tend to increase less than proportionately when a credit union expands, with the result that large credit unions can offer services cheaper and more efficiently than small credit unions can. However, NCUA has done nothing to slow down the trend. At various times, NCUA spokespeople have said that they welcome the decline in the number of credit unions since it is not cost effective for the agency to devote resources to examining small credit unions. Their view has been that members can be as well or better served in large credit unions. Over the last decades the agency has frequently increased the barriers to groups seeking new charters.

This position may be defensible in the case of most mainstream credit unions serving a middle-class membership, although even here the decline in the number of credit unions means less member participation and less genuinely democratic control. It is not defensible, however, in the case of CDCUs serving low-income neighborhoods. Many CDCUs have disappeared, and their members have not been well served in the aftermath.

Chapter 4 discussed the reasons why CDCUs are needed. As banks pull out, many poor communities have no conventional financial institutions, and residents are forced into the hands of check cashers, liquor stores, pawnshops, and loan sharks. Even when bank branches are present, they tend not to lend very much in the local area, and therefore serve to funnel resources out of the community.

When a small mainstream credit union with a middle-class membership closes its doors, most of its members can find another credit union which they are eligible to join. In the case of mergers, the charter of the new credit union is explicitly changed to include the members of the closed institution. But in a poor neighborhood, when the CDCU closes, there is usually no other credit union nearby, and no credit union for which the members could qualify.

The question of whether large mainstream credit unions can operate effectively, and produce needed services, in poor communities is one which is unclear and in need of further research. Certainly there are obstacles. As Chapter 5 showed, CDCUs suffer higher loan losses and higher expenses than do mainstream credit unions, and they therefore charge somewhat higher interest rates on their loans and offer lower dividend rates on savings. Under these circumstances, it is not necessarily to the advantage of a middle-class credit union to expand into a poor neighborhood. There may be sound economic reasons for the relative absence of large credit unions in poor areas. Therefore, the premise behind NCUA's view is faulty: When a CDCU closes, its members probably cannot be picked up by an existing credit union.

Even if they can join a larger credit union, that credit union may not provide the same level of services. Chapter 4 showed that branches of banks in poor areas typically accept deposits and provide other customer services, but they do not make very many loans. They find it more profitable and less risky to lend in middle-class communities. Consequently, they siphon funds away from the area. No studies exist on the question of whether mainstream credit unions with branches in poor neighborhoods operate in the same way as banks do, but until the case is proven otherwise, one ought to be suspicious. When a CDCU closes, its members might be able to find a new credit union, but one cannot be certain that the new credit union will be as predisposed to lend to them as the old CDCU was.

It follows that the NCUA policy of permitting and encouraging a decline in the number of small credit unions, including CDCUs, operates to the detriment of low-income people in a way quite different from the way it affects more affluent groups.

It is possible that NCUA is changing its policy on new charters. As Table 7.1 shows, new charters of federal credit unions almost disappeared in 1991, but they rebounded somewhat in 1992. The 33 new charters in 1992 included 7 CDCUs. Nevertheless, the number of liquidations continues to be high, and these include CDCUs. In May of 1992, the NCUA board met with the National Federation of CDCUs and heard its Executive Director, Clifford Rosenthal, propose a program of 10 new CDCU charters a year for three years, plus a temporary moratorium on CDCU liquidations. While the agency has not accepted the second part of the proposal, it may have been influenced by the first part.

New Federal Legislation

CDCU leaders argued for years that new federal legislation was needed if the promise of banking in poor communities was to reach its full potential. They prepared numerous position papers and draft bills and argued their case strenuously in Washington. In 1993, their persistence was rewarded when President Clinton proposed the Community Development Banking and Financial Institutions Act. While the exact terms of the legislation were likely to change, the importance of the President's action was that it restored the federal government's initiative in the development of financial services for the poor.

The President came into office with a commitment to what he called "community development banking" as a strategy to improve living conditions and combat poverty in low-income areas of the country. In a series of speeches and interviews, both during the campaign and after taking office, he praised small, private-sector financial institutions that made credit available to poor people for housing and business development.

The inclusion of credit unions in the President's policy was a victory for the efforts of the National Federation of CDCUs. Although Clinton was aware of CDCUs—as a presidential candidate he had visited one in Texas—he did not talk much about them in his speeches on community development banking. Instead, he focused on two models of low-income financial institutions, the Grameen microenterprise lenders in Bangladesh and the South Shore Bank in Chicago (with, not incidentally, an affiliate in Arkansas).

The microenterprise lenders were described in Chapter 3. First developed in Bangladesh, they identify a group of people, typically five women, to form a "circle" for the purpose of planning small business ventures. The group picks one of its members to take the first small loan from the bank. When that loan is paid back, or partially paid back, the next woman can qualify for a loan to start her business, and so forth until all the members are engaged in new activities. The achievements of South Shore Bank were described in Chapter 4. Owned by an inter-racial group of civic minded activists and bankers, with considerable capital from foundations and churches, it exists for the twin purposes of making a profit and promoting community economic development. Over a twenty year period, it has brought sufficient capital into its neighborhood on the south side of Chicago and made enough mortgage loans to transform what was once a nearly destroyed area of the city into a thriving, lower-middle-class residential and business community.

Upon assuming office, the Clinton administration initially proposed that the federal government help establish 1,000 microenterprise lenders on the Grameen model and 100 development banks like South Shore. As the proposal was debated in Washington in the first few months of the administration, however, it was criticized from several different perspectives, and as a consequence changes were made in the program.

The first criticism came from the existing community development credit unions and loan funds, from institutions and people who already had a track record of providing financial services for economic development in poor areas. They objected to the exclusive focus of the program upon new institutions, and argued that the government should reinforce successes that had already been achieved in the field. As early as 1985-86, the National Federation of CDCUs had developed a proposal for a public "National Neighborhood Banking Corporation" that would provide equity funding for CDCUs, and in 1991 the National Association of Community Development Loan Funds had joined the proposal as a cosponsor.[20] The two national organizations now argued that something like this neighborhood banking corporation should be incorporated into the President's proposal.

The second principal criticism came from people who thought that the focus on small, alternative financial institutions was counterproductive and harmful; the real emphasis should be on the large banks and thrifts, the institutions that controlled most of the country's money. Interestingly, this criticism came from both the right and the left of the political spectrum. From the right, Republicans argued that banks should be given incentives to encourage them to lend in low-income neighborhoods. From the left, organizations such as ACORN (Association of Community Organizations for Reform Now), argued for much tougher provisions and enforcement of the Community Reinvestment Act (CRA). Currently, they argued, CRA was toothless and ineffective; even banks that did little lending to low- and moderate-income people in their local communities received high ratings. The Act needed both amendment and tough enforcement in order to force the banks into a constructive relationship with central cities and other poor areas.

The criticism from the left represented a danger to the interests of the CDCUs and the loan funds. At their most extreme, the proponents of a tougher CRA seemed to argue that the very existence of small alternative lenders was harmful because it allowed the banks to back off from their responsibilities. The issue was brought into the open at a meeting of bank critics with the board of the National Federation of CDCUs in February of 1993.

The CDCUs' representatives responded to the bank critics that there was no necessary conflict between the two groups, and that if there were to be an open fight on the issue, the likelihood of defeat for both sides would be increased. There was no need to choose, they said, between a CDCU strategy and a strong CRA strategy. They are compatible and even mutually supportive. The argument seems persuasive. In fact, CDCUs have been among the strongest supporters of CRA enforcement in their cities. In numerous cases—for example at Austin/West Garfield FCU in Chicago and at the Lower East Side People's FCU in New York—credit union organizers have

---

[20] National Federation of Community Development Credit Unions. "The Neighborhood Banking Corporation."

used the leverage provided by the CRA to persuade, cajole, or even force banks that were in the neighborhood, or banks that were departing from the neighborhood, to make contributions to them. The contributions have included buildings, technical assistance, staff, deposits, and grants. But CDCUs and their spokespeople at the National Federation have been careful not to argue that banks could meet their CRA responsibilities solely by contributing to alternative financial institutions; the main responsibility of the banks, they maintain, is to lend. CDCUs have frequently protested the lax enforcement of CRA requirements, and have spoken out in favor of making the requirements more explicit.

In any case, the administration took account of some of these criticisms as it developed its policy for investment in low-income communities. In July, 1993, the President announced a two-part program, the first part dealing with public investment in community development financial institutions, and the second with the Community Reinvestment Act. He proposed $382 million over four years to be given to community financial institutions in the form of seed money and equity grants. Referring to CRA, he asked government regulators to draft a new set of rules that would reduce paperwork but tighten the standards for compliance.

The administration refused, therefore, to accept the argument that a conflict exists between encouraging small community lenders on the one hand, and requiring larger banks to do business in poverty areas on the other. It took the position that the two thrusts were compatible, that they were twin components of the same initiative.

Whether because government officials had studied the history of the OEO credit unions in the 1960s, or because they simply had good sense, they structured the new program to avoid some of the problems of the earlier period. As Chapter 3 showed, one of the mistakes made in the OEO period was that the government subsidized salary and other expenses, encouraging the credit unions to increase their expenses beyond a sustainable level. Then when the funding was cut off, the credit unions could not meet their budgets, and many failed. Under the terms of the new legislation, federal support will be in the form of grants, equity investments, deposits, loans, and shares, but not subsidies for expenses.

Equity grants will be of the most help to CDCUs. They will improve the financial condition of the credit unions by increasing their reserve ratios, and at the same time, under NCUA's member business loan regulations, will increase the size of business loans that can be made. But capital grants will not entice the credit unions into thinking that they can operate beyond their means. Describing the importance of this sort of funding, the National Federation of CDCUs wrote:

> Our greatest need is for equity capital, i.e., reserves. For a number of years, low-income credit unions have been limited by NCUA in their ability to do community development lending (especially, housing and small business lending) because they are, by NCUA standards, insufficiently capitalized...
>
> We don't necessarily agree with NCUA's policies in this regard. But we do recognize for a fact that financial institutions with below-peer capital ratios will always encounter regulatory difficulties when they conduct lending perceived as 'high risk'—e.g., lending to low-income people, lending for small businesses, nonconforming mortgage lending. This kind of lending is absolutely essential to our mission as CDCUs.
>
> ... It is extremely difficult for CDCUs to generate internally an 'adequate' level of capital (peer-level or higher) to carry on community development lending without intense regulatory scrutiny. There are several reasons for this. By nature, serving the poor is very labor-intensive and costly. Loan losses do tend to be higher than in non-CDCU credit unions. Also, CDCUs are often constrained from making the larger, more profitable loans (e.g., mortgage lending) either because of regulatory pressure or because of our asset size. To make a quantum leap in capacity, we believe CDCUs need an external infusion of capital.[21]

The President's proposal was the most ambitious federal government initiative in the area of community development finance since the Depression. If successful, it will stabilize community development credit unions and other similar institutions, and promote their growth both in number and size, so that they will be capable of making a much greater impact on poor communities throughout the country. At the same time, the CDCUs will remain private sector cooperatives, still under the control of their members.

A Community Reinvestment Act for Credit Unions?

Closely related to the issue of whether the Community Reinvestment Act should be tightened for banks is the question of whether the CRA, or something like it, should be applied to the country's credit unions. At present it is not, and credit unions are therefore not required to show to a public agency that they are making a contribution to the needs of the poor

---

[21] National Federation of Community Development Credit Unions. "Response of the National Federation of CDCUs to NAFCU's 'A 12-Point Plan for Community Development Credit Unions.'"

and other groups within their communities. Representative Henry Gonzalez of Texas, Chairman of the House Banking Committee, said in August, 1993, that the CRA should be expanded to include credit unions and also nonbank financial entities such as mortgage and insurance companies.[22]

Spokespeople of the mainstream credit union industry would prefer that the question not be raised. They have long argued that it would be inappropriate to apply the CRA to credit unions, since credit unions are constrained by their charters to lend only to people who have a common bond within their field of membership. Credit unions simply cannot be held to a standard that would require them to do business with people outside their charter. Credit union representatives also argue that CRA regulations are unnecessary for them since they are member-owned, non-profit cooperatives, and as such they voluntarily meet the most pressing needs of their members.

The credit unions' argument about not being allowed to do business outside their field of membership is valid, as far as it goes, but it ignores the fact that charters can be amended, and that fields of membership are in fact being expanded substantially. Many credit unions which began with a limited, well-defined field of membership have expanded that field so much that almost anyone who lives close to the credit union or one of its branches can find a way to qualify. In some cases, associational fields have been converted to geographical fields, meaning that absolutely everyone in a defined area is eligible to join. The expansion in the field of membership has gone together with other changes in credit union regulations and practices which have had the effect of making credit unions functionally much more like banks than they used to be. Since many credit unions operate like banks, the question arises with increasing force, why they should not be held to CRA standards, as banks are.

Similarly, with respect to the cooperative structure of mainstream credit unions, it is no longer clear that this ensures a socially responsible attitude on the part of credit union managers. As Chapter 3 showed, over time credit union members in the United States have become more affluent and comfortable, and credit union staffs have become larger and more professionalized. The sense of a "movement" that once pervaded credit unions has been converted gradually into one of an "industry."

Under these circumstances, it would seem appropriate for the government to require credit unions to show that they are providing financial services to the less fortunate within their fields of membership. Without new legislation, NCUA could impose something like CRA requirements on credit unions, in a tailored, individualized way. The broader and more inclusive the

---

[22] *Credit Union Newswatch* (August 30, 1993).

field of membership, the stronger the requirements should be. Credit unions which have charters that give them the opportunity to serve poor people would need to show to NCUA that they have made good faith efforts to do exactly that. Under such a standard, community development credit unions would be subject to CRA-type requirements, since most of them have geographic fields of membership that certainly include poor people. They would have no trouble demonstrating compliance. Difficulties might arise, however, for credit unions which have broad charters but which concentrate upon their more affluent potential members.

Recent research by *Credit Union Magazine*[23] shows that many credit unions have a great deal of opportunity to respond to the needs of poor people. Although the majority of credit union members in the country are reasonably well-off, a survey of 1,200 credit unions showed that 29 percent of member households had less than $20,000 annual income. Some credit unions have seized this opportunity, in some cases by developing programs that are designed specifically for low-income people. Some, for example, grant loans of very small amounts. But some credit unions do little or nothing to respond to the particular needs of their low-income members, and for these credit unions a little public accountability for their actions might go a long way.

The question becomes more pointed in the case of credit unions asking for expanded charters specifically in order to draw low-income communities into their fields of membership. In early 1993, the Governmental Affairs Committee of CUNA passed a resolution asking that NCUA facilitate such charter amendments. The Board of Directors of the National Federation of CDCUs responded rather negatively to the proposal, and scheduled a major panel on the issue several months later at its annual meeting. The lack of enthusiasm from the CDCUs is a reflection of their skepticism that large credit unions will operate in their communities in any way differently from the banks. As has been seen, banks in poor neighborhoods tend to provide a place for people to deposit their money, earn interest, cash checks, and buy money orders, but they are reluctant to lend money in the local community. CDCUs are particularly worried that large credit unions might squeeze them out of local communities and then refuse to supply the local people with adequate lending.

If NCUA is to permit mainstream credit unions to expand their charters into low-income neighborhoods, therefore, it should require performance standards of them that bear some relationship to the CRA. It is not enough for the credit unions simply to set up shop, accept deposits, and cash checks.

---

[23] Reported in *Credit Union Magazine* (May 3, 1993).

They should show that they can make loans in the neighborhood, even if this requires some adjustment in their normal underwriting policies. Otherwise they will just be a conduit drawing funds out of the area. They should show that they have assessed the financial needs of the area and are capable of making the appropriate contributions. Furthermore, in the spirit of a cooperative, they should show that they are drawing neighborhood people into the organization in positions of responsibility, on the staff, committees, and board of directors. Credit unions that expand into low-income areas in this manner would likely be welcomed enthusiastically by the local communities. They can bring both financial and technical resources that are needed. If their intent is to operate like typical banks, however, NCUA would be well-justified in denying their applications for charter expansion.

Policy at Other Levels

Not all policy that affects community development credit unions is formulated at the level of the federal government.[24] State and local governments have an influence, as do a multitude of private sector groups.

The principal influence that state governments have on CDCUs is through their authority to charter, examine, and regulate credit unions. Most states do not have a specialized regulatory agency that parallels NCUA, but rather embed their credit union oversight within a more general department or agency that regulates all types of businesses. In California, for example, state-chartered credit unions are supervised by the Department of Corporations. The states do, however, have separate laws providing for credit union charters. Many CDCUs have chosen a state rather than a federal charter for a variety of reasons, including the fact that personal associations have sometimes been closer with state officials than with federal ones. Typical is the Vermont Development Credit Union in Burlington, which chose a state charter in 1989 because some of the credit union's organizers had worked for years with people in the state government and trusted them. Even when credit unions have state charters, however, they must comply with most of the NCUA regulations because this is a condition of insuring their deposits with the National Credit Union Share Insurance Fund.

In recent years, most of the states have been no more active in chartering credit unions in general, and CDCUs in particular, than has NCUA. There is no reason, however, that states cannot follow and cooperate with President Clinton's community development banking initiative, reinforcing it on their own. They can actively solicit CDCU charters, and they can find ways of assisting them with infusions of capital to promote their stability if the fed-

---

[24] Tholin and Pogge have a particularly strong section on policy towards CDCUs at the non-federal level.

eral funding is not sufficient.

State and local governments can contribute to community economic development by depositing funds in CDCUs. Public deposits throughout the country in private financial institutions are enormous, and a small portion of these funds directed towards CDCUs can make an important difference to the ability of those institutions to lend and to make ends meet. It must be recognized, however, that several barriers often stand in the way of this type of partnership. From the public side, state and local governments are often constrained by law, or by constitution or charter, to place their funds where they receive the highest possible rate of return. They are often not able to offer deposits to CDCUs at concessionary rates, and the high market rates they must hold out for are unattractive to the credit unions. The credit unions in turn may not wish to deal with large blocks of money that flow in and out quickly, as government deposits often do. Furthermore, they may not be able to accept the funds because of the NCUA limit on non-member deposits. Several examples exist, however, of public bodies making below-market-rate deposits in CDCUs, which in turn permit below-market-rate loans to members for economic development purposes.

Private as well as public sector bodies can make deposits in and grants to CDCUs. A large number of socially responsible investors want to place their funds where they will get a reasonable return and at the same time will contribute to human welfare and social change. Many churches find themselves in this position, as do some foundations, educational institutions, and even corporations. They can make deposits in individual CDCUs directly, or they can lend money to the National Federation of CDCUs which packages deposits to individual credit unions.

Finally, and importantly, is the role that the rest of the country's credit unions can play in nurturing the growth of CDCUs. Historically, a certain tension has frequently existed between CDCUs and their more established sisters. As explained in Chapter 3, however, that tension was dissipated, at least somewhat, in the early 1990s. At the national level, the National Federation of CDCUs joined the Credit Union National Association, for reasons of advantage to both groups. The Federation benefited by having access to the technical resources and financial support of CUNA; CUNA in turn benefited by being able to represent itself publicly as embracing those credit unions most committed to the welfare of poor people and to social change.

CDCUs have a testier relationship to the other principal trade association of credit unions, the National Association of Federal Credit Unions. NAFCU is an association of the largest federally chartered credit unions. As such it has had little to do with CDCUs, but in late 1992 and 1993 it began promoting a 12-point program regarding CDCUs and community development banking. While some of the points were supportive of CDCUs (for example, point 10: "Urge the Clinton Administration to support CDCUs as the key to financial self-help and the cornerstone of community development initiatives"), others were hostile or self-serving. Point 1, for example, was hostile: "Urge the NCUA to conduct a study and issue a report on why CDCUs have failed in the past."[25] Number 6, among others, was self-serving: "Establish a mentor credit union program; mentor credit unions will receive credit towards their NCUA operating fee for active participation (fees could be derived from technical assistance funds.)" While leaving the door open for future discussion, the National Federation of CDCUs in effect responded that if this was NAFCU's idea of help, they could keep it to themselves.

The picture varies at the state level. A few states' credit union leagues (the trade associations of the credit unions, which are organized by state) have been very helpful to CDCUs, providing technical assistance and welcoming them into the credit union family. The CDCUs in some states report, however, that their leagues have been unhelpful, even hostile.

One of the main projects ahead of CUNA over the next decade, Operation Moonshot, has a goal of increasing the number of credit union members in the country from the existing level of a little over 60 million to 100 million. It is an ambitious goal, and it is unlikely to be achieved unless the credit unions can attract a substantial number of new members from low-income parts of the country. This may occur in part through the expansion of mainstream credit unions into central cities and other poverty areas, but as noted earlier, some obstacles lie in the way of such expansion. Middle-income people may not choose to join in a financial institution with the poor, since they would have to bear some of the burden of the higher loan default and expense ratios associated with banking among the poor. In turn, the low-income communities may not welcome the outside credit unions if those institutions do not demonstrate a commitment to lending in the area and supporting the local people in other ways. So at least in part, the success of

---

[25] In its rejoinder, the National Federation of CDCUs noted:
> Certainly there have been failures among CDCUs. But it is not at all clear that failures among CDCUs have exceeded those of other credit unions. Since 1980, we have witnessed a sharp decline in the number of credit unions of all kinds. Among 'mainstream' credit unions, there have been large-scale failures resulting from fraud and insider dealing. There have been failures at the level of corporate credit unions. Moreover, there has been a steady 'upscaling' of the credit union industry, so that median credit union household income in fact exceeds the median for all US households. Yet, we have not called for a study of the 'failures' of the credit union industry at large, nor of the industry's failure to serve low-income people.

Op. cit., "Response of the National Federation of CDCUs."

Operation Moonshot will depend upon the success and growth of CDCUs, institutions nurtured within low-income communities and intended principally for the welfare of the poor. It is strongly in the interest of the credit union industry as a whole, therefore, to support CDCUs.

The possible types of support are almost endless and have only begun to be explored. While cooperation has become quite close at the national level, a great deal more remains to be done at the state level and at the level of individual credit unions. CDCU staff members are often in urgent need of training and technical assistance; these can be provided by state leagues or even by single, more-established credit unions that are located nearby. Leagues can develop marketing material for CDCUs, advocate for CDCUs with state governments, and encourage brother/sister credit union relationships. Large credit unions can place below-market-rate deposits in CDCUs.[26] A most encouraging example of this sort of cooperation occurred at the South Central People's Federal Credit Union in Los Angeles, chartered in 1993, where credit unions pledged $5 million in deposits even before the institution opened its doors to the public.

Conclusion

Whether consciously or not, the community development credit union movement is returning credit unions to the roots of cooperative banking. While rejecting the racism and other reactionary ideas that sometimes characterized the early German people's banks, they have breathed new life into some of the basic ideas of those institutions. Like the Schulze-Delitzsch and Raiffeisen societies, they have shown that disadvantaged people can band together to support each other, that they can attract resources from outside their communities, and that they can use funds for productive business investments that create jobs and provide people with an ownership stake in their own neighborhoods. Like the early American credit unions, they have shown that credit unions can make personal loans that help struggling, marginalized people get out of debt traps and claim more control over their lives. Like all of the early credit unions, the CDCUs rely on volunteer and low-paid work by people who are dedicated to a cause that is greater than themselves. While most American credit unions have moved away from these commitments as their memberships have become increasingly affluent, CDCUs have stayed true to their goal of trying to provide a way for low-income communities to revitalize their economic structures, and for low-income people to transform their lives.

---

[26] Ideas such as these are explored in more detail in Tholin and Pogge.

As the middle years of the 1990s approach, a new sense of optimism is creeping at least slowly through the community development credit union movement. Five or ten years earlier, a disinterested observer could have been forgiven for wondering whether CDCUs were not an idea whose time had come and gone. Most of the OEO credit unions had failed, liquidations and mergers of low-income credit unions were proceeding regularly, surviving CDCUs were growing only slowly, they were burdened with serious financial problems, and few new CDCUs were appearing. CDCUs are a good idea in the abstract, such an observer might have concluded, but not one which is going to make much of a contribution to the resolution of America's great poverty problem.

Both questions and obstacles still remain, and much of this book has been concerned with documenting them in detail. But they are balanced by a renewed faith in the future. New CDCUs are appearing in somewhat larger numbers, and because of NCUA's increasingly rigorous chartering requirements, they are on the whole better prepared to conduct business successfully than their predecessors had been. Existing CDCUs are improving their balance sheets, increasing their memberships, and expanding into new areas such as business and mortgage lending. Non-member deposits in CDCUs are growing, as churches and foundations learn more about this way of contributing to human welfare. NCUA has taken a new interest in encouraging CDCUs. The Clinton administration has proposed a major initiative in community development banking which holds the promise of injecting significant capital into CDCUs. And the Credit Union National Association has forged a new partnership with the CDCU movement.

More important than all the national changes is the spirit of confidence in the individual community development credit unions. It cannot be documented or measured with precision, but it can be felt. Attendance at the annual meetings of the National Federation and at regional meetings has risen sharply; the people new to these meetings are just as committed as the old-timers, and often more enthusiastic. No one embodies the new spirit of the CDCU movement better than Mark Griffith, the 30-year-old organizer of Central Brooklyn Federal Credit Union, chartered in January 1993 in the African American Bedford Stuyvesant area of New York. Griffith is a poet as well as an activist. "People in the traditional banking community question our background," he says, "but I am convinced it has helped. We do not represent business as usual, and we bring a certain freshness....There is a new generational consciousness."[27]

---

[27] Lueck.

Individual credit unions and the movement as a whole are sure to face setbacks in the years to come, but there is every reason to believe that the CDCUs will grow, that they will draw more people into the cooperative saving and lending process, and that they will make increasingly important contributions to their communities.

BIBLIOGRAPHY

Aschhoff, Gunther, and Eckart Henningsen. *The German Cooperative System: Its History, Structure and Strength.* Frankfurt am Main: Fritz Knapp Verlag, 1986.

Association of Community Organizations for Reform Now (ACORN). "Take the Money and Run: The Siphoning of Deposits from Minority Neighborhoods in 14 Cities." New York: 1992.

Atlanta Journal-Constitution, "The Color of Money." (May 1-16, 1988).

Ayres, Ian. "Pride and Prejudice." *The New Republic* 207 (July 6, 1992): 30-34.

Becker, Gary S. *The Economics of Discrimination.* Chicago: University of Chicago Press, 1957.

Becker, Gary S. *Human Capital: A Theoretical and Empirical Analysis, With Special Reference to Education.* 2d. ed. Chicago: The University of Chicago Press, 1975.

Bentson, George J., Dan Horsky, and H. Martin Weingartner. *An Empirical Study of Mortgage Redlining.* New York: New York University, Graduate School of Business Administration, Salomon Brothers Center for the Study of Financial Institutions, Monograph Series in Finance and Economics, Monograph 1978-5, 1978.

Bonner, Arnold. *British Cooperation.* Manchester: Cooperative Union Ltd., 1961.

Brown, Jonathan, with Charles Bennington. *Racial Redlining: A Study of Racial Discrimination by Banks and Mortgage Companies in the United States.* Washington, D.C.: Essential Information, Inc., 1993.

Calem, Paul S. "The Community Reinvestment Act: Increased Attention and a New Policy Statement." *The Business Review* (July-August 1989): 3-16. Philadelphia: Federal Reserve Bank of Philadelphia.

California Council of Urban Leagues. *Redlining in the Bay Area: A Call to Action*. Sacramento: Report to the California Assembly Committee on Consumer Protection, Governmental Efficiency and Economic Development, August 5, 1992.

Canner, Glenn B., and Dolores S. Smith. "Home Mortgage Disclosure Act: Expanded Data on Residential Lending." *Federal Reserve Bulletin* (November 1991): 859-881.

Credit Union National Association. *Operating Ratios and Spreads, Year-End 1991*. Madison, WI: CUNA Economics and Research Department, 1992.

Detroit Free Press, "The Race for Money." (June 24-27, 1988).

Dublin, Jack. *Credit Unions: Theory and Practice*. Detroit: Wayne State University Press, 1979.

Ely, Richard T. "German Cooperative Credit Unions." *Atlantic Monthly* (February 1881): 207-223.

Episcopal General Convention. "Taking Action for Economic Justice." Detroit, July 1988.

Fairbairn, Brett. "Social Bases of Co-operation: Historical Examples and Contemporary Questions." In *Co-operative Organizations and Canadian Society: Popular Institutions and the Dilemmas of Change*, edited by Murray E. Fulton. Toronto: University of Toronto Press, 1990, 63-76.

Flax-Hatch, David. "Tracking Chicago's Business Bucks: Commercial Lending and the Chicago Municipal Depository Ordinance." Chicago: The Woodstock Institute, 1987.

Gore, Harold, Clifford Rosenthal, and Ward Smith. "An Analysis of the Role of Credit Unions in Capital Formation and Investment in Low- and Moderate-Income Communities." New York: National Federation of Community Development Credit

Unions, 1986 (presented to the Executive Office of the President—Office of Policy Development).

Gurley, John G., and Edward S. Shaw. *Money in a Theory of Finance*. Washington, D.C.: Brookings Institution, 1960.

Haas, Gilda. Testimony before the Subcommittee on Housing and Community Development and the Subcommittee on Consumer Affairs and Coinage of the U.S. House of Representatives Committee on Banking, Finance and Urban Affairs, May 7, 1992.

Henderson, Perry E., Jr. *The Black Church Credit Union*. Lima, Ohio: Fairway Press, 1990.

Herrick, Myron T. *Rural Credits: Land and Cooperative*. New York: D. Appleton and Co., 1914.

Houghton, Mary. "Adaptation of Bank Holding Company Structure for Economic Development of Disinvested Urban Communities." Testimony before the U.S. House of Representatives Committee on Banking, Finance and Urban Affairs, July 22, 1992.

Hoke, Linda. "Community Development Credit Unions: A Powerful New Vehicle for Southern Economic Development?" *Southern Growth Reports*. Research Triangle Park, North Carolina, March 1991.

Isbister, John, with the assistance of Robert Thompson. "The Lending Performance of Community Development Credit Unions." Davis, California: Center for Cooperatives, University of California, 1992.

Jerving, Jim. *Changing Youth: Starting a Youth Credit Union and Learning Center*. Dubuque, Iowa: Kendall/Hunt Publishing Company, 1993.

Liebowitz, Stan. "A Study That Deserves No Credit." *The Wall Street Journal* (September 1, 1993): A14.

Livingston, Peter. "The Crisis in Limited Income Credit Unions." Madison, WI: Credit Union National Association, 1973.

Lueck, Thomas J. "Into the World of Banking Comes a Hip-Hop Credit Union." *The New York Times* (April 25, 1993).

McLenighan, Valjean, and Jean Pogge. *The Business of Self-Sufficiency: Microcredit Programs in the United States*. Chicago: The Woodstock Institute, 1991.

McNally, Ginger. "Income Generation Programs: Financial and Social Impact on the Poor." Master's thesis, Monterey Institute for Foreign Study, Monterey, California, 1992.

Moody, J. Carroll, and Gilbert C. Fite. *The Credit Union Movement: Origins and Development 1850-1980*. 2d ed. Dubuque, Iowa: Kendall/Hunt Publishing Company, 1984.

Moore, Barrington. *Social Origins of Dictatorship and Democracy: Lord and Peasant in the Making of the Modern World*. Boston: Beacon Press, 1966.

National Credit Union Administration. Annual Report. Washington D.C.: annual.

National Federation of Community Development Credit Unions. *CDCU Report*. New York: 1991.

National Federation of Community Development Credit Unions. "Interim Report: Church-Based Credit Union Study." New York: 1990.

National Federation of Community Development Credit Unions. "Final Report: Church-Based Credit Union Study." New York: 1991.

National Federation of Community Development Credit Unions. "Interim Report: Church Credit Union Development Project." New York: 1992.

National Federation of Community Development Credit Unions. "The Neighborhood Banking Corporation." New York: 1991.

National Federation of Community Development Credit Unions. "The OEO Credit Union Experiment: Implications for Community Development Banking." New York: 1993.

National Federation of Community Development Credit Unions. "Response of the National Federation of CDCUs to NAFCU's 'A 12-Point Plan for Community Development Credit Unions.'" New York: 1993.

Neunlist, Lindsay L. "Limited-Income Credit Unions." Washington, D.C.: National Credit Union Administration, Research Study No. 17, 1992.

Neunlist, Lindsay L. "Low-Income Credit Unions: 1992 Year-End Report." Washington: National Credit Union Administration, 1993.

Ols, John M., Jr. "Secondary Mortgage Market: Home Loans in the Atlanta Area." Statement before the Subcommittee on Consumer and Regulatory Affairs, U.S. Senate Committee on Banking, Housing, and Urban Affairs, February 28, 1991.

Peal, David. "Antisemitism by Other Means? The Rural Cooperative Movement in Late Nineteenth-Century Germany." *Leo Baeck Institute Yearbook*, 32 (1987): 135-153.

Quint, Michael. "A Bank Shows It Can Profit and Follow a Social Agenda." *New York Times* (May 24, 1992): 1, 14.

Robinson, Ceretha, and Anne Gilson. *Government Involvement with Community Development Credit Unions: Lessons Learned from the OEO Experience*. Chicago: The Woodstock Institute, 1993.

Rosenthal, Clifford N., and Joseph Schoder. "People's Credit: A Study of the Lending of the Lower East Side People's Federal Credit Union." New York: National Federation of Community Development Credit Unions, 1990.

Rudin, Ronald. *In Whose Interest? Quebec's Caisses Populaires, 1900-1945*. Montreal and Kingston: McGill University Press, 1990.

Satin, Mark. "Citizen Bankers Would Rebuild the United States—Community by Community." In *When Workers Decide: Workplace Democracy Takes Root in North America*, edited by Len Krimmerman and Frank Lindenfeld. Philadelphia: New Society Publishers, 1992, 91-97.

Schaaf, Michael. *Cooperatives at the Crossroads: The Potential for a Major New Economic and Social Role.* Washington, D.C.: The Exploratory Project for Economic Alternatives, 1977.

Stevens, Judy, and Kathryn Tholin. *Lenders of First Resort: Community Development Loan Funds.* Chicago: The Woodstock Institute, 1991.

Tholin, Kathryn. *Putting it All Together: The Birth of the Austin/West Garfield Federal Credit Union.* Chicago: The Woodstock Institute, 1989.

Tholin, Kathryn, and Jean Pogge. *Banking Services for the Poor: Community Development Credit Unions.* Chicago: The Woodstock Institute, 1991.

Trimble, Martin Paul. "Public-Purpose Financial Institutions: Models for Democratic Financial Reform." Philadelphia: National Association of Community Development Loan Funds, 1991.

Tucker, Donald S. *The Evolution of People's Banks.* New York: Columbia University Press, 1922. Reissued, New York: AMS Press, 1967.

Wolff, Henry W. *People's Banks: A Record of Social and Economic Progress.* 2d ed. London: P. S. King and Son, 1896.